Risk and Resilience

What enables individuals to overcome adverse childhoods and move on to rewarding lives in adulthood? Drawing on data collected from two of Britain's richest research resources for the study of human development, the 1958 National Child Development Study and the 1970 British Cohort Study, Schoon investigates the phenomenon of resilience – the ability to adjust to and overcome adverse conditions. Comparing the experiences of over 30,000 individuals in two birth cohorts born twelve years apart, Schoon examines the transition from childhood into adulthood among individuals born in 1958 and 1970 respectively. The study focuses on academic attainment among individuals exposed to high versus low levels of socio-economic deprivation, but also considers behavioural adjustment, health and psychological well-being, as well as the stability of adjustment patterns in times of social change. This is a major work of reference and synthesis, that makes an important contribution to the study of life-long development.

INGRID SCHOON is Professor of Psychology and Director of the Centre for Human Development and Well Being at City University, London.

Risk and Resilience

Adaptations in Changing Times

by

Ingrid Schoon

CAMBRIDGE UNIVERSITY PRESS
Cambridge, New York, Melbourne, Madrid, Cape Town, Singapore, São Paulo

Cambridge University Press
The Edinburgh Building, Cambridge CB2 2RU, UK

Published in the United States of America by Cambridge University Press,
New York

www.cambridge.org
Information on this title: www.cambridge.org/9780521541565

First published 2006

Printed in the United Kingdom at the University Press, Cambridge

A catalogue record for this publication is available from the British Library

Library of Congress Cataloguing-in-Publication data

Schoon, Ingrid.
   Risk and resilience: adaptations in changing times/Ingrid Schoon, – 1st ed.
     p. cm.
   Includes bibliographical references and index.
   ISBN 0-521-83374-4 (hardback) – ISBN 0-521-54156-5 (pbk.)
   1. Resilience (Personality trait) 2. Child development – Great Britain –
   Longitudinal studies 3. Children with social disabilities – Great Britain –
   Longitudinal studies 4. Childern with social disabilities – Education –
   Great Britain – Longitudinal studies. I. Title.

BF698.35.R47S36 2006
155.2′4 – dc22   2005016926

ISBN-13 978-0-521-83374-5 hardback
ISBN-10 0-521-83374-4 hardback
ISBN-13 978-0-521-54156-5 paperback
ISBN-10 0-521-54156-5 paperback

To Brian and Mary Low

Contents

Contents   ix

Figures

Tables

Foreword by Glen H. Elder, Jr

Over the past half century, a contextual view of human lives has emerged in the social and behavioural sciences. This perspective represents a major shift in orientation from age-specific domains, such as adolescence and young adulthood, to the full life course of human careers and development. Questions relate the developing organism to lived experience in a changing world. Distinctive of this change is the evolution of life-course theory and methods, the integration of biological models, and the rapid growth of longitudinal studies and their data archives. Few books better reflect these advances than Schoon's *Risk and Resilience: Adaptations in Changing Times* – an illuminating study of the life course, from birth to middle age, in two British birth cohorts. The two cohorts are distinguished by people who were born at different times.

In important respects, the framework of this project dates back to the longitudinal studies of Americans born in the 1920s. These studies generated fresh thinking about the life course by following study members into the Great Depression, World War II and the postwar era. The developmental effects of each life trajectory depended on whether they were marked by hardship, military service or higher education. Over the years a set of principles have come to define the life course framework which informs Schoon's study, life-long development, human agency, the timing of events, linked lives and historical context. The life course consists of age-graded trajectories and their life transitions, involving work and family, along with other domains. Transitions are embedded in trajectories, such as job entry in work careers.

These early studies of human development were quickly followed by an ambitious British initiative at the end of World War II. James Douglas launched a national longitudinal study of children born in one week in 1946. Twelve years later this study was followed by a national sample of the 1958 birth cohort, and then by another national sample of the 1970 birth cohort. A fourth national cohort was launched in 2000. The first three birth cohorts, equally spaced, provide an exceptional opportunity to assess the impact of social change on British lives, and the studies that have done so have documented an increasing social inequality and its adverse effects on families and lives.

Risk and Resilience: Adaptations in Changing Times is based on two British birth cohorts with markedly different life histories. The childhood of the 1958 cohort coincided with a time of extraordinary economic growth and social transformation, a 'Golden Age' in the words of Eric Hobsbawm, whereas the 1970 cohort grew up in an era of dislocation, instability and uncertainty. The two cohorts experienced the recessionary decade of the 1980s (the worst economic recessions of the past fifty years), but at very different times in their lives. The older cohort was more established in careers and in marriage. Comparisons of the two cohorts at the same age show many changes, including greater economic well-being and higher education for the 1970 cohort, but also an increase in socio-economic inequality, less marital stability and a higher level of emotional malaise. Gender differences tend to favour females, though life has become noticeably more stressful across the two cohorts for the least educated men and women.

The two longitudinal cohorts in this study provide a rare opportunity to investigate socio-economic change, social risks and their life-course effects on academic achievement and resilience in school, socio-economic status and psychological well-being in adulthood. But as any user of longitudinal data knows, the investigator has to make the best of available measurements and their timing. This is especially difficult in comparisons of two or more cohorts or samples. However, the 1958 and 1970 British cohorts offer an unusually good match, and Schoon has made the best of some inadequate measures, especially in relation to protective factors and to school achievement. Both cohort studies provided similar data for a multiple item index of social risk (e.g. parent social class, housing tenure, overcrowding, receipt of state benefits, amenities) and three times of measurement into adolescence. To minimise the construction of a risk index in which the components have differing effects on behavioural outcomes, the analysis used discrete groupings of indicators – with a focus on socio-economic disadvantage. In quantitative models, multiple social risks adversely influenced adult socio-economic status and psychological well-being through impaired academic achievement, though educational resilience minimised this outcome.

The study focuses on two types of life courses in adolescence with origins in social disadvantage, a trajectory of resilience in which the study member does better than expected and one characterised by increasing risk or vulnerability. The popularity of resilience as a developmental concept reflects a contemporary movement towards more positive psychologies, but its widespread use and diverse meanings have prompted critical appraisals and doubts about the concept's usefulness. Schoon addresses some of the key issues in this literature and proposes a commonly accepted definition – to wit, resilience is a process that relates positive adaptations to disadvantaged origins. She also makes a compelling case in favour of this theoretical approach to the life course and human development.

One of the challenges in following young people from childhood to the later years is that their characteristics are interrelated. A person is not a composite of isolated attributes, but instead resembles a system of characteristics. With this in mind, Schoon employs both person-centred and variable-centred analyses. Each method is appropriate for different questions. Children who displayed an above-average reading ability in childhood, despite a high-SES risk, were classified as following a trajectory of 'educational resilience'. Protective social ties proved to be an important source of this resilience. Vulnerability depicts the trajectory of the lower achievers. In adulthood, analyses compare the life-course experiences of these disadvantaged groups with those of a high SES-risk group. Some children of privileged circumstances also lost their advantage and became vulnerable, while others fared well across the adolescent years.

A pathway of resilience is frequently assumed to surmount the adverse developmental effects of 'growing up in a disadvantaged environment', but Schoon makes clear that very few of the disadvantaged escaped the limitations of their family origin. The 'hidden injuries' of their background are apparent in the middle years. As she observes, the 'experience of early social disadvantage has life-long consequences', in many cases even for the most resilient. Pathways of resilience from early family disadvantage have notable policy implications for social intervention but, as the study indicates, they seldom enable the young to completely escape the scars of a deprivational childhood.

The men and women in this longitudinal study were born only twelve years apart in Great Britain, but in many respects they grew up in different social worlds which shaped their lives. *Risk and Resilience: Adaptations in Changing Times* tells this story and concludes that a background of social disadvantage does not ensure a life of disadvantage. Some men and women who followed a pathway of resilience into the middle years have managed well the deprivations of the past, whereas others are handicapped by them. Such different experiences bear upon the quality of life in the later years, the next phase of this groundbreaking study.

Preface by John Bynner

Secondary analysis of large-scale longitudinal survey data enable hypotheses to be tested about the specifics of life, as in economists' studies of 'returns to learning', but rarely the testing of comprehensive developmental theory as a whole. The vagaries of question selection and design means that operationalisation of key theoretical concepts and the specification of their relationships can be weak in any given study employing secondary data. Such data is more often used to contextualise theoretical development rather than fit the models to which it translates to empirical data. Karl Joreskog's pioneering work on the development of structural equation modelling was a breakthrough in offering through the LISREL programme a solution to the statistical modelling problem but examples of applying it or its many variants, such as AMOS, in a comprehensive theory testing programme are relatively rare.

Ingrid Schoon's work using the 1958 and 1970 British birth cohort studies, datasets to test and develop further a 'Developmental-contextual model' of human development is a superb example of such theory testing in action. She starts from a life-course perspective that sees human development, as a dynamic process – part constructed through human agency and part shaped through the changing (proximal and distal) contexts through which the individual moves. From this she builds a developmental model, embracing the key concepts of risk and resilience, turning points and escape from adversity through the deployment of personal and social resources. The key focus is on youth transitions: what determines the form the pathways to adulthood take and what are their consequences for achievement and fulfilment in later life.

The birth cohort study data is the perfect empirical counterpart to the theory in supplying the lifetime information against which to test and develop the model through a number of stages and in different domains. The result is a rich amalgam of research review, theoretical formulation and cumulative evidence from statistical analysis. The final chapters draw the work together with an overview of the contributions to knowledge that have come from it and a consideration of the policy implications to be derived from them.

With a background of long-standing interest in the 1958 and 1970 birth cohorts studies and the responsibility for directing them from 1989 to 2003, it is a particular pleasure for me to see their scientific potential realised so comprehensively and to have small part in the research programme itself. Howard Newby, when Chief Executive of the UK Economic and Social Research Council, described longitudinal studies as the equivalent of the large-scale facilities such as 'atom smashers' in the physical sciences that supply the acid test of theoretical propositions. Their closest counterpart in the social sciences are large-scale longitudinal studies that supply the key means of understanding the processes through which human beings flourish or decline in interaction with their environment. The design of each new follow-up of the birth cohorts starts from the premise of adding to the knowledge base in ways that will best help achievement of this goal, drawing on as wide a range of advice as possible from the scientific user community about the critical variables to include. Ingrid Schoon sets new standards in drawing out of the data the key resources for testing her theoretical ideas. The book is a major step forward in the secondary analysis of longitudinal data that will be a key reference text for many years to come.

Acknowledgements

This book would have been impossible to compile without the help and input of many people, and I am very grateful for their support. First of all I want to thank the participants of the cohort studies who have supplied the information on which this book is based. Their continued commitment to the studies throughout their lives is greatly appreciated. The research reported here would also not have been possible without the funding from numerous charitable foundations, government departments and agencies, in particular the Economic and Social Research Council (ESRC) who made it possible to establish and maintain a continuous programme of data collection.

The analysis and approach adopted here has been shaped by the many ways in which I am connected to others in the field, and I feel deep gratitude to the following for their help, advice, wise counsel and support: Mel Bartley, David Blane, John Bynner, Neville Butler, Liza Catan, Rosemary Crompton, Glen Elder, Elsa Ferri, Peter Flügel, Jutta Heckhausen, Uwe Hentschel, Steven Hope, Heather Joshi, Peter Martin, Barbara Maughan, Samantha Parsons, Alan Porter, Andy Ross, Amanda Sacker, Katariina Salmela-Aro, Jaqueline Scott, Rainer Silbereisen, Kate Smith, Dick Wiggins and Dieter Wolke.

I am also very grateful for the funding I have received from the Economic and Social Research Council (ESRC) to carry out the research supported by grants R000238051, L326253061 (Project 1) and RES225-25-2001 (Project 2). Data from the National Child Development Study and the British Cohort Study were supplied by the ESRC Data Archive. Those who carried out the original data collection bear no responsibility for its further analysis and interpretation.

Introduction

This book is about the factors and processes that promote escape from disadvantage. What is it that enables some individuals to overcome adverse childhoods and move on to rewarding lives in adulthood? The study is not about those with exceptional achievements. It is about individuals whose childhood circumstances were characterised by socio-economic hardship, but who developed and maintained good psycho-social adjustment, and who as adults in their early thirties live relatively comfortably. There is increasing evidence from studies across many nations demonstrating the human capacity to overcome even extreme privation and trauma and to show positive adaptation in the face of that adversity, a phenomenon also referred to as resilience (Elder, 1974/1999; Garmezy, 1971; Pilling, 1990; Rutter & Madge, 1976; Rutter, 1998a; Werner & Smith, 1982, 1992). This study will advance our knowledge of resilience by comparing experiences of individuals growing up in a changing socio-historical context.

The focus of the study lies on academic attainment, but also considers behavioural adjustment, health and psychological well-being, as well as the stability of adjustment patterns over time, covering the transition from childhood into adulthood and the assumption of work and family related roles. It is argued that it is the combination of individual re-sources, the support provided by the family and significant others, as well as experiences and opportunities within the wider environment that facilitate successful adaptation to challenging situations. Life chances and opportunities are shaped by socio-historical and economic circum-stances, gender and one's location in the social structure. Therefore, the study sets out to investigate the multiple levels of influence on individual development over time, and to examine the nature of the linkages between experiences of socio-economic adversity, adaptive responses to these experiences and long-term outcomes.

What is unique about this study is that it compares the lives of over 30,000 individuals in two cohorts born twelve years apart, mapping the pathways linking childhood experiences to adult outcomes. The study draws on data collected for two nationally representative cohort studies, the 1958 National Child Development Study (NCDS) and the 1970 British Cohort Study (BCS70), two of Britain's key resources for the study of human development. For more than forty years cohort members were followed in their development from birth to adulthood, at a cost of millions of research money, the perseverance and skill of a large team of research staff, the inspiration, foresight and leadership of key investigators associated with the studies through their most for-mative years, and the commitment of the cohort members to their continued participation.

The comparison of two birth cohorts offers a unique opportunity to gain a better understanding of the context dependency of resilience, and to examine change as an experiment of nature. While cohort members born in 1958 grew up in a period of extraordinary growth and social transformation, a period described by Eric Hobsbawn (1995) as the 'Golden Age' the cohorts born in 1970 experienced their childhood in an evolving new age of uncertainty and instability, portrayed by Hobsbawn as the 'Crisis Decades', including changes in labour market opportunities, changing patterns of educational participation, patterns of family formation, as well as general well-being and health (these changes will be described in more detail in Chapter 3).

A period of economic depression lasting from 1979 to 1987 and again between 1991 and 1994 brought with it the sharpest rise in umemploy-ment since World War II. Most cohort members born in 1958 completed their full-time education just before the onset of the depression, while the later born cohort reached the minimum school leaving age right in the midst of the depression. The cohort data thus allows the comparison of experiences of individuals born before and after the onset of the 'Crisis Decades', offering the opportunity to investigate how a changing context influences adjustment processes and resilience. Furthermore, the longitudinal approach makes it possible to investigate the antece-dents and long-term consequences of different adjustment patterns across the life course.

This is not the first study focusing on the lives of disadvantaged young people, aiming to illuminate the experiences and conditions that enable individuals to successfully withstand potentially devastating effects of adversity over time. Research on resilience has burgeoned over the last thirty years, following early ground-breaking studies of schizophrenic patients and their children. These identified subgroups of individuals who showed relatively adaptive patterns, who managed to achieve competence at school, work, and in social relations includ-ing marriage, despite their high-risk status (Bleuler, 1911, English translation 1978; Garmezy, 1970; Luthar et al., 1997; Masten et al., 1990; Rutter, 1966). This work was carried forward to develop the field of developmental psychopathology, an interdisciplinary approach for the study of human functioning (Cicchetti, 1984, 1990, 1993; Rutter & Garmezy, 1983).

Another milestone in resilience research is Emmy Werner's pioneering series of studies on high-risk children born in Hawaii who were followed from early childhood to now mature adulthood (Werner & Smith, 1977). Despite being exposed to serious risk factors, such as perinatal stress, poverty, parental psychopathology and disrupted family environments, one-third of these high-risk children made satisfactory adjustments in adult life (Werner & Smith, 1982, 1992, 2001).

Vital insights into the factors and processes involved in individual variations in response to exposure to risk were gained by the landmark studies conducted by Michael Rutter, comprising among others a comparative survey of all ten-year-old children living in an inner London borough and children of the same age with homes on the Isle of Wight (Rutter et al., 1970; Rutter et al., 1975a; Rutter et al., 1975b; Rutter et al., 1975c), a follow-up study of girls reared in institutions (Rutter & Quinton, 1984) and a follow-up study of Romanian orphans who had been brought to England before the age of two years (Rutter, 1998b). These investigations demonstrated the importance of long-range longitudinal research for investigating the experiences contributing to the emergence of resilience in adverse circumstances, laying the foundation for the study of the origins and course of individual patterns of adaptation in the face of socio-economic adversity.

Of particular importance for the approach adopted in the present study is the seminal work of Glen Elder on *Children of the Great Depression* (1974), in which he identified the profound effects of historical change on human development. By comparing the experiences of children born in Berkeley and parts of Oakland, California, in the early and late 1920s, he could show that children born at the beginning of the 1920s were not as susceptible to the effects of family disruption and hardship caused by the Great Depression as children born in the late 1920s (Elder, 1974/1999). The findings illustrate that developmental processes should be viewed not only in relation to individually lived time, but also in relation to the socio-historical context in which they take place. With his theory of the life course (Elder, 1985, 1994, 1998) is offering an approach towards a contextual understanding of developmental processes, which has inspired the current study.

Outline and structure of the book

Key assumptions underlying the conceptualisation and operationalisation of resilience are discussed in Chapter 1. A theoretical framework conceptualising the dynamic interactions between individual and context is outlined and developed in Chapter 2. In Chapter 3, the specific socio-historical conditions experienced by cohort members born in 1958 and 1970 are described. The developmental-contextual model of adjustment, which has been formulated in Chapter 2 is then tested, examining the context, timing and duration of risk effects in shaping individual development over time (Chapter 4), the protective factors and processes facilitating adjustment in the face of adversity (Chapter 5), the stability of early adjustment over time (Chapter 6), as well as the role of life plans in moderating the experience of early social disadvantage (Chapter 7). The findings are critically reviewed (Chapter 8), and their implications for interventions and social policy are discussed in Chapter 9.

A detailed description of the two birth cohorts and the different sweeps of data collection is given in Appendix A. Issues related to response bias and the handling of missing data are discussed in Appendix B, and a description of measures and test instruments used for analysis can be found in Appendix C.

1   Risk and resilience: definitions

> What we really want to understand are the processes of human development in different times and places, for individuals with varying risks and assets, and for individuals developing in a variety of social contexts.
>
> (Rigsby, 1994, p. 91)

Why study the occurrence of resilience, and how to conceptualise and measure the phenomenon? In this chapter, issues concerning the definition and operationalisation of resilience will be reviewed and discussed. The concept of resilience is examined, laying out underlying assumptions about the processes and conditions that are assumed to give rise to the manifestation of resilience. Concerns regarding the value of the concept, the way it is measured, and how it had been used in the explanation of behaviours and outcomes will be addressed.

Why does the study of resilience matter?

A growing concern in social policy over the last decade has been the increasing marginalisation of less privileged individuals and relatively disadvantaged social groups. The foundations of 'social exclusion' processes are laid down early in life through exposure to socio-economic risk factors identified with adverse circumstances at home and at school (Atkinson & Hills, 1998; Bynner, 2001a; Duncan & Brooks-Gunn, 1997; Luthar, 1999; McLoyd, 1998). Children reared in disadvantaged or deprived circumstances are at increased risk of adverse developmental outcomes ranging from educational underachievement and behavioural problems to adjustment problems in later life, such as low occupational status and poor health (Duncan & Brooks-Gunn, 1997; Essen & Wedge, 1978; Rutter & Madge, 1976). Yet the outcomes of early risk experiences are by no means entirely predictable. Not all individuals experiencing socio-economic adversity fail to achieve, and it is well documented that some children exposed to adverse conditions appear to avoid developing consequent problems of adjustment.

5

The aim of this study is to gain a better understanding of the factors and processes facilitating or hindering young people in fully developing their potential. Through access to longitudinal data covering the period from birth to adult life, it is possible to analyse the cumulative effect of experiences and circumstances operating over a continuous period of time. Moreover, outcomes assessed early on in the individual's life can be included as factors in processes accounting for what happens later, enabling a better understanding of the vicious and virtuous circles that characterise human development across the life course. By comparing the experiences of two nationally representative birth cohorts, covering the entire life span from birth to adulthood, it is furthermore possible to assess how changing times have influenced individual lives and the ways in which individuals respond to adverse experiences. Knowledge about the factors and processes involved in positive adaptation despite the experience of adversity can bring new impetus to the development of social policies aiming to promote the well-being of disadvantaged high-risk children and their parents.

The particular focus of this study lies on academic attainment in the face of socio-economic adversity. Academic attainment is vitally important in our culture, and success or failure in school can have serious long-term individual and social consequences. Academic or educational attributes, especially as reflected in school qualifications, are becoming increasingly important in securing adult employment, but are also associated with adult health and well-being (Bynner et al., 2000c; Keating & Hertzman, 1999; Shanahan, 2000). Therefore academic resilience, i.e. the development and maintenance of average or above average levels of academic attainment despite the experience of socio-economic adversity has been chosen as a key focus of this study.

Conceptualising resilience

Resilience is generally defined as a dynamic process whereby individuals show adaptive functioning in the face of significant adversity (Luthar et al., 2000; Masten, 1994; Rutter, 1990). The instigation of the concept of resilience during the 1970s brought with it a paradigmatic shift in how scientists began to view the causes and course of development of individuals experiencing significant adversity or trauma, moving away from the constancy model portraying the developmental course as deterministic either through the effects of genetics, or by the predetermining role of early experiences (Clarke & Clarke, 2003; Sroufe & Rutter, 1984). The need for a new orientation arose because of accumulating evidence of studies showing positive developmental outcomes despite the experience of significant adversity in different contexts (Anthony, 1974; Garmezy, 1974; Rutter, 1981; Werner et al., 1971).

Historically, most studies on the development of at-risk individuals have tried to understand adjustment problems or the reverse: the avoidance of academic failure, behaviour problems, motivational deficits, ill health or mental disorder. A shift of focus from the pathogenic paradigm centring on a deficit or disease model towards a prime focus on adaptive outcomes was advocated by Antonovsky (Antonovsky, 1979; Antonovsky, 1987) who coined the term 'salutogenesis' to describe developmental processes that lead to 'wellness' outcomes. Rather than asking 'What prevents individuals from getting ill?' he asks 'How can individuals become healthier?' Such a 'wellness framework' calls for the study of the health pole of 'the health ease/dis-ease continuum, (Antonovsky, 1979) but also takes into account the social structural sources of the forces that make for well-being (Antonovsky, 1994). The shift of focus from adaptational failures to positive outcomes in adverse conditions also implies a new impetus for research aiming to inform the design of social policy interventions aiming to create opportunities for development and to promote the chance of positive chain reactions.

Central assumptions in resilience research

The concept of resilience has been used to refer to:

(a) a positive outcome despite the experience of adversity;
(b) continued positive or effective functioning in adverse circumstances; or
(c) recovery after a significant trauma (Masten et al., 1999).

Resilience is a two-dimensional construct defined by the constellations of exposure to adversity and the manifestation of successful adaptation in the face of that risk (Luthar et al., 2000; Masten, 2001; Rutter, 1999). Resilience is generally not directly measured. The identification of resilience is based on two fundamental judgments: (a) is a person 'doing ok'? and (b) is there now, or has there been any significant risk or adversity to be overcome? (Masten & Coatsworth, 1998). A central assumption in the study of resilience is that some individuals are doing well, despite being exposed to an adverse risk situation, while others fail to adapt. The very definition of resilience is therefore based on an expectation of successful or problematic adjustment in response to risk factors that are assumed to effect adaptations:

Resilient individuals are those whose adaptations represent extreme positive residuals from a prediction equation where adaptations are predicted from a linear combination of risks and assets. In other words, determination of resilience depends on (a) judgements about outcomes and (b) assumptions about the causes of adaptations that may not have been explicitly described or consciously examined. (Rigsby, 1994, p. 88)

In order to identify resilience it has to be established whether the circumstances experienced by individuals do in fact affect their chances in life. If there is no association between the experience of adversity, access to resources and opportunities, and consequent adjustment, the phenomenon of resilience would be a mere chance event, a random occurrence.

Resilience differs from other terms such as general positive adjustment, or competence, insofar as it takes into consideration the circumstances and processes under which positive adjustment takes place. One cannot talk about resilience in the absence of adversity. Positive adjustment occurring with (versus without) conditions of adversity often has different correlates and thus reflects different constructs (Luthar, 1999). Furthermore, several studies have found varying antecedents of positive adjustment in general versus resilience in the face of adversity (Rutter, 1990).

The two-dimensional definition of resilience brings with it the challenge of defining our understanding of risk and adversity, as well as positive adjustment. It has been argued that the identification of resilience involves value judgments about differences between expected and observed outcomes, as well as the causes of success and failure (Bartelt, 1994; Kaplan, 1999; Masten, 2001; Rigsby, 1994; Ungar, 2004b). In the following, I will review and respond to concerns raised regarding the conceptualisation of risk and adjustment in resilience research.

Identifying risk

The notion of risk used in resilience research stems from epidemiological research, identifying expected probabilities of maladjustment (Cicchetti & Garmezy, 1993; Masten et al., 1990a; Rutter, 1988). Fundamental to the idea of risk is the predictability of life chances from earlier circumstances. Resilience has been attributed to individuals who beat the odds, who avoid the negative trajectories associated with risks even though they:

(a) were members of high-risk groups, such as children from deprived family backgrounds characterised by material hardship and poverty;
(b) grew up in violent or deprived neighbourhoods;
(c) were born with or acquired major disabilities, injuries or illnesses;

(d) have endured stressful experiences, such as individuals from dysfunctional families or children with mentally ill parents; or
(e) have suffered trauma, such as sexual or physical abuse, or exposure to war-time experiences.

Risk or adversity can comprise genetic, biological, psychological, environmental or socio-economic factors that are associated with an increased probability of maladjustment (Luthar & Cicchetti, 2000; Masten et al., 1990b). Premature birth, mental illness in a parent, divorce, family violence, civic unrest or war – many kinds of adversity and their impact on individual adjustment have been investigated (Garmezy & Rutter, 1983; Haggerty et al., 1994; Rolf et al., 1990). A major risk factor however influencing individual adjustment across domains, affecting children's cognitive competences as well as social-emotional functioning, is socio-economic adversity (Duncan & Brooks-Gunn, 1997; Luthar, 1999; Robins & Rutter, 1990; Rutter & Madge, 1976), which has been chosen as the main focus of this book. The term socio-economic adversity is used here as a descriptor of living conditions characterised by low social status, poor housing, overcrowding and lack of material resources.

Variability in risk exposure

While early studies on resilience focused on a single risk factor, such as maternal psychopathology or experience of a stressful life event such as divorce, it soon became apparent that individual risk factors do not exert their effect in isolation, but in interaction with other influences. The relationship between any single risk factor and subsequent outcomes tends to be weak and usually many variables are involved in determining an outcome (Garmezy & Masten, 1994; Rutter, 1979, 1990; Sameroff & Seifer, 1990; Sameroff, 1999). What distinguishes a high-risk individual from others is not so much exposure to a particular risk factor, but rather a life history characterised by multiple disadvantages. Serious risk emanates from the accumulation of risk effects (Robins & Rutter, 1990), and it has been suggested that it is the number of these factors and their combined effect that exert a deleterious impact on developmental outcomes (Sameroff et al., 1993; Rutter, 1979).

Statistical versus actual risk

Concerns have been raised regarding the difficulties in determining whether all individuals identified as resilient have actually experienced comparable levels of adversity. The issue of defining risk is not a trivial matter, as the risk factor must be a potential cause or precursor of the specified outcome in question and represent a high risk within the sample under consideration. Treating a particular event or experience as reflecting adversity if it shows a significant statistical association with maladjustment or disorder does, however, not account for the many other probabilities of a given event. Risks describe probabilities and not certainties and it has been argued that we have to clearly differentiate between statistical and actual risk (Richters & Weintraub, 1990). Even in circumstances where significant associations have been established between risk exposure and adjustment problems, questions may remain about the specific living conditions of different individuals in a particular sample (Cicchetti & Garmezy, 1993; Kaplan, 1999; Masten, 1994).

Individuals exposed to particular adverse life circumstances are treated as homogeneous groups, despite possible variations in the degree to which their lives are actually shaped by the influence of the particular risk factors in question. Social class, for example, has been widely used as a risk indicator, although it conveys little information about specific experiences to which children within a given level of social class are exposed (Richters & Weintraub, 1990). A child raised by working-class parents will not necessarily experience poor quality care-giving or scarcity of material resources. Moreover, the experience of adversity might only be temporary and not long-lasting. Without more comprehensive information about the risk situation, it cannot be assumed that there actually is a significant risk exposure. The identification of resilience might sometimes be more appropriate for resilient families than for the child within them – or a well-functioning child may not be resilient at all, but may actually have experienced a low-risk situation.

The variability in risk exposure does, however, not necessarily invalidate resilience research based on global risk indices such as social class (Luthar et al., 2000). Knowledge about potential risk factors has been helpful in stimulating research into the processes and mechanisms by which these global risks influence individual adjustment clarifying conditions in which they show their effect and where they don't.

Plurality of meaning

Another related concern addresses the plurality of meaning in evaluations of risk (Bartelt, 1994; Gorden & Song, 1994; Ungar, 2004b). It has been argued that the meaning of the constructs used for the identification of risk as well as the conceptualisation of resilience and adjustment are relative, situational and attributional, whereby the constructs may have a greater significance to the researchers who define or investigate resilience, than for the person who experiences it (Gordon & Song, 1994). It could be possible, for example, that a person identified by a researcher as 'being at-risk' might not consider this label appropriate to describe him- or herself. There are indeed serious concerns regarding stigmatisation and exclusion, predetermining the failure of individuals exposed to severe hardship. Yet, adverse living conditions do exist and it is vital to know what can be done to create environments within which individuals, families and communities can strive. Gordon and Song (1994), for example, focused their research on acts of defiance of negative predictions, and Ungar (2004) demonstrated the multiplicity of pathways leading to adjustment, emphasising the need to appreciate the heterogeneity of outcomes in response to adversity.

Thus, despite concerns regarding the variability of risk exposure, or the dissonance between interpretations of the situation by the individual experiencing it and the researcher, the investigation of the factors and processes associated with variations in response to adversity appears still worthwhile. For example, if most individuals perceived a specific experience as difficult and harmful while others interpret it as relatively neutral, their interpretations could be useful for identifying protective factors or adaptive processes (O'Connor & Rutter, 1996).

Positive adjustment

There is an ongoing debate about what constitutes adaptive functioning and definitions of successful adaptation differ in relation to historical, cultural and developmental contexts (Luthar, 1999; Luthar et al., 2000; Masten et al., 1999; Masten, 2001; Masten & Coatsworth, 1998; Rutter, 2000). The criteria by which positive adaptation is determined have varied considerably between studies. A focus on positive outcomes may not only consider the maintenance or return to adequate functioning after the experience of adversity or trauma, but may also seek to understand how individuals achieve optimal functioning, involving enhanced psychosocial resources and the development of new coping skills (Kaplan, 1999). Positive adjustment has been defined not only in terms of a lack of pathology, the attainment of psychosocial developmental milestones, the statistical average, the utopia of self-actualisation, but also as the ability to negotiate life's developmental crises (Ogbu, 1981; Masten, 2001; Ungar, 2004; Walsh, 1998).

There is some debate as to whether positive adjustment should be reserved for exceptional attainments or for more ordinary achievements.

It has been argued that positive adaptation describes that which is substantially better than what would be expected, given exposure to the risk circumstances being studied (Luthar & Zelazo, 2003). The definition of positive adaptation should also reflect the seriousness of the risks under consideration. For example, for children facing serious trauma it is entirely appropriate to define positive adjustment simply in terms of the absence of psychiatric diagnoses or adequate functioning, rather than superiority in everyday adaptation (Masten, 2003).

It has been stressed that the assessment whether a person is 'doing ok' generally does not require outstanding achievements, but rather refers to behaviour within or above the expected average for a normative cohort (Masten, 2003). In the majority of cases, resilience arises from ordinary adaptive processes rather than rare or extraordinary ones. As Ann Masten has put it: resilience arises from 'ordinary magic' (Masten, 2001). This view offers a far more optimistic outlook for action aiming to promote competence and human capital in individuals and society than the assumption of outstanding capabilities. The criterion of 'doing ok' is, however, itself culturally determined. The identification of positive adjustment implies normative expectations for adaptations and involves judgments about the quality of developmental functioning which have an historical, cultural and developmental reference point.

Context dependency

The outcomes used to define resilience change as a function of age and vary across contexts and cultures. Outcomes are generally defined in terms of judgments regarding appropriate responses that meet societal expectations associated with developmental milestones to be passed at particular life stages (Masten, 1994). Age-dependency, for example, is reflected in measures of children's general competence that include assessments of academic attainment and behavioural adjustment, which have been established as the most consistent childhood predictors of adult adjustment in the world of work, family life and health (Garmezy et al., 1984; Masten et al., 1988; Werner & Smith, 1992). Adjustment in adolescence is concerned with emotional maturation, adjustment to pubertal change and formation of a coherent identity (Erikson, 1959), while positive adjustment in old age has been linked to mastery of daily demands or satisfaction with one's own ageing (Baltes & Mayer, 1999).

It has been argued that existing definitions of resilience are socially constructed and reflect biases grounded in the internalisation of the predominant order we participate in (Ungar, 2004). Concerns regarding the question of who decides the criteria of positive adaptation may become more and more pressing as the number of cross-cultural studies across and within nations increases (Ogbu, 1985). Researchers must become aware of the normative values underlying the identification of successful or unsuccessful outcomes, and learn to distinguish between their own values and interests and those of others who may have different or even opposing values (Kaplan, 1999). For example, among teenagers growing up in persistent and severe poverty, in households where the day-to-day needs of the family for additional resources is strongly present, the wish to leave school and gain full-time paid employment as soon as possible might be the resilient strategy, rather than struggling to stay on in further education (Bartelt, 1994). In defining positive adaptation, the question whether successful development should only be defined within a specific cultural context has to be asked – as well as what perspective has to be adopted when subcultural norms differ from the majority culture (Masten, 1999). Thus, the choice of criteria for identifying positive adjustment has to be made explicit, as it has important implications for the definition of resilience. The following chapters examine academic resilience within two general population samples, focusing on attainments at or above the average within these populations.

Multiple domains of adjustment

Another issue to be considered in defining resilience is the wide variety of outcomes across domains. The range of outcomes encompasses academic, emotional, behavioural or physical adjustment. Not all children respond to adversity in the same way and there are variations in adjustment. For example, it is possible that a child exposed to economic hardship shows good academic performance, but at the same time has behavioural problems (Luthar, 1991). Positive adaptation should be defined across multiple spheres, to avoid overly narrow definitions that can convey a misleading picture. It should be noted that success in a particular domain cannot be assumed to generalise to other spheres – as resilience is not an all-or-nothing phenomenon. It has been suggested that we should identify and differentiate between specific domains of adjustment, i.e. academic, emotional or social resilience, and avoid notions of overall resilience (Luthar, 1993). However, unless multiple domains of adjustment are assessed, only a partial picture of adaptation can be formulated (Cicchetti & Garmezy, 1993). Thus, in the following the associations between academic attainment, behavioural adjustment and adult psychosocial well-being will be examined.

Risk and protection

Protective factors play a role in modifying the negative effects of adverse life circumstances and help to strengthen resilience. Some individuals succeed despite the odds and break the vicious cycle. Previous research has revealed three broad sets of variables operating as protective factors that may impede or halt the impact of adverse experiences. These factors include: characteristics of the individual, the family environment and the wider social context (Masten et al., 1990b; Rutter, 1987; Werner & Smith, 1992). The triarchic set of factors has also been confirmed in studies using the British Cohort data (Bynner et al., 2000c; Joshi et al., 1999, Osborn, 1990, Pilling, 1990; Sacker & Schoon, 2002; Schoon & Parsons, 2002b; Schoon et al., 2004):

- *Individual attributes*: individuals demonstrating early academic resilience despite the experience of socio-economic hardship generally also performed better in most other school tests, demonstrated fewer persistent behaviour problems and had more hobbies and social contacts than their more vulnerable peers. They enjoyed school, showed a strong belief in their own ability, and were academically motivated, i.e. they wanted further education after the minimum school leaving age. They furthermore showed good planning in their partnership and career choices, and had a positive outlook on life.
- *Characteristics of their families*: factors associated with positive adjustment during childhood and adolescence included a stable and supportive family environment, characterised by parents who read to their child, who took an active interest and involvement in their child's education and career planning and who took their children out for joint activities. Another important factor was a supportive father who helped the mother with the household chores.
- *Aspects of the wider social context*: not only parents, but also significant others in the wider social context provide vital sources of support, as for example teachers who recognised the children's capabilities and who encouraged and supported their educational and occupational strivings. Generally, the characteristics of the school environment played a significant role in fostering adaptive development. There was also evidence to suggest the importance of positive community forces, such as support and cohesion among neighbours and a sense of belonging to the community.

This triarchic set of factors can be understood as psychosocial resources that support or promote adaptive development. Individuals who can draw on many, or high levels of personal and social resources are more effective in coping with adversity than individuals with fewer (or lower level) resources.

It has been argued that protective factors are simply the opposite of risk factors (Stouthamer-Loeber et al., 1993) and that the same variable could be categorised as a protective factor or in its reverse as a risk factor. Family harmony, for example, can be a protective factor, while family conflict would act as a risk factor. Yet, some variables show curvilinear instead of linear effects, such as parental control, where both excessive strictness or indulgence may carry risks (Rutter, 1990). Other variables might show their effect more strongly at one end of the dimension, as for example mother's age, where teenage motherhood is associated with increased risk effects, although being born to a relatively elderly mother does not necessarily provide benefits (Schoon & Parsons, 2002b). Furthermore, the risks associated with mother's age might not derive from the biological age of the mother as such, but from some other linked features, such as social disadvantage. Resilience is a relative phenomenon, depending on complex interactions between constitutional factors and life circumstances. What is needed is a better understanding of the person–environment interactions, the underlying mechanisms and processes that enable individuals to develop and maintain psychosocial resources despite the experiences of adversity. Issues related to protective factors and processes and their dynamic person–environment interactions are discussed in more detail in the following chapters, especially in chapter 5.

Critique of the resilience concept

The conceptualisation of resilience and its various implementations in research are not without criticism and serious concerns have been raised about the value of the concept – about how it has been measured and how it has been used in the explanation of behaviours and outcomes (Glantz & Sloboda, 1999; Rutter, 1990). In particular, concerns have been identified regarding the subjective and often unarticulated assumptions underlying the identification and operationalisation of resilience (Kaplan, 1999; Tarter & Vanyukov, 1999). There is no consensus on the referent of the term. A major limitation of the concept is that it is tied to the normative judgments of what constitutes positive or desirable outcomes (Bartelt, 1994). Issues relating to what it means to be successful, and who defines success have already been discussed, highlighting concerns regarding expectations and value judgments involved in deciding what constitutes an adaptive outcome. To avoid arbitrary or ethnocentric values becoming reified and universal, researchers must make clear the values and context-dependency of criteria underlying the identification of successful or unsuccessful outcomes and specify the outcome variable of interest as well as its evaluative significance for representatives of different segments of society. Furthermore, the prediction model specifying the causes of adjustment or maladjustment must be explicit and as complete as possible, taking into account the multilevel influences involved in shaping individual development (Richters & Weintraub, 1990).

Resilience as trait or process

A focus on adaptive functioning bears the danger of identifying resilience in terms of the characteristics of individuals who succeed in life, following the assumption that everyone can make it if they only try hard enough (Kaplan, 1999; Tarter & Vanyukov, 1999). Personality traits such as hardiness, stress-resistance, ego resilience and ego strength (Block & Block, 1980; Kobasa, Maddi & Kahn, 1982) have been used synonymously to characterise individuals who due to this attribute are able to withstand stress without permanent damage. Yet, although individuals may manifest resilience in their behaviour and life patterns, resilience is not a personality characteristic. Adaptive functioning in the face of adversity is not only dependent on the characteristics of the individual, but is greatly influenced by processes and interactions arising from the family and the wider environment. Individual development is continually produced, sustained and changed by the socio-historical context experienced.

To conceptualise resilience as a personality trait bears the danger of blaming the victim, of rendering individuals personally responsible for their problems, instead of investigating the underlying processes that allow some individuals to succeed in life despite the experience of adversity, or investigating the barriers to their development (Tarter & Vanyukov, 1999). Terms such as resiliency should be used with caution as they carry a misleading connotation of a discrete personality attribute (Masten, 1994; Luthar et al., 2000). Likewise use of the term resilient as an adjective for individuals should be avoided. It should instead be applied to profiles of person–environment interactions (Luthar & Zelazo, 2003).

While personality characteristics are useful to explain individual differences in response to stress or adversity, the fact that some individuals show positive outcomes despite the experience of serious and prolonged adversity, while others not exposed to adversity do not, cannot be attributed to having a high or a low score on a trait such as resilience. What is vital for a better understanding of the phenomenon is the consideration of dynamic person–environment interactions reflecting adaptive responses to adversity. The same stressor can either strengthen or attenuate a behavioural disposition, depending on the interaction with other factors (Masten et al., 1990b; Rutter, 1990). It has now been widely recognised that positive adjustment in the face of adversity is dependent on the person–environment interactions that bring about adaptation, and resilience has been described as a dynamic process (Luthar & Cicchetti, 2000; Garmezy & Rutter, 1983; Masten, 1999; Rutter, 1990, 1999).

Conclusion

Despite the significant conceptual problems raised here, the study of resilience should not be abandoned and we should strive towards a better understanding of adaptive functioning in the face of risk or adversity. A more detailed knowledge of the factors and processes enabling individuals to withstand and overcome adversity might be helpful to other individuals facing similar adverse circumstances and might help them to redirect development in a more adaptive direction, improving the odds of a desired outcome. There may as well be benefits in bringing issues of variations in individual response to adversity to the attention of policy makers. In particular, the shift from a deficiency or disease model to a more optimistic focus on strengths, assets and adaptive functioning will bring new impetus to the design and development of preventive and treatment interventions. What is needed is not the abandonment of the concept but to salvage the useful aspects, and difficulties in conceptualisation, operationalisation and measurement should be addressed. For resilience to be a useful concept in a progressive research tradition, it must be embedded in a theoretical framework that guides the investigation and understanding of the multilevel causal structures and processes that shape individual development across time and contexts.

2 Towards a developmental-contextual systems model of adjustment

> The ecology of human development involves the scientific study of the progressive, mutual accommodation between an active, growing human being and the changing properties of the immediate settings in which the developing person lives, as this process is affected by relations between these settings, and by the larger contexts in which the settings are embedded.
>
> (Urie Bronfenbrenner, 1979, p. 21)

This chapter presents a developmental-contextual systems model of adaptation across the life course. The model aims to integrate findings of previous research regarding factors and processes implicated in positive adjustment of individuals facing socio-economic deprivation into a guiding framework for research. The basic proposition underlying the approach is that human development takes place in a socio-historical context. It is argued that for a better understanding of the processes leading to positive adaptation despite the experience of adversity it is necessary to identify the interplay between individual and environment over time. Existing theoretical propositions for the study of resilience will be reviewed and integrated into a developmental-contextual systems model for the empirical study of adaptations in context and time.

The adopted person-process-context-time perspective is informed by assumptions formulated within the ecological theory of human development with its emphasis on multiple interacting spheres of influence (Bronfenbrenner, 1989; Bronfenbrenner, 1995; Bronfenbrenner & Ceci, 1994), as well as life-course theory with its focus on the temporal dimension and developmental effects of social change and transitions (Elder, 1998). The model specifies multiple levels of influence shaping individual variations in response to adversity, the dynamic interactions between a developing individual and a changing context, the developmental integration of earlier levels of adjustment into later ones, the directedness and human agency of developmental processes, as well as continuities and variations in adjustment, reflecting the embeddedness of human development in socio-historical change.

Multiple levels of influence

In the early studies of children experiencing parental psychopathology, family disruptions or poverty it became apparent that positive adjustment in the face of adversity is associated with a number of protective factors leading to the amelioration of or protection against risk factors (Garmezy, 1985; Werner & Smith, 1982; Werner & Smith, 1992). These protective factors were found to operate at three broad levels, including influences from the individual, the family and the wider community (as already discussed in Chapter 1). The so-called triarchic framework of resilience (Luthar et al., 2000) has been tremendously influential and the three broad sets of protective influences have been shown to be highly robust predictors of resilience in a variety of domains (Fergusson & Lynskey, 1996; Luthar, 1999; Masten et al., 1988; Seifer et al., 1992; Wyman et al., 1991). Knowledge about the wide range of protective factors associated with adaptive functioning in high-risk conditions does, however, not explain how some individuals are able to overcome adversity while others are not. What is needed is a better understanding of the mechanisms and processes underlying positive adjustment in the face of adversity, linking the different spheres of influence in time and place.

Ecological approaches in the study of resilience

The ecological perspective of human development provides a heuristic for understanding how multiple factors influence individual development and adjustment. Bronfenbrenner (1979) introduced the notion of development-in-context, which postulates that developmental outcomes are shaped by the interaction of genetic, biological, psychological and sociological factors in the context of environmental support. The theory was inspired by the 'awareness of the resilience, versatility, and promise of the species *Homo sapiens* as evidenced by its capacity to adapt to, tolerate and especially create the ecologies in which it lives and grows' (Bronfenbrenner, 1979, p. xiii). According to this approach, resilience is based on the complex and bi-directional transactions between individual and context. Different contexts such as culture, neighbourhood and family are conceptualised as nested spheres of influence varying in proximity to the individual ranging from micro to macro. The developing child, for example, is rooted within many interrelated systems, such as families, schools and neighbourhoods, as well as the wider socio-historical context.

Bronfenbrenner's conceptualisation of context provides a crucial contribution for a better understanding of the different sources of influence on individual development and is vitally important for this study. He differentiated between the proximal environment, which is directly experienced by the individual (as for example, the family environment) and more distal cultural and social value systems that have an indirect effect on the individual, often mediated by the more proximal context. The conceptualisation of multiple spheres of influence and the transactional interchanges between individual and context has become greatly influential in guiding and informing studies of resilience in at-risk populations (Cicchetti & Lynch, 1993; Cicchetti, 1993; Egeland et al., 1993; Sameroff & Chandler, 1975).

Bronfenbrenner also recognised that a better understanding of the forces and experiences shaping human development allows us to bridge the gap between empirical research and the application of knowledge. Based on research evidence, guiding principles for the design and implementation of specific, developmentally appropriate interventions can be obtained for improving the well-being and development of human beings by influencing the conditions of their lives.

Structural-organisational perspectives of human development

Another issue emerging from the early studies was the importance of a developmental perspective for research on risk and resilience. Development constitutes a patterning of adaptation across time. Only by understanding the nature of the underlying developmental processes can we achieve a better understanding of why certain individuals remain well adjusted despite the experience of adversity, while others don't. It has been argued that early patterns of adaptation provide a framework for, and are transformed and integrated into, later levels of functioning (Glantz & Sloboda, 1999; Egeland et al., 1993; Sroufe & Rutter, 1984). Developmental outcomes at a particular life stage are rarely final endpoints but are themselves positive or negative influences contributing to subsequent outcomes and stages.

The structural-organisational perspective, conceptualising development as a hierarchical integrative process, has gained increasing popularity in the risk and resilience literature, especially in the field of developmental psychopathology (Cicchetti & Schneider-Rosen, 1986; Sroufe, 1979). The focus on positive outcomes despite experience of adversity is not considered to be at all inconsistent with conceptions developed within developmental psychopathology which is concerned with the investigation of 'the origins and time course of a given disorder, its varying manifestations with development, its precursors and sequelae, and its relation to non-disordered patterns of behaviour' (Sroufe & Rutter,

1984). It is assumed that knowledge of normal development can inform the study of deviant outcomes and conversely, that knowledge of deviant and at-risk populations can enhance understanding of normal development, promoting our understanding of atypical development, but also of normal development, especially regarding individual differences in development and the risk and protective processes associated with different types of developmental outcomes (Cicchetti, 1990; Cicchetti & Garmezy, 1993; Luthar, 1993; Masten et al., 1990; Rutter, 1987).

Current adaptational patterns are viewed as the product of a transactional process between the developing person and the environment (Cicchetti & Schneider-Rosen, 1986; Egeland et al., 1993; Sroufe, 1979) which, in turn, become predictors for future developmental outcomes. The assumption of hierarchical integrative processes asserts consistency and coherence of individual adaptation across time as it implies that future adaptation and developmental outcomes can be predicted from knowledge of earlier adaptation patterns (Sroufe, 1979). Yet, the very definition of resilience predicates changes in trajectories and deviation from predicted relationships. What is needed is a better understanding of why certain individuals are beating the odds.

Self-active developing systems

The notion of self-regulating developing systems, which are open to and interact with their environments has been developed by Ludwig von Bertalanffy in his formulation of systems theory. This was conceptualised as a counterpoint to mechanistic preconceptions, arguing for an historical, developmental and organismic concept of social behaviour (von Bertalanffy, 1968). The idea of developing systems is informed by theoretical biology and attempts to differentiate living from non-living matter. Living systems are understood as a unified whole where most levels are interrelated and are characterised by self-activity and historicity. Likewise in his ecological systems theory, Bronfenbrenner (1979) emphasises the need for the non-reductionist analysis of individual behaviour requiring the simultaneous description of several spheres of influence, thereby moving beyond simple cause and effect explanations of behaviour.

In this regard, the notions of equifinality and multifinality, derived from systems theory, are relevant for a better understanding of risk and resilience processes. Equifinality refers to varied pathways leading to similar outcomes. Multifinality assumes that a single component or risk factor may act differently depending on the organisation of the system in which it operates (Bronfenbrenner, 1989; Bronfenbrenner, 1979; Cicchetti & Rogosch, 1996; von Bertalanffy, 1968). Multiple pathways can lead to similar manifest outcomes and different outcomes may spring from the same source. Some individuals appear to escape the potential adverse effects of disadvantage. Changes in development are possible at many points across the life course, illustrating the potential diversity in onto-genetic outcome, regardless of similarity in risks experienced (Cicchetti et al., 1993; Lerner, 1996).

Furthermore, living systems strive actively to continue functioning, i.e. surviving, under various conditions by purposively changing the environment and themselves (von Bertalanffy, 1968; Bronfenbrenner, 1995). The goal-directedness of self-active systems is historically situated in time and space, and includes the accommodation to external conditions and at the same time the adaptation to internal needs. Since environment and individual are in transaction, it follows that developmental outcomes at consequent time points not only reflect previous levels of adaptation but also intervening environmental inputs. As such, changes in the level of adaptation at later time points can be expected, based on changes in the environment, or changes guided by active individual choice and self-organisation involving reciprocal person–environment interactions.

The life course as organising principle

The principles of human agency, bi-directional person–environment interactions and historicity are also central to the assumptions for-mulated within life-course theory, which emphasises the embedded-ness of human development in social structures and historical change (Bronfenbrenner, 1995; Elder, 1985; Elder, 1998; Lerner, 1984; Lerner, 1996; Sameroff, 1983). The critical contribution of life-course theory is to incorporate the component of socio-historical time into the ecological person-process-context model (Elder, 1998). The developing person is viewed as a dynamic whole, involving person–environment transactions over time. Research of the life course is concerned with the description, explanation and modification of constancy and change of behaviour throughout the life course, underscoring the link between contextual change and individual development (Elder, 1974/1999; 1998).

The life-course perspective emerged in the 1960s from within the intellectual traditions of sociology and psychology, both trying to breach disciplinary boundaries.[1] It has to be differentiated from the more rigidly

---

[1] In the following the terms life span and life course are used interchangeably. Yet, there are field-specific preferences, and since the origin of the West Virginia Conference Series (Goulet & Baltes, 1970), psychologists tend to prefer life span, whereas sociologists prefer the term life course.

defined life-cycle approach (Giele & Elder, 1998) which conceptualises human development as a series of fixed, normative stages through which individuals pass during their life course. The life course approach instead describes the transitions from one life stage to another as movements involving the interaction between a changing individual and a changing context, allowing for many diverse events and roles that do not necessarily proceed in a given sequence. It acknowledges the influence of structural change over historical time, and accounts for variations in individual experience according to socio-historical and geographical locations (Elder, 1974/1999).

Today the life-course approach is widely accepted as providing a set of background assumptions that guide and provide common ground for research on a great number of issues (Colby, 1998; Mortimer & Shanahan, 2003). The assumption of mutual embeddedness of individual and context, and the conceptualisation of development as the dynamic interaction between a developing or changing individual and a changing context is recognised across disciplines (Baltes, 1987; Cicchetti & Lynch, 1993; Cicchetti & Aber, 1998; Elder, 1998; Lerner, 1984; Moen et al., 1995; Sameroff et al., 1993). The notion of dynamic interaction implies that individuals influence the contexts that influence them, that no one level of analysis in isolation can be considered the sole cause of change. The notion of embeddedness addresses the multiple levels of analysis, e.g. the biological, psychological, social and historical context contributing to human functioning. The levels do not function in parallel, as independent domains, but there are dynamic bi-directional interactions between the levels. Each level may be both a product and a producer of the functioning and changes at all other levels. Furthermore individual development is shaped by conditions and events occurring during the historical period lived through by the individual. Different contextual conditions will lead to different development when different individuals interact in them and the same attributes in individuals will lead to different developments when they interact in different socio-historical contexts.

Key principles of the life-course approach

Life-course theory is based on five key principles:

1 Human development is a life-long process.
2 Individuals construct their own life course through the choices and actions they take within the opportunities and constraints of history and social circumstances, a principle also referred to as human agency.

3 The life course is embedded and shaped by social structures and the historical times and places experienced by individuals over their lifetime.
4 The developmental antecedents and consequences of life transitions, events and behaviour patterns vary according to their timing in a person's life.
5 Lives are lived interdependently, and social and historical influences bear on this network of linked lives (Elder, 1998).

According to the *principle of linked lives*, the misfortune and success of a family, for example, is shared through its members. Lives are lived interdependently and individual experiences are connected to the lives of significant others. Another key theme of life-course analysis concerns the *timing* of developmental transitions. The impact of earlier experiences and attainments on later outcomes cannot be understood without reference to issues of timing and transition patterns. For example, early life transitions such as entry into the labour market directly after minimum education, or early parenthood can affect subsequent transitions even after many years. Furthermore, lives are embedded and shaped by the socio-historical context in which they occur, described by the *principle of historical time and place*. Events beyond individual control can influence later outcomes, such as the Great Depression during the 1920s, which brought severe hardship for members of the Oakland Growth Study and their families (Elder, 1974/1999). Yet, when confronted with mounting economic pressures individuals and their families often worked out successful adaptations, conceptualised by the *principle of human agency*. Through the choices made and actions taken, individuals were able to take advantage of opportunities and to tackle constraints imposed through the socio-historical circumstances. Individuals are not passively exposed to experiential factors, but can become producers of their own development in that they affect the context that affects them. Yet, life chances and opportunities are not equally distributed. They vary according to social origin, gender, race, age and the wider socio-historical context experienced (Duncan & Brooks-Gunn, 1997; Elder, 1998; Rutter, 1988).

The importance of the life-course perspective for this study lies in its scope to investigate how individual lives are mutually shaped by personal characteristics and the socio-historical environment. The life-course approach allows us to integrate process and structure and to link individual time with historical time.

A developmental-contextual model for the study of resilience

Insights formulated within a life-course perspective are unfortunately easier to appreciate than to operationalise. The actual practice of life-course research has lagged behind the conceptual advances, partly because the long-term longitudinal studies needed to investigate its assumptions are resource-intensive methods (Colby, 1998). The developmental-contextual systems model outlined in the following will form the basis for the consequent empirical testing of various assumptions about the dynamic interactions between individual and context in developing and maintaining positive adjustment despite the experience of socio-economic adversity during the transition from dependent child to independent adult.

Figure 2.1 illustrates the different spheres of influence shaping individual adjustment. Notably the varied spheres do not exist in isolation, they are interrelated and mutually interdependent. Furthermore, the model advocates a systems view to resilience (Garmezy, 1985; Haggerty et al., 1994; Rutter, 1990) postulating a holistic approach incorporating multi-level person–context interactions. The model also captures the transactional nature of development over time, focusing on the

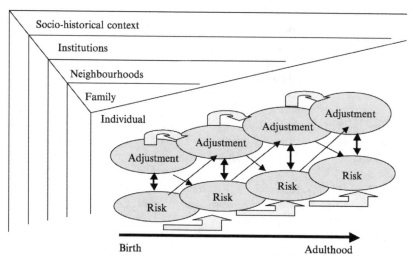

Figure 2.1. A developmental-contextual model of resilience.

reciprocal interactions between risk experiences and individual adjustment, which are embedded in the wider socio-historical context.

The model is an explicit developmental model, allowing us to assess the dynamic interactions between individual and context. Any point in the life span has to be understood as the consequence of past experience and as the launch pad for subsequent experiences and conditions. For example, early adjustment patterns influence later adjustment, and early risk experiences are linked to the experience of risk at later life stages. Early experiences and the meanings attached to them are carried forward into consequent situations. Yet, life-long development may also involve processes that do not originate at birth or early childhood but in later periods.

Transitions and turning points

One of the key concepts of life-course theory concerns transitions or changes from one state to another, such as moving from primary into secondary education, entry into paid employment, or forming a family (Elder, 1998). Transitions are embedded in trajectories that describe the dynamic state of behaviour and achievements extending over a substantial part of, or the entire, life span. While trajectories imply cumulations of experience stretching over the life course, transitions refer to changes in state or states, such as leaving full-time education. Transitional events have been distinguished from life events in that transitions require reorganisation at either the structural or functional level during entry into and exit from a particular state (Rutter, 1996). Different influences may operate at each phase of the transition process and each transition phase might involve a choice point with its options and constraints (Elder & Shanahan, 2006).

While most transition experiences, as for example entry into further education, marriage or parenthood, generally promote continuity and stability, accentuating existing features of development (Elder & Caspi, 1988b), it might also be the case that transitional events result in life-long change. A substantial and enduring change in the course of development, often occurring during transitions, represents a turning point (Elder, 1985; Rutter, 1996). It has been argued that understanding how individuals navigate developmental transitions and choices is the crux of understanding risk and resilience across the life span (Graber & Brooks-Gunn, 1996).

A basic principle of the life course is that human development extends over the entire life span and that behaviour cannot be fully explained by restricting analysis to specific life stages, such as mid-childhood, adolescence or mid-life (Baltes, 1987; Elder, 1998). It is only by following children from birth into and through the adult years that we can chart their developmental trajectories and pathways. Individual differences in the experience of negotiating a transition are associated with a variety of conditions, including development before the transition, the timing of the transition and the wider socio-historical context in which the transition occurs with its opportunities and constraints. The potential for development is shaped by the reciprocal influences of person–environment interactions that differ in terms of timing (onset, duration, termination), direction, order, or the socio-historical context in which they take place. The developmental impact of events is contingent on when they occur in a person's life, and the influence of an event at a particular life stage is shaped within the context of personal biography.

The research presented here focuses on academic adjustment in the face of socio-economic adversity, as well as other life accomplishments, thereby reflecting the complexity of interlinking life transitions. In almost all Western cultures, academic attainment has been established as the most consistent childhood predictor of adult achievement in the world of work, family life and health (Garmezy et al., 1984; Masten et al., 1988; Werner & Smith, 1992, 2001). Without general and specialised forms of education and training, individuals will be excluded from a number of occupations or opportunities, regardless of their abilities and aptitudes. To concentrate on one outcome only, however, would oversimplify the lives of people, as transition outcomes are rarely final endpoints and are intrinsically linked. They themselves have to be understood as positive and/or negative influences shaping subsequent outcomes and stages. Developmental functioning has to be considered as continuously evolving states of being, where outcomes or consequences are themselves precursors to subsequent experiences and events.

Educational transitions, as well as the transition from school to work, are shaped by the opportunities and constraints of social structure and historical context. Socio-economic adversity in particular, which is the risk factor under investigation here, has been shown to have a vital influence on individual adjustment. The aim of this study is to investigate how individual attainments and socio-economic adversity are linked over time. The factors influencing individual development are not seen in isolation, but as embedded in a wider social and historical context.

Spheres of influence

The model shown in Figure 2.1 differentiates between characteristics of the individual, the family, neighbourhoods, institutions, and the wider socio-historical and cultural context. It takes into consideration the distinction between a proximal and distal environment ranging from micro to macro, introduced by Bronfenbrenner (1979). The proximal context is directly experienced by the individual, while the distal context reflects the cultural and social value systems that have an indirect effect on the individual, often mediated by the more proximal context. Proximal processes reflect the immediate day-to-day experiences that most directly shape individual development, as for example, in the family environment. The form, power, content and direction of the proximal processes affecting development vary systematically as a joint function of the person, the environment (both immediate and more remote) in which the processes are taking place and the nature of the developmental outcome under consideration (Bronfenbrenner & Ceci, 1994).

Individual characteristics

Individual characteristics clearly play a role in determining the life path and the notion that individuals are active agents that take control over their environment is central to the life-course perspective (Bronfenbrenner, 1979; Elder, 1985; Elder, 1998). Individuals adjust their behaviour to a changing context and variations in life-course patterns can be understood as differences in adaptation to circumstances in order to achieve control over the environment (Elder, 1985; Giele & Elder, 1998).

Specific aptitudes and skills, such as intellectual, creative, socio-affective, sensory–motor and other abilities, are a necessary but not a sufficient precondition for successful adaptation. These person characteristics have been described by Bronfenbrenner (1995) as psychological resources and liabilities. He differentiates these from a more dynamic set of person attributes: the developmentally instigative characteristics that also affect the course and character of psychological functioning and growth. During infancy, such dynamic tendencies are expressed through selective response to stimuli. These early initiatives become increasingly guided by emergent conceptions of the environment and the self and are subsequently expressed through differential interests, values, beliefs and goals in relation to persons, objects and symbols of the environment (Bronfenbrenner, 1995, p. 634).

Human agency By recognising and exercising their own compe-tencies, interests and values, individuals formulate expectations by projecting themselves into the future. The formulation of ambitions, aspirations, or a life plan helps to direct and guide the transition from present to the future (Bühler, 1933/1959; Clausen, 1993; Ginzberg et al., 1951; Heckhausen, 1999; Little, 1983; Nurmi, 1993; Schneider & Stevenson, 1999; Schoon & Parsons, 2002a). Tenaciousness and persist-ence in pursuing an ambition, or willingness to work hard at realising one's potential are key factors in developing competences when striving to gain control over a changing environment (Heckhausen, 1999). Teenage aspirations, for example, can act like a compass to help chart a life course and provide direction for spending time and energy and have been shown to influence educational attainment, career choices and future earnings (Clausen, 1993; Elder, 1968; Elder, 1974/1999; Schneider & Stevenson, 1999; Schoon & Parsons, 2002a). Yet, expectations and aspirations might have to change and will have to be modified depending on the social reality the individual encounters. Inevitable experiences of failure and defeat may endanger motivational determination. Compromises might be necessary, adjusting aspirations and self-evaluations that were either too high or too modest (Baltes, 1987; Ginzberg & Herma, 1964; Gottfredson, 1981; Heckhausen, 1999; Heinz, 2002).[2]

Bounded agency The long-range planning of a life not only involves individual-based phenomena, but individual life projects have to be synchronised with the desires and goals of others. Lives are lived interdependently and the social relationships in people's lives can be thought of as a 'developmental context' (Hartup & Laursen, 1991). Life planning can include others as co-actors (either indirectly or directly), take significant others into consideration by constructing life plans for others, or attempt to convince others to follow (Smith, 1996). It thus can be argued that the origin, content and context of life plans generally has a social base (Cantor et al., 1987). Furthermore, human agency is always expressed in circumstances that are more or less limited by available options and real world constraints, a phenomenon referred to as 'bounded agency' (Evans 2002; Heinz, 2002; Shanahan, 2000). Social origin, gender and ethnicity circumscribe the range of options available to the individual as do historical events beyond individual control, such

---

[2] Ginzberg & Herma (1964) emphasise the importance of recognising when to adjust one's expectations: some individuals are more adept than others in profiting from their experi-ences and in adjusting their expectations when necessary, while others may waste much of their energy running after illusions, while still others might settle for too little.

as changes in the labour market, economic downturn, or the outbreak of war (Elder, 1974/1999).

Biological dispositions

Another factor to be considered is the role of biological dispositions as an underpinning of human development. Biological influences on development are typically reflected in age-related and relatively universal patterns of change, which include maturational processes as well as age-related decline (Heckhausen, 1999). Proponents of behavioural genetics see the course of human development as a function of genetically controlled maturational sequences (Scarr, 1992). Yet, findings show that in no case is the genetic determination so strong that there is no room for environmental effects (Plomin & Daniels, 1987). More recent developmental bioecological approaches have conceptualised genes and other biological variables as contributors to reciprocal, dynamic processes which can only be fully understood in relation to the socio-cultural environment in which they take place (Bronfenbrenner & Ceci, 1994; Gottlieb et al., 1998; Horowitz, 2000; Moffitt & Caspi, 2001; Elder & Shanahan, 2006).

Family influences

Throughout the whole life course, human development takes place through processes of progressively more complex reciprocal interaction between the developing individual and the persons, objects and symbols in his or her immediate environment. These interactions have been referred to as proximal processes, which must occur on a fairly regular basis over extended periods of time in order to be effective (Bronfenbrenner & Ceci, 1994).

Family origin is assumed to have a direct effect on attainment through a wide range of mechanisms and interactions that begin at birth or even prenatally. Individuals born into more privileged families will encounter more educational opportunities, greater access to financial resources, role models and informal/kinship networks than their less privileged peers (Bourdieu & Passeron, 1977; Coleman, 1988; Featherman & Lerner, 1985; Keating & Hertzman, 1999; Schulenberg et al., 1984). Getting off to a good start can mean an increased likelihood of encountering opportunities and of developing successful adjustment patterns. The same effect, though in the opposite direction, can occur for those who are not born so lucky and who consequently acquire an enhanced likelihood of risk experiences. This principle of cumulating advantages or disadvantages is sometimes referred to as the 'Matthew effect' due to its link to the Gospel passage that says: 'Unto every one that hath shall be given, he shall have abundance: but from him that hath not shall be taken away even that which he hath.' (Matthew 25:29)

Caregiver relationship Longitudinal studies of children and adolescents who developed competences despite the experience of severe adversity emphasise the importance of caregiver relationships for successful adaptation (Masten, 1994; Rutter, 1999; Werner & Smith, 1982; Werner & Smith, 1992). Beyond the provision of physical care, including the soothing and stimulation of emotions, the caregiver is providing a secure base for young children to explore the environment. There is evidence that the quality of early parent–child relationships had predictive significance for success in later development tasks (Carlson & Sroufe, 1995). Parental warmth, involvement and moderate control have been associated with children's adjustment and achievement (Baumrind, 1978; Macoby, 1980). Family factors associated with educational resilience include parenting styles, parental involvement and expectations for the child's education (Clark, 1983; Coleman, 1988; Eccles & Harold, 1993; Epstein, 1990; Lee & Croninger, 1994; Schneider & Stevenson, 1999). Parents influence the development of educational achievement by encouraging their children to succeed academically (Reynolds & Walberg, 1991), or through direct involvement with schools (Steinberg et al., 1996).

The quality of parent–child relationships, parental involvement and parental expectations for their child can be influenced by socio-economic adversity. For example, the experience of economic hardship, income loss and unemployment may reduce parental responsiveness (Conger et al., 1993; Elder, 1974/1999; Elder & Caspi, 1988a; Sampson & Laub, 1994). It has also been argued that characteristics of the child, such as a difficult temperament, play a role in determining parenting styles, and that there is evidence of a two-way interaction (O'Connor & Rutter, 1996; Rutter, 1999).

Linked lives Individual development is not only influenced by experiences within the family environment. Throughout the life course, lives are lived interdependently within networks of shared relationships (Elder, 1985; Elder, 1998). The principle of 'linked lives' extends beyond the family to friends, peers, neighbours, teachers and employers. It describes the interconnections among individuals, the family, the community and the institutions in which individual development is embedded. A confluence of influences interacts to shape individual development. The conceptualisation of social structures and context beyond the immediate family context allows for a more comprehensive incorporation of the multiple environmental settings influencing individual development, and also for the investigation of how the more distal environments impact on the more proximal, microsystemic environments that mediate the effects of the distal ecological system. The principle of linked lives also informs a better understanding of social transitions and the notions of role sequence and synchronisation (Elder, 1998).

Neighbourhoods

In recent years there has been an increasing interest in the effects of neighbourhoods on individual adjustment, following the recognition that neighbourhoods are the primary social contexts for many young people in contemporary society. It has been argued that neighbourhoods can be considered as the cradle of risk shaping the lives of children, their family and the wider community (Booth & Crouter, 2001). The effects of neighbourhoods are considered to be particularly pronounced in inner-city settings characterised by poverty, crime and violence (Luthar, 1999). Children and young people growing up in neighbourhoods with a high proportion of low-income families are at an increased risk of behavioural problems, such as aggressive behaviour and academic maladjustment (Duncan et al., 1994), while living in more affluent neighbourhoods would result in better outcomes for children and families. Brooks-Gunn (1995) for example, drawing on research by Jencks (Jencks & Petersen, 1992) and Wilson (Wilson, 1991; Wilson, 1987), argues that adaptive development can be fostered through improved social organisation involving good neighbourhood resources (such as libraries, community centres, high-quality child care and local parks), collective socialisation involving norms, sanctions and reciprocity among neighbours, as well as a general participation in the mainstream economy. Thus, research on the factors and processes enabling young people to fully develop their potential should not stop at the family level, but aim to identify how to diminish the risks individuals are exposed to in their everyday lives, and how to improve and build up supportive structures in the wider environment.

Institutions

The school environment, in general, is a powerful shaper or a deterrent to the development of individual potential. When children enter school they encounter a new world of expectations outside the family (Masten & Coatsworth, 1998). School activities, both inside and outside the classroom; interpersonal relations with teachers, students and other staff; various roles and role expectations; physical, structural and material features, all render the school environment a most important context for shaping the expectations and outlook of young people (Vondracek et al., 1986). In the school context, young people have their first encounter with a structured social arena within which to experience the 'sense of industry', the consequences of social and academic competence, competition and power relationships (Erikson, 1959). It can be argued that children's experience in this new environment is important in at least three respects: the notions they acquire about themselves as academic performers in the subject matters they 'learn'; exposition to the principles, rules and values such as achievement motivation that regulate selection, placement, as well as promotion in our society, and also the experience of interacting with friends and acquaintances – learning to get along with teachers and peers.

Teacher expectations, for example, have been shown to influence not only teacher–student interactions, but also student performance (Brophy & Good, 1974; Cooper, 1979). Teachers develop preferences for certain students who are perceived as college bound and motivated, generally children from privileged families (Alexander et al., 1987; Finley, 1984; Heyns, 1974; Kerckhoff, 1993; Rist, 2000; Spring, 1976). Children from disadvantaged families, in contrast, are given less positive attention, fewer learning opportunities and less reinforcement for instances of good performance (McLoyd, 1998). Students, in turn, are influenced by their teachers' feelings about their abilities (Eccles & Wigfield, 1985; Parsons et al., 1982).

The school setting also prepares the young person for the world of work, providing information, advice and experience relevant to the impending transition from school to work. Within the workplace, employers have expectations about their employees and expect collaboration towards achieving a common goal (Warr, 1999). The experience of the world of work requires the developing person to become an active participant. Finding a job, changing jobs, losing jobs, or changing careers are major transitions in the life course of every individual. The reason why some individuals are more likely to achieve than others lies often in the nature of the chosen occupations, the necessary requirements for entry, the structure of the organisations in which people work, and also the general economic climate. If there are no jobs available, and unemployment rates are high, it is particularly difficult to establish a successful career. Transitions are shaped by the opportunities and constraints imposed by social structures and the wider socio-historical context in which they are embedded (Elder, 1994).

The wider socio-historical context

Life-long development underscores the need for investigating the impact of a changing socio-historical context on individual development. The impact of social change in childhood interacts with subsequent forms of social change across the life span, linking historical time with individual time (Elder et al., 1993; Modell, 1976; Shanahan, 2000). Societal circumstances beyond the control of the individual, such as economic depression or the outbreak of war, contribute considerably to the development of potential. A major task confronting the individual throughout the life course is: how to cope effectively with the changing social reality. For a comprehensive understanding of individual development we cannot isolate individuals and their immediate context from the wider socio-historical context in which their actions are carried out. The following analysis is based on data collected from two birth cohorts born twelve years apart. Both data sets are of immense value for investigating the embeddedness of human development in a changing socio-historical context, which is described in more detail in Chapter 3.

Cross-cohort comparison

The cohort data enable the assessment of long-term influences of early experiences, tracing antecedent factors and processes that influence present circumstances and characteristics of individuals and groups. Unlike cross-sectional studies, which compare developmental changes in different age groups each observed once at the same point in time, longitudinal studies follow individuals as they develop over time. In comparison to retrospective studies, the prospective approach has a number of methodological advantages, minimising problems of memory error and distortion. Reports of early life events are not influenced by knowledge of the subsequent personal history, the cohorts include appropriate controls and the conjoined impact of different factors experienced at different time points can be analysed in a multivariate, multicausal model. Being able to draw on longitudinal data collected for two cohorts of individuals born at different time points, permits inter-cohort comparisons and allows for the control of age and cohort effects to which any single longitudinal study is subject (Baltes et al., 1988; Giele & Elder, 1998; Schaie, 1965).

Age, cohort and period effects The birth year of cohort members locates them in an historical time and related social changes. Cohort members encounter the same historical events at different ages and stages in their life course. Developmental changes, such as changes in height or weight or in individual behaviour, associated with the biological or developmental time elapsed since the births of individuals are referred to as *age effects*. Studying only one cohort of individuals bears the danger of confounding age changes and cohort specific differences. For example, differences in behavioural adjustment at different ages may be confused with differences that result not from age but from the effects of membership in different birth cohorts. *Cohort effects* refer to the socially shared experience of age peers, which might be different for individuals born at different times. A cohort is defined as an aggregate of individuals within a geographically or otherwise delineated population who experience the same significant life event within a given period of time (Glenn, 1977; Ryder, 1965; Menard, 2002). Cohort effects can thus be regarded as the interaction of age and period effects. If only one cohort is studied, the cohort effect cannot be determined. By comparing two cohorts at the same or similar age it is, however, possible to show whether developmental change is different at that age for individuals born at different times. Differences between the two cohorts in age-related behaviour (for example, leaving full-time education or becoming a parent) can thus be studied. Such comparisons give a better understanding of the impact of social change on the lives of cohort members. Comparing two birth cohorts for which data have been collected at different historical periods, also allows us to reflect on *period effects*. These are the product of distinctive historical and cultural events experienced by persons of a given age and cohort (Giele & Elder, 1998). Period effects describe the influence of historical change that is relatively uniform across successive birth cohorts. Unlike a cohort, which is an aggregate of individuals or cases, periods and ages are aggregates of time, variables rather than units of analysis (Menard, 2002). Period effects refer to the effect of history, specific to years or periods rather than to ages. They describe the prevailing socio-economic context at the time of data collection. For example, while the 1958 cohort grew up in times of relative economic affluence and stability, the 1970 cohort was born into a period of increasing instability and economic downturn. These contemporary events may have an immediate effect on behavioural adjustment, regardless of age.

Conclusion

The aim of this chapter was to develop a framework for investigating the emergence, as well as the continuity and change of constellations of risk and adjustment in the life course. The adopted ecological person-process-context-time approach offers a developmental perspective that captures the dynamic interaction between individual and context, contributing to a better understanding of human development and the nature of the forces that shape and stimulate the realisation of individual potential in a changing socio-historical context.

Key spheres of influence include individual characteristics, proximal processes with 'significant others' such as parents, siblings, peers, neighbours, teachers and work colleagues, as well as the interactions within the wider socio-historical context (Bronfenbrenner, 1995). As the comprehensive analysis of all these levels is beyond the scope of this study, the following analyses will focus on characteristics of the individual and the family, as well as their embeddedness in a changing socio-historical context. The model provides a framework for investigating how constellations of individual and contextual factors develop across the life span.

The model raises questions that have not yet fully been addressed and answered by research, especially regarding the pathways and processes linking individual and context over time. Comprehensive, longitudinal, multi-wave studies are necessary in order to gain a better understanding of the factors and processes that shape developmental pathways. Unlike cross-sectional studies that can measure inter-individual differences at one point in time, or retrospective studies that have to rely on subjective reports that can be distorted by hindsight, prospective longitudinal studies allow us to explore the processes of change. They provide causal explanations for intra-individual change and for inter-individual differences in intra-individual change, and they enable the researcher to describe the interactions of developmental variables. By including individual and contextual variables in the same model, the relative importance of various factors can be assessed in various settings. Furthermore, by measuring relevant variables at several time points, the interrelations among these variables can be investigated.

Results and findings emerging from studying one cohort only have been criticised for being context-specific and not generalisable across cohorts. However, by comparing experiences in two birth cohorts born twelve years apart it is possible to gain a better understanding of unique and general patterns and principles, advancing our understanding of positive adaptation despite the experience of adversity by focusing on a changing individual in a changing socio-historical context.

3   Persisting inequalities in times of social change

> . . . there can be no serious doubt that in the late 1980s and early 1990s an era in world history ended and a new one began . . . From the vantage-point of the 1990's the Short Twentieth Century passed through a brief Golden Age, on the way from one era of crisis to another, into an unknown and problematic but not necessarily apocalyptic future.
>
> (Eric Hobsbawm, 1995, pp. 5–6)

During the lifetimes of the 1958 and 1970 birth cohorts, British society witnessed considerable changes in almost every aspect of its way of life. The aim of this chapter is to describe transformations in the labour market, the provision of education and training opportunities, as well as changing family forms and life styles experienced by young people growing up in Great Britain between the late 1950s and the turn of the new Millennium. The effect of historical events on the lives of cohort members born in 1958 and 1970 will be outlined, focusing on outcomes in educational and occupational attainment, family life and psychological well-being of cohort members in mid-adulthood, i.e. in their early thirties. At that age most cohort members will have completed their education and training, established their occupational careers and household and family formation will have begun.

According to the principles of life-course theory the impact of any historical event is contingent on the cohort's life stage. Figure 3.1 gives the age of cohort members at different historical events. When different cohort members encounter the same historical event, they do so at different life stages, bringing with them different experiences. The impact of historical changes varies among cohort members who are drawn from two large-scale population samples, comprising individuals from all strands of life.

After the end of World War II, there had been a period of extraordinary economic growth and social transformation, described by Hobsbawm (1995) as a 'Golden Age'. Following the food and fuel shortages immediately after World War II, a wide range of legislation was implemented,

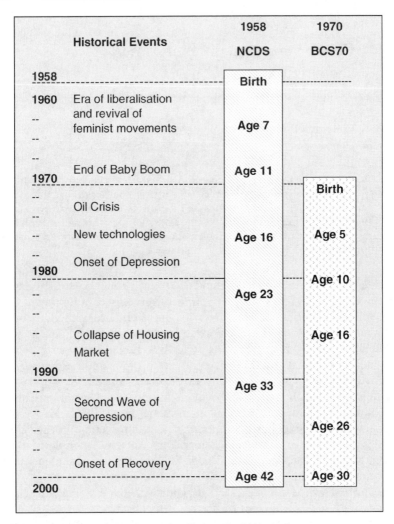

Figure 3.1. Age of cohort members by historical events.

aiming to bring greater equity and opportunity for all (Marwick, 1982). In 1944, the Education Act was established to increase the proportion of highly trained people in the country, introducing the selective allocation of children to grammar and other secondary schools on the basis of their capabilities. A National Health Service was set up in 1948 providing free health care for all citizens, and the social security system was expanded. The majority of the population experienced increasing living standards and growing affluence, fuelled by rising personal income, purchasing power, individual ownership of financial capital and housing (Dilnot & Emmerson, 2000). The end of World War II was also followed by a massive baby boom (Coleman, 2000a).

This period came to an end in the early 1970s, and was followed by an evolving new age of uncertainty and instability, the 'Crisis Decades' (Hobsbawm, 1995). The recessions in the 1980s were the most serious for fifty years and brought with them increasing levels of unemployment and poverty. Between 1979 and the end of the 1990s, the proportion of households living below 50 per cent of the mean equivalent disposable household income increased from 8 per cent to about 20 per cent (Atkinson, 2000). Since the mid-1990s, however, a period of recovery has set in.

Britain in international perspective

There have been sustained attempts to describe the changing character of society in terms of internationally comparable statistics. The Human Development Index (HDI) provides such a summary measure. It can be used to indicate progress across countries in terms of access to essential capabilities, measured by the distribution of income, education and health (Halsey, 2000). The HDI is based on the simple average of three indicator components: longevity, knowledge and income (UNDP, 1998, p. 107). Longevity is measured by expectations of life at birth. Knowledge is measured by the adult literacy rate and the gross enrolment ratios at primary, secondary and tertiary level. Income is measured by real GDP per capita in purchasing power parity.

Among the 173 countries identified by the United Nations Development Programme all regions have made progress in the past forty years, each at a different pace and reaching different levels. In the year 2000 the UK ranked thirteenth in human development, identifying it as a highly privileged country in terms of longevity, knowledge and income. Between 1960 and 2000 life expectation at birth rose from 71 years to 77.7 years. This compares to a life expectancy of 74.5 years in the industrialised countries and 64.7 years in the world as a whole. The British real GDP per capita also rose, and in the year 2000 was above average in both the European Union and among OECD (Organization for Economic Co-operation and Development) countries. Britain's combined primary, secondary and tertiary gross educational enrolment ratio is the highest of all countries.

Human development is, however, about more than just the rise or fall of national incomes; it is rather concerned about the range of things people can do or be in their lives (UNDP Human Development Report,

1998). It is about building human capabilities, to enable individuals to lead long and healthy lives, to be knowledgeable and to have access to the resources needed for a decent standard of living. The HDI assesses only average achievements, and may mask inequalities within countries. Since the late 1970s there has been a widening inequality in the UK arising from insecurity of employment, an increased proportion of families without work and lack of access to opportunities in education and its consequent benefits (Atkinson & Hills, 1998; Atkinson, 2000). Among OECD countries the United Kingdom and the United States have, in comparison to Denmark or Sweden, relatively high levels of income inequality, yet in global terms these are still relatively low (UNDP Human Development Reports, 2001). The ways in which Britain has made and maintained its wealth and how this has affected individual lives will be described below, focusing on changes in the labour market, in education and training, in commitment to personal relationships and psychological health and well-being.

The changing labour market

During the second half of the twentieth century, the United Kingdom witnessed a far-reaching transformation of the nature of work and the necessary skills to succeed (Gallie, 2000). At the beginning of the century Britain's manufacturing industries were flourishing and expanding. Yet, after the mid-century the pattern of economic development changed dramatically. Employment in manufacturing declined and was superseded by a rapid growth in the service industries. While in 1951 most work was manual (64 per cent), by 1991 only 38 per cent of the labour force was occupied in manual work. Employment in the service industries, on the other hand, increased from under half of all employment in 1951 to more than two-thirds at the turn of the century (Gallie et al., 1998). There was an increase first in clerical occupations and then in professional and managerial jobs, indicating a fundamental transformation of the occupational structure of the British workforce (Gallie, 2000; Routh, 1981). While manual employment declined, employment in professional and managerial occupations tripled between 1951 and 1991 (Gallie, 2000).

Unemployment

The most central issue with respect to employment trends is the rise in unemployment since the late 1970s. From about 1948 until the beginning of the 1970s there was relatively low unemployment in most developed countries (White & Smith, 1994). In the UK the years between

1945 and the early 1970s saw unprecedentedly low levels of unemployment, with an unemployment rate as low as 3 per cent until 1971 (Gallie, 2000). From the time of the first 'oil crisis' in 1973, unemployment rates increased sharply, fuelled by two recessions during the early 1980s and the early 1990s. Between 1979 and 1987 the UK witnessed the sharpest rise in unemployment since World War II (Gallie, 2000). During the mid-1980s unemployment rates in the UK rose to about 11 per cent, following a dramatic loss of employment in heavy manufacturing, mining and textile industries. In particular, youth unemployment rates soared to record levels, with about a third of sixteen- to nineteen-year-old males and about a quarter of females of the same age being without work (Hart, 1988; White & Smith, 1994).

While most cohort members born in 1958 completed their full-time education just before or at the onset of the recession, the later born cohort reached minimum school leaving age right in the midst of it. When cohort members born in 1958 left school at sixteen in 1974, employment prospects were still relatively good. Cohort members born in 1970, however, were directly hit by the increasing rates of unemployment. Between 1991 and 1994 Britain witnessed a second period of economic decline, this time affecting employment across all occupations. Since the mid-1990s, however, a period of recovery set in and declining unemployment rates returned to a level close to that at the end of the 1970s (Gallie, 2000).

Another economic indicator to be considered is the relative distribution of income, as assessed by the Gini coefficient, which gives a summary measure of the distribution of income in the population. Between 1980 and 2000 income inequality rose in the UK, although income inequalities fell in the immediate aftermath of the periods of economic decline and remained stable after 1996 (Lakin, 2001).

Female participation in the labour market

The transformation of the labour market was accompanied by a dramatic change in the participation of women in the labour force. In the second half of the century the life of women has been transformed enormously and feminism has advanced the narrowing of gender gaps in educational and occupational opportunities, health and welfare. In 1951 only about a third (31 per cent) of women were economically active. In 2000, this has increased to nearly half (47 per cent). Figure 3.2 illustrates that the overall workforce in the UK has remained relatively stable between the 1960s and the 1980s, followed by a small growth in the mid-1990s. We can also see the continuous rise of women

Figure 3.2. Workforce in the UK (in thousands: seasonally adjusted).
Source: Office for National Statistics (ONS), 2003.

entering the labour market, while male participation in the labour market has fallen. This trend might be associated with the increasing rates of unemployment since the 1980s. Unlike in most other EU countries, men in Britain are considerably more likely to experience unemployment than women (Gallie, 2000). During the recession, craft, operative and non-skilled workers, who are proportionately more likely to be male, were more vulnerable to the risk of unemployment, while white-collar and professional workers were less likely to be unemployed.

Did the increase in women's participation in the labour market lead to a decline in sex differences in types of employment? Table 3.1 shows the changes in employment structure for each cohort and their parents. Occupational status was assessed using the Registrar General's measure of Social Class (RGSC) (see Appendix C). The RGSC is defined according to job status and the associated education, prestige, or life style (Marsh, 1986). It is coded on a six-point scale: I professional; II intermediate; IIInm skilled non-manual; IIIm skilled manual; IV partly skilled; and V unskilled (Leete & Fox, 1977). Class I represents the highest level of prestige or skill and class V the lowest. Parental social class was assessed at birth. Own social class was assessed in mid-adulthood.

Table 3.1 indicates the secular change in employment structure, giving the occupational social class of men and women in employment at age 30 in BCS70 and ages 33 and 42 in NCDS and that of the fathers of each cohort, as ranked by the Registrar General's Social Class (adapted from Woods et al., 2003). Information about women in employment is separated by whether they work full-time or part-time, since occupations of women who work part-time are often of lower grades

Table 3.1. *Occupational status of cohort members in adulthood: men and women and their fathers*

	Occupational social class of father						
	I	II	IIInm	IIIm	IV	V	N (100%)
1970 cohort							
Fathers	7	20	9	46	14	4	9,083
1958 cohort							
Fathers	6	15	11	45	18	5	9,588

	Occupational social class of current job						
	I	II	IIInm	IIIm	IV	V	N (100%)
1970 cohort at 30 in 2000							
Male workers	8	34	13	32	11	2	4,835
Female full-time	6	43	37	7	7	0	2,945
Female part-time	2	19	44	9	21	6	1,299
1958 cohort at 33 in 1991							
Male workers	8	34	11	33	12	3	4,725
Female full-time	4	45	32	7	11	1	2,010
Female part-time	1	21	38	7	23	10	1,797
1958 cohort at 42 in 2000							
Male workers	7	40	10	32	8	3	5,042
Female full-time	4	45	31	7	11	1	2,570
Female part-time	2	22	38	7	23	8	1,976

than occupations of women in full-time work. There is a decrease in the proportion of men in manual occupations (classes IIIm, IV and V). On the other hand, there is an increase of men and women working full-time, who are employed in social class II, i.e. intermediate occupations. Only relatively small numbers of cohort members or their fathers are recorded as having occupations in social class I, and there are generally more men in this occupational group than women. Professional occupations held by women who work part-time are very rare, and women part-timers are generally concentrated in semi- and unskilled jobs.

Intergenerational social mobility

There is a considerable change in the proportion of men in manual occupations, i.e. social classes IIIm, IV and V, between the generations. Sixty-eight per cent of the fathers of the 1958 cohort compared to 48 per cent of sons (i.e. male cohort members) at age thirty-three and 43 per cent of sons at age forty-two were in a manual occupation. For the 1970 cohort the changes are similar with 64 per cent of fathers and 45 per cent of sons at age thirty being in a manual occupation. There is also a dramatic increase of intermediate occupations,[1] which are occupied by about a fifth of the fathers and about a third of sons. The changes in professional positions are not as striking and about the same proportions of fathers and sons are in a professional job.[2] The analysis of social mobility, the transition from class of origin to own occupation, shows that in both cohorts about one in three men in their early thirties were in the same position as their fathers (Woods et al., 2003). The chances of experiencing upward mobility from a given background were somewhat diminished for the more recently born cohort. While 45 per cent of men in their early thirties in the 1958 cohort increased their social position, only 39 per cent of thirty-year-old men in the 1970 cohort managed to do so. Downward social mobility among men also increased slightly from 22 per cent in the 1958 cohort to 26 per cent in the 1970 cohort (Woods et al., 2003).

For women in the two cohorts the chances of social mobility remain remarkably similar. Twenty-two per cent of women in their early thirties in NCDS versus 20 per cent of thirty-year-old women in BCS70 remain in the same position as their fathers. Twenty-eight per cent of women in both cohorts experienced downward mobility, and 51 versus 52 per cent increased their social status. Generally, for both men and women, the occupational change is mostly between adjoining categories and extreme moves from 'rags to riches' or vice versa are rather uncommon in the two cohorts (Woods et al., 2003).

The influence of parental social class on own occupational attainment remains apparent in both cohorts. Children born into a professional family (social class I) were about eight times more likely than those with parents in social class V to be in a professional job in their early thirties. Educational attainment has generally become more important for the later born cohort to succeed in their occupational career. Yet, even when controlling for ability tested at school and final qualifications attained, the influence of social background remains significant, and children from social class I were twice as likely than children from social class V to enter a professional or managerial career (Woods et al., 2003).

---

[1] This group includes a wide range of white-collar jobs, including teaching, nursing and management, which are not professional, or junior clerical or sales occupations.
[2] Professional status refers to occupations in medicine, law, etc., or senior civil servants.

New technologies

The shift in the occupational structure (decline in manual work and expansion of jobs in the service industries) was closely linked to the changing structure of industry, yet also involves a far-reaching process of upskilling the British labour force (Gallie, 2000; Routh, 1981). The introduction of automation and then during the 1970s of new computer technologies, required a smaller manual workforce, and replaced the old craft skills by new, more readily learned and transferable skills associated with the new methods of production and management. Automatisation and computerisation not only changed manufacturing processes, but also affected the service industries. The traditionally secure, non-manual occupations have become increasingly more vulnerable. It has been argued that these changes lead in effect to a de-skilling of the work-force (Ainley & Corney, 1990; Coles & Macdonald, 1990). There is however also evidence that those who use the new technologies are more likely to report that the skill requirements for their jobs have actually increased (Gallie et al., 1998). Generally the rapid spread of information technologies and the changes in the labour market involved increasing demands by employers for highly qualified recruits, and required new policies in education and training. Successive governments responded to these fundamental changes in the labour market by expanding higher education (Halsey, 2000)and by implementing new programmes of vocational training.

Changing patterns of participation in education

In Britain the legal minimum school leaving age was raised in 1972 from fifteen to sixteen years, making the 1958 cohort the first generation to encounter this change. The average lengths of schooling continued to rise among all social groups from then onwards (Furlong, 1997; Halsey, 2000). While in the 1970s the predominant pattern was to leave school at the minimum age and to move directly into a job, by the 1990s most young people continued in full-time education after the age of sixteen years (Bynner & Parsons, 1997; Furlong, 1992; Roberts, 1995; Surridge & Raffe, 1995). Increasing qualification levels have been observed in most developed countries in the post-war period and the age when young people enter employment has been effectively delayed. In most other Western societies, the timing of transitions into adult roles has extended as more education and skill development is required to take on adult roles and to balance the increasingly complex and challenging demands (Arnett, 2000; Banks et al., 1992; Furlong, 1997; Fussell & Greene, 2002; Mortimer & Larson, 2002; Shanahan et al., 2002).

In the UK the rate of seventeen- and eighteen-year-olds participating in full-time education more than doubled between 1973–74 and 1993–94 (DFE, 1983; DFE, 1993). The average length of schooling continued to rise, and a growing number of young people participated in further and higher education, once the preserve of a privileged minority (Blossfeld & Shavit, 1993; Bynner & Parsons, 1997; Egerton & Halsey, 1993). Youth training schemes were introduced in the UK from the mid-1970s onwards, in an attempt to encourage higher rates of educational participation among the less privileged. By the mid-1980s the numbers of young people leaving school without qualifications fell steeply and for those who traditionally sought to move from education to employment at sixteen, attendance at training schemes became a necessary precursor (Bynner, 1998; Furlong & Raffe, 1989).

The period between the mid-1970s and the end of the 1980s when the NCDS cohort and the BCS70 cohort entered the labour market was marked by rising unemployment risks and less certainty than in previous times. An increasing proportion of young men and women stayed on in full-time education. Not all of the increase in education participation consists of continuous spells, as some cohort members returned to education after some time in the labour market. Among the later born cohort there has been an increase of young people involved in government youth training schemes, especially young men.

Continuing inequalities of educational opportunity

One might expect that the educational expansion, reinforced in many countries by educational reforms, would reduce social inequalities in educational opportunity (Boudon, 1974). Yet, empirical studies on educational attainment in different countries have shown that inequality of educational opportunity between social strata has remained quite stable over time and that the effects of social origin on the final transition patterns have tended to increase (Blossfeld & Shavit, 1993; Erikson & Jonsson, 1996; Müller, 1996). It has been argued by Blossfeld & Shavit (1993) that the marked educational expansion in most countries has not been uniform across all educational levels. The educational systems expanded much more rapidly at the primary and secondary levels than at the post-secondary levels, leading to severe bottlenecks in the transition to tertiary education. In some countries, including Great Britain, the expansion of secondary education has been accompanied by a growing

Table 3.2. *Highest qualifications attained in the two birth cohorts*

	None	NVQ1	NVQ2	NVQ3	NVQ4	NVQ5	N
1970 cohort at 30							
Men	9.6	8.3	24.3	23.4	30.5	4.0	5,450
Women	8.7	7.9	30.9	17.7	31.3	3.6	5,773
1958 cohort at 33							
Men	11.1	13.4	27.8	18.8	25.1	4.2	5,455
Women	13.2	12.9	34.7	13.2	22.7	3.3	5,685
1958 cohort at 42							
Men	11.1	10.7	20.3	24.5	28.4	5.0	5,562
Women	13.1	11.2	30.0	14.6	27.0	4.1	5,725

differentiation into academic and vocational tracks, whereby the increase of vocational or non-college education allowed for the incorporation of growing proportions of children from lower social strata who would complete secondary education but would not be considered for further academic education. This expansion of vocational training has 'led to an opening up of secondary education without disturbing the basically exclusive character of higher education' (Blossfeld & Shavit, 1993, p. 20).

Table 3.2 illustrates educational attainment in terms of a broad classification of academic and vocational qualifications based on a scale related to National Vocational Qualification[3] (NVQ) levels (Makepeace et al., 2003). BCS70 cohort members born in 1970 are less likely to leave school without any or only some qualifications than NCDS cohort members born twelve years earlier. On the other hand, they are more likely to gain A-levels (NVQ3) and first degree qualification (NVQ4). The percentage of young men and women in their thirties with a postgraduate degree (NVQ5) has remained more or less the same. There is however, some indication that further qualifications are obtained between thirty-three and forty-two.

Young people from working-class backgrounds were less likely than their middle-class peers to remain in school beyond the minimum leaving age, to leave school with recognised qualifications, or to enter higher education (Blossfeld & Shavit, 1993; Halsey et al., 1980). Figure 3.3 suggests that the degree of inequality in educational attainment has somewhat increased especially for women. Yet in both cohorts, young people from working-class families are more likely to leave school without qualifications and are less likely to obtain further qualifications than their more privileged peers (Bynner, 1998). Family background factors

---

[3] See Appendix C for a more detailed description.

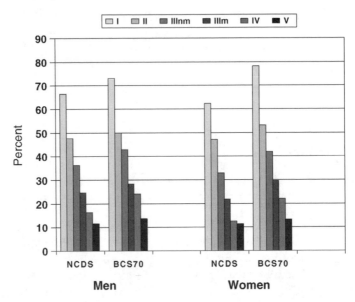

Figure 3.3. The attainment gradient: percentage with degree-level qualifications by parental social class.

were also strongly involved in the crucial post-sixteen transitions when decisions were made about whether to stay on in education or to leave. In both cohorts over two-thirds of young people coming from unskilled families and just over half from skilled or partly skilled manual background had left education by the age of sixteen, compared to one-tenth of those with fathers in the professions and one-quarter from managerial backgrounds. Young people from a working-class background were more likely than middle-class youths to join youth training schemes (Furlong, 1992; Roberts, 1992; Schoon et al., 2001). Yet, in comparison to the NCDS cohort, where training led to full-time employment, the experience of training in the later born cohort is associated with the repeated experience of unemployment (Schoon et al., 2001). The structural changes in the economy seemed to be too pervasive for the youth training schemes to succeed.

The findings indicate that social inequalities in the patterns of youth transitions have continued over the last two decades, and suggest a persistent link between social origin and educational opportunities. While the overall level of qualifications has increased, the relative chances of young people from different social backgrounds obtaining these qualifications remain associated with parental social class. There is also evidence that the not so able children from middle-class families have benefited most from the expansion of education (Schoon et al., 2001; Machin, 2003).

Changing gender differentials

While educational inequalities associated with social class have persisted, inequalities associated with gender have altered considerably. In the early 1970s young women tended to gain fewer formal qualifications and were underrepresented at university. By the early 1980s the situation started to change. Girls were more likely than boys to have obtained school-leaving qualifications and were increasingly participating in higher education (Department of Education and Science, 1983; Department of Education and Science, 1993). During the 1990s these gains have consolidated and attention has turned to male underachievement in the education system (Roberts, 1995). Young women tended to remain in full-time education, while young men were more likely to have entered full-time jobs after minimum schooling age. In recent years there has also been a disproportionate increase in unemployment among young males, a change that has been largely attributed to the decline of the manufacturing sector and the growth of the service industry (Hammer, 1997). It has been pointed out by Bynner & Parsons (1997) that during the 1990s much wider opportunities for education and training after school-leaving became available to young women and that the huge gender gap that dominated the experience of the 1958 cohort is gradually disappearing. On the other hand, there is evidence of an increasing polarisation among women. Educated women are doing better than ever before, but the situation of those without qualifications remains the same (Joshi & Paci, 1998).

Gender differences become especially apparent after the completion of full-time education. In both cohorts, the employment histories of men are dominated by full-time work, while women's experience is characterised by longer spells of being out of the labour force and working part-time, reflecting their multiple roles as both mother and worker and suggesting a greater effect of emerging family responsibilities (Schoon et al., 2001).

Partnership and parenthood

The changes and uncertainties experienced in education and the world of work are mirrored in personal and intimate relationships which have become increasingly fragile and impermanent. One of the major demographic trends in Britain since the 1950s is the postponement and reduction of commitments relating to marriage and parenthood. Since the 1970s the popularity of marriage has fallen to an all-time low, and the proportion of those married at each age has fallen for both sexes (Coleman, 2000a). As the number of marriages has plummeted, there has been a continuous rise in cohabitation, which by the end of the century had to some extent replaced the formal arrangement of marriage, as it has become the most common form of first liaison (Kiernan & Estaugh, 1993; McRae, 1999; Ermisch & Francesconi, 2000). Cohabitations are more fragile relationships than marriage and are between three and four times more likely to break up than marriages at equivalent ages, even when children are present (Ferri & Smith, 2003a). The trend towards increasingly transient and unstable relationships has been underlined by a dramatic increase in divorce rates. These have risen from about 27,000 petitions for divorce during 1956–60 to nearly 160,000 at the end of the century (Coleman, 2000a). Since the introduction of the Divorce Law Reform Act in 1971, divorce rates have kept on rising. Today over 40 per cent of marriages will end in divorce. This statistic has not stopped the desire for marriage among some. At the beginning of the 1990s, over 40 per cent of weddings involved at least one formerly married person, and 12 per cent, two divorced persons (Coleman, 2000a). The break from traditional family transition patterns is also reflected in the growth of single-person households. More individuals of all ages are living alone. The mean household size has been shrinking continuously and the number of single-person households had been increasing, with the largest increase since 1971, especially among men and women under retirement age and particularly those aged under forty (Coleman, 2000a).

Partnership arrangements in the two cohorts

The trends in partnership relationships which have emerged in the UK during the past decades are clearly reflected in the living arrangements reported by the cohort members in mid-adulthood (see Figure 3.4). There is a dramatic increase of individuals living without a partner. In their early thirties one in three men and women born in 1970 were single compared to one in five cohort members born in 1958 (these include cohort members who never lived with a partner, were divorced, separated or widowed). In NCDS the great majority of men and women were married at the age of thirty-three, while in BCS70 the proportion of married couples has nearly halved. About a fourth of men and women born in 1970 were living with partners to whom they were not married,

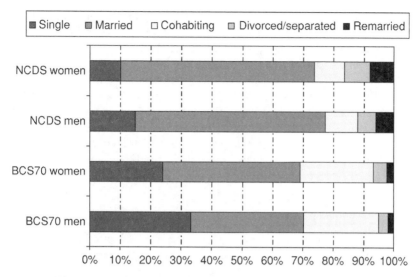

Figure 3.4. Partnership situation of cohort members in their early thirties.

compared to only about 10 per cent in NCDS, reflecting the increasing popularity of cohabitation. Most men and women in BCS70 and NCDS who currently cohabit at age thirty and thirty-three respectively had never been married before. Among the married couples born in 1970, 70 per cent had cohabited before they got married, in comparison to a third of men and women born in 1958 (Ferri & Smith, 2003a).

Implications for parenthood

The average family size of all ages of women at all durations of marriage during 1951–5 was 2.2 children. This increased to 2.8 during 1961–5, the time of Britain's 'baby boom', but, since 1972, has fallen constantly, remaining below the level required to replace the population, reaching 1.7 in the year 2000 (Coleman, 2000a). Childlessness has been increasing to levels not seen for decades, and more and more women delay having children until their thirties. Delaying childbirth, however, does not mean postponing it forever. While birth rates for women aged under thirty have been falling for about twenty years now, those for women aged over thirty have been increasing.

In NCDS, 24 per cent of women and 41 per cent of men were childless at thirty-three, in comparison to 46 per cent of women and

64 per cent of men in BCS70 at age thirty (Ferri & Smith, 2003a). Advances in family planning, increasing use of contraception, and the rising number of women participating in further education and the labour market are arguably among the reasons behind this trend (Murphy, 1993). Family formation in the UK is generally taking place significantly later in life, particularly for those who continue further education (Allan, 1999). Yet, in comparison to other European countries, the UK has relatively low rates of birth to women aged over thirty. On the other hand, it has the highest rate of teenage pregnancies. The number of births to teenage mothers in the UK is about four times the Western European average (Coleman, 2000a).

Family type

Partnership arrangements and patterns of family formation have profound implications for children (Haskey, 1996). There has been a dramatic increase in children being born outside marriage. Until the 1950s less than 5 per cent of births were outside marriage. Since the 1960s this rate has increased continuously and today, with 36 per cent of babies born outside marriage, Britain is top of the European league outside Scandinavia. Furthermore, the rate of children born to a lone parent has almost tripled since the 1970s, rising from 8 per in 1971 to 21 per cent in 1996 (McRae, 1999). Initially this rise was mainly among divorced lone parents, yet since the mid-1980s it has been argued that the main growth in lone parents stems from never-married lone mothers (Murphy & Wang, 1999). With the increasing rates of re-partnership and remarriage, a phenomenon also described as serial monogamy, there is an increase in the numbers of children experiencing life in a reconstituted family (Ferri & Smith, 1996).

Among cohort members with children the 'nuclear' family has nevertheless remained by far the most common arrangement among parents. At thirty-three, over 80 per cent of parents born in 1958 were living with a spouse and their children. This has reduced to about 60 per cent of married parents at thirty in BCS70. There has, however, been a steep increase in the proportion of cohabiting parents living with their children, which has tripled for parents born in 1970. If they are included in the 'nuclear' family group, the difference between the two cohorts is smaller, but still remains (Ferri & Smith, 2003b).

In comparison to NCDS, nearly twice as many men in BCS70 who were bringing up children by the time they were thirty were stepfathers (17 per cent in BCS70 versus 9 per cent in NCDS). In both cohorts the number of women who were stepmothers in their early thirties was tiny (below 3 per cent), reflecting that most children remain with their mothers after a partnership breakdown (Ferri & Smith, 2003b).

Another major family type is the single-parent family, usually headed by the mother. This family type increased in the aftermath of the rising divorce rates and the growing number of children born to single, unsupported mothers. The proportion of lone mothers in their early thirties increased from 12 per cent in NCDS to 19 per cent in BCS70. All single mothers born in 1958 had previously had a partner and only 4 per cent of mothers born in 1970 were never partnered, undermining the suggestion that lone mothers are typically young women choosing single, unsupported parenthood (Ferri & Smith, 2003a).

Theses trends reflect a growing diversity of living arrangements, and dramatic changes in the patterns of intimate relationships. In comparison to cohort members born in 1958, for individuals born in 1970, a delayed entry into partnership and parenthood, rising rates of partnership breakdown and serial monogamy have become increasingly common experiences. In many respects, these changes can be seen as a consequence of the transformations in the overall socio-historical context described earlier. The changes in the economic context have led to an increasing participation of women in the labour market and to generally increased advances in educational attainment. However, the overall gains in educational and occupational attainment have not been universal. There is an increasing polarisation of opportunities, especially for those men and women without higher qualifications. The traditional pathway into early partnership and parenthood (often unsupported) is more common among women without qualifications, while men and women who participated in further education are more likely to delay partnership and parenthood. Highly educated women, in particular, have remained childless or delayed childbearing until after they have established their careers (Joshi & Paci, 1998).

Generally the trends in patterns of partnership and family arrangements indicate the increasing instability and transitory nature of personal relationships. The growing fragility of personal and emotional commitment in conjunction with the increasing insecurity in the labour market and the greater complexity of work, may have increased certain types of health problems, in particular psychological distress.

Psychological well-being and health

The changes and uncertainties in work and intimate relationships seem to have taken their toll and levels of depression and stress-related problems among the younger cohort have increased. In both cohorts the Malaise Inventory (Rutter et al., 1970) has been used to measure levels of psychological distress, or depression.[4] In comparison with the earlier born cohort, the prevalence of distress among the younger cohort has nearly doubled. In BCS70, 10.4 per cent of men and 14.1 per cent of woman reported high levels of distress, compared to 4.5 per cent of men and 8.6 per cent of women in NCDS. Higher rates of depression are invariably reported for women (Jenkins et al., 1997; Nolen-Hoeksema, 1990). Overall, the prevalence of psychological distress increased over the period 1980–2000 and the level of overall depression is lower in NCDS than in the later born BCS70 cohort (Montgomery & Schoon, 1997; Sacker & Wiggins, 2002; Schoon et al., 2003; Wadsworth et al., 2003).

In a study using multilevel modelling to examine the effects of social class, gender, age, period and cohort on psychological health as measured by the Malaise Inventory, Sacker & Wiggins (2002) found that age and cohort effects are the most important determinant of psychological well-being, while period effects contribute least. They showed that psychological health improved slightly between the early twenties and early thirties, followed by a decline in the forties. The later born cohort reported generally poorer psychological health than the earlier born cohort. Furthermore, the study indicates that the difference in psychological health between men and women has narrowed over the period 1981–2000. Women's psychological well-being has been improving over time, but that of men's has not, which the authors attribute to the increasing participation of women in the labour market which benefits their psychological well-being.

Other indicators of psychological well-being used in the cohort studies include questions about life satisfaction and feeling in control. In their early thirties, cohort members born in 1958 appeared to be slightly more satisfied with their lives than cohort members born in 1970. Being asked to indicate on a scale from zero to ten how satisfied they are about the way their life has turned out so far, 57 per cent of cohort members in NCDS and 53 per cent in BCS70 had a score of eight and above, indicating that the majority of cohort members are generally satisfied with their lives so far. A question asking whether they generally have free choice and control over their lives was affirmed by 88 per cent of cohort members in NCDS and 90 per cent in BCS70. Thus, in both cohorts men and women in their early thirties feel highly satisfied and in control

---

[4] For a more detailed description of the Malaise Inventory, see Appendix C.

of their lives. The level of life satisfaction has remained more or less stable between the 1990s and the year 2000, although there is a slight drop in life satisfaction among the later born cohort. This finding confirms the study by Blanchflower & Oswald (2004) who compared trends in well-being over time in Britain and the US. They found that over the last quarter of a century reported levels of well-being have declined in the US, but that life satisfaction in Britain has not changed much, running approximately flat through time. They furthermore established that well-being is U-shaped in age, and that it reaches a minimum around the age of forty.

In both cohorts we find strong evidence of social class inequalities in psychological well-being and health. The risk for psychological distress is higher for those in manual jobs than for those in professional occupations (Montgomery & Schoon, 1997; Wadsworth et al., 2003). There is also a persisting influence of social origin on the level of psychological well-being. Cohort members born into disadvantaged families are more likely to experience psychological distress in mid-adulthood than their more privileged peers. They are also less satisfied with their lives and feel less in control than cohort members born into more privileged families.

Conclusion

Despite the dramatic economic and social advances witnessed in the UK during the second half of the twentieth century, inequalities of opportunities and life chances have remained, or have even become greater. Britain's real GDP per capita is above average among European and OECD countries and has increased steadily over the past decades. But has the nation's economic performance increased the well-being of its citizens? The changes described above lend support to hypotheses that economic growth does not bring happiness to society (Easterlin, 1974; Easterlin, 1995). By the early 1990s a mood of insecurity and resentment had begun to spread and brought with it the disintegration of the old patterns of human social relationships (Hobsbawm, 1995). Britain is currently Europe's leader in teenage pregnancies, lone-parenthood and divorce (Halsey, 2000). Intimate personal relationships have become increasingly unstable, as have prospects at work. The impact of these changes affected the two cohorts differently. There is an increasing polarisation between those who are able to benefit from the economic and social advances and the ones who are excluded, largely because of their relatively disadvantaged socio-economic circumstances, lack of access to opportunities in education and insecurity of employment. Despite the striking differences in the way the two cohorts live their lives, the persistence of family social class as a driver of life chances has been a recurring theme for outcomes in education, work, family formation and psychological well-being. The processes by which the social structure influences individual adaptation will be investigated in the next chapters.

4   Selection, causation and cumulative risk effects

Time present and time past
Are both perhaps present in time future,
And time future contained in time past

T. S. Eliot, 1936

The aim of this chapter is to investigate the long-term influence of socio-economic adversity on individual adjustment, taking into account the timing, duration and context in which the developing individual experiences adversity. The question of how individuals and environments are linked across the life course, i.e. the developmental-contextual systems perspective formulated in Chapter 2, will be re-cast in terms of a testable model of continuities in social disadvantage and individual adjustment and their reciprocal effects over time.

There is now consistent evidence that early and persistent experience of socio-economic disadvantage is a reliable predictor for the occurrence of adjustment problems in childhood and adulthood. Children growing up in socio-economically disadvantaged families are at an increased risk for a wide range of adverse outcomes including poor academic achievement and adjustment problems in later life, as reflected in own occupational attainment, social position and poor health (Bynner et al., 2000; Luthar, 1999; Rutter, 1998; Schoon et al., 2002; Schoon et al., 2003; Werner & Smith, 1982, 1992). The consequences of growing up in a disadvantaged family environment can continue into adulthood or even into the next generation (Birch & Gussow, 1970; Duncan & Brooks-Gunn, 1997; Garmezy, 1991; Rutter & Madge, 1976). The extensive knowledge about social inequalities in individual adjustment is, however, not matched by a comparable understanding of the pathways and processes through which socio-economic factors influence individual development (Brooks-Gunn et al., 1999). The focus of this chapter lies in the investigation of how constellations of risk and adjustment emerge and develop across the life course, specifying the processes by which socio-economic risk influences individual adjustment.

Theoretical perspectives

The role of early and persisting socio-economic adversity in shaping individual adjustment has been discussed from three different theoretical perspectives: social-causation, social-selection and pathways models emphasising the cumulative effect of life events throughout the life course. These three perspectives have their origin in discussions about the aetiology of health inequalities (Bartley, 2004; Keating & Hertzman, 1999) and can be useful for a better understanding of the processes linking the social context to individual adjustment in general, as well as for understanding the processes influencing academic adjustment during childhood and adolescence and consequent adult psychosocial functioning. In the present context, academic attainment is considered as a marker of developmental health (Power & Hertzman, 1999) which is likely to be related to adult social position and adult psychological well-being.

According to the *social causation hypothesis*, socio-economic circumstances such as social position and related financial and material resources influence individual adjustment. It is argued that social inequalities experienced throughout the life course generate adjustment problems. This approach is partially supported by evidence that social position at birth predicts both social position and psychological distress in adulthood (Kuh et al., 1997; Power et al., 1998).

According to the *selection* hypothesis, adjustment problems in childhood are causally related to adjustment and socio-economic status in adulthood. It is argued that own social position and adjustment in adulthood is a consequence of earlier adjustment problems. Evidence in support of this perspective suggests that less healthy children are less likely to attain high social status and more likely to be ill as adults, a phenomenon which has been described as direct health selection (Townsend et al., 1982). Here this would mean that low academic attainment in childhood is associated with lower social status and lower psychological well-being in adulthood. *Indirect social selection* hypotheses describe the possibility that some children may have characteristics, such as adverse coping styles for example, that are not illness in themselves, but which may contribute to both later ill-health and disadvantaged social position (West, 1991; Wilkinson, 1996).

The *pathways model* emphasises the role of continuities in both social circumstance and individual adjustment over time, and draws attention to the reinforcing effect of differing psychosocial and socio-economic circumstances throughout the life course (Bartley, 2004; Hertzman, 1999; Kuh & Ben-Shlomo, 1997; Power & Hertzman, 1999; Rutter, 1989). It is argued that the cumulative effect of life events along developmental trajectories creates a vicious cycle with short-term as well as long-term implications. Socio-economic status in childhood affects the likelihood of both material and psychosocial risks for psychosocial functioning. The differential aggregation of these risks leads to inequalities in adult psychosocial adjustment. In this model, the occurrence of disadvantage at any one time point is seen to be predictive of further disadvantage at a later time. Any instance of disadvantage adds to the likelihood of adjustment problems at future times.

Timing of risk experiences

A number of studies have demonstrated the extent to which any inequalities in an adult's psychosocial adjustment originate during childhood and adolescence (Brooks-Gunn et al., 1999; Lundberg, 1991; Peck, 1994; Power, 1991; van de Mheen et al., 1997; Kuh & Ben-Shlomo, 1997). The experience of early socio-economic disadvantage may severely strain the adaptational abilities of children and is thus a potential risk factor for development. However, the experience of early socio-economic disadvantage does not always have a direct impact on individual development. There is evidence of great diversity in the temporal dimension of socio-economic adversity, much of which is only short-term, but still a great amount can last for most of childhood (Duncan & Rodgers, 1988). Early experience of adversity may be overcome by improved circumstances, but may nevertheless leave the individual potentially more vulnerable to any disadvantage experienced at a later stage (Cicchetti & Tucker, 1994). There is evidence that adversity during early childhood, as opposed to later developmental periods, has a crucial impact on later adjustment (Duncan et al., 1998; Haveman & Wolfe, 1994; Luthar, 1999). There is also evidence that current contextual adversity determines current adjustment (Campbell et al., 1996; Feiring & Lewis, 1996; Tizard, 1976). A number of studies have also shown that persistent hardship has stronger effects than transitory adversity on individual outcomes (Ackerman et al., 1999; Bolger et al., 1995; Duncan et al., 1994; Pungello et al., 1996; Schoon et al., 2002; Schoon et al., 2003) and it has been argued that chronically stressful environments hinder the development of successful adaptation (Hammen, 1992; McLoyd, 1998).

Differences in findings can be explained by methodological variations in the studies, involving different developmental periods, different indicators of adversity and developmental outcomes and different analytical strategies. It has been argued that persistence effects may vary for different aspects of environmental adversity in relation to specific outcomes or may vary for the same aspect for different outcomes (Ackerman et al., 2004). The effect of early and persistent risk on the developmental process and on later functioning is probably the most difficult issue to investigate, not only because of the problems of separating the effects of early risk experiences from those of later years. The relative contribution of early, concurrent or persistent effects can only be assessed by drawing on longitudinal studies, as these provide detailed information about individuals who have been followed over time.

A developmental-contextual model of psychosocial adjustment

To assess the influence of timing and duration of socio-economic adversity on individual adjustment in the two birth cohorts, a developmental-contextual model of psychosocial adjustment has been formulated, reflecting the person-process-context-time dimensions of the life-course approach (Schoon et al., 2002; Schoon et al., 2003; see also Chapter 2). Here the model is used to investigate the pathways linking social disadvantage and individual adjustment across the life course and to assess the role of family socio-economic disadvantage and academic adjustment in explaining adult social inequality in psychological well-being. Figure 4.1 gives a diagrammatic representation of the model, linking early life experiences to adult outcomes. It is expected that socio-economic background factors are associated with both early academic attainment and consequent adult psychosocial adjustment. Continuity between early academic attainment and later adult psychosocial adjustment lies with the influence of socio-economic background factors that are associated with both academic attainment during childhood and adolescence and later outcomes. The contribution of early socio-economic risk to adult psychosocial adjustment is modelled by the different pathways suggested by social causation, social selection and cumulative pathway models. In addition, the model is an explicit developmental model, assessing the timing and duration of the interactions between individual and context.

The association between *concurrent* risk and psychosocial adjustment is indicated by correlations 'a'. These correlations give us an indication of the magnitude of inequalities in adjustment, i.e. social variations in educational attainment during childhood and adolescence as well as social variations in psychological adjustment in adulthood. The notion

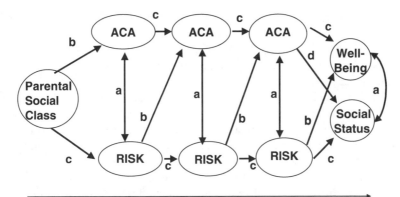

Figure 4.1. The developmental-contextual model of psychosocial adjustment.

of *social causation* is modelled here by the paths labelled 'b', testing the influence of socio-economic circumstances experienced during childhood on later academic and psychological adjustment. The paths labelled 'c' test the *continuities* in both socio-economic circumstances and individual adjustment over time. The combination of paths 'b' and 'c' describe continuities of both social circumstances and individual adjustment over time as well as the cumulation of risk effects along developmental trajectories (as specified in the pathways model) in that the 'b' paths assesses the additional incremental time-lagged effects of socio-economic adversity (in early childhood, late childhood and adolescence) on individual adjustment at subsequent time points. The combination of pathways gives an example of the way in which the developmental approach forces us to consider the complexity underlying the ideas of social causation and cumulative risk effects over time.

The path labelled 'd' is assessing selection effects, i.e. the effect of individual adjustment on consequent own social position and psychological well-being. Previous research has shown that children's academic or behavioural adjustment has a negligible effect on subsequent socio-economic conditions in the family household (Schoon et al., 2002; Schoon et al., 2003) and it can be assumed that these conditions are out of their control. There is, however, evidence that indirect selection effects predict to some extent adult psychosocial adjustment (Schoon et al., 2003; West, 1991; Wilkinson, 1996). Path 'd' is testing the causal effect of academic adjustment at sixteen on individual psychosocial adjustment in adulthood, taking into account previous academic attainment.

The approach adopted here not only investigates the developmental pathways linking experiences in childhood to adult outcomes, it furthermore considers the effects of a changing socio-historical context on these influences, which is not shown in the diagram but is taken into account in the analyses by applying the model to the two birth cohorts growing up twelve years apart. Contexts are changing over time, and different cohorts of individuals will experience their effects differently. The importance of the developmental-contextual perspective for this study lies in its scope to integrate process and structure and to link individual time with historical time.

Selection of indicator variables

The variables shown in the diagram are all latent variables, measured by observed indicator variables, which were collected at different time points. The latent variables capture the socio-economic conditions experienced by the family household from birth to adolescence, academic attainment at different ages throughout childhood and adolescence, as well as own social status and psychological adjustment in adulthood. For a description of the variables used in the analysis see Appendix C. Table 4.1 gives a summary of the indicator variables included in the model.

Assessing socio-economic risk

Socio-economic disadvantage is associated with a variety of co-factors, such as poor quality of housing or lack of material resources that pose risks for adaptive development (Conger et al., 1993; Duncan & Brooks-Gunn, 1997; Fergusson et al., 1990; Huston et al., 1994). These different factors interact and usually it is not one, but the number, the accumulation and the continuity of risks that determine an outcome. Multiple risk models have generally been shown to be better predictors of individual outcomes than single risk models (Ackerman et al., 1999; Caprara & Rutter, 1995; Fergusson et al., 1994; Sameroff et al., 1993) and in the following, a multiple risk indicator will be used.

Table 4.1. *Variables and observed indicators used in the model*

Variables	Observed Indicators
Social Risk (RISK)[1]	
Parental Social Class	Registrar General's Social Class (RGSC)
Material Conditions Scale	Housing Tenure Overcrowding (>1 person per room) Amenities (sole use of bathroom) Receipt of state benefits
Academic Adjustment (ACA)	
Academic Achievement	Age 7: Copy Test, Draw-a-Man, Reading (NCDS and BCS70), Arithmetic (NCDS only) Age 11: Reading, Mathematics Test (NCDS and BCS70) Age 16: Exam scores (NCDS and BCS70)
Psychological Well-being in Adulthood (Well-being)	
Psychological Adjustment at age 30 (BCS70) and 33 (NCDS)	Malaise Inventory, Feeling in Control, Life Satisfaction
Social Position in Adulthood (Social Position)	
Social Position at age 30 (BCS70) and 33 (NCDS)	Registrar General's Social Class (RGSC) Cambridge Scale (CS)

[1] The indicators of parental social class and material conditions in the family household were measured at ages seven, eleven and sixteen for NCDS and ages five, ten and sixteen for BCS70.

Most multiple risk studies use a single risk index, summing the number of risk factors present. Summing the number of risk factors in a single index, however, gives equal weight to all of them and does not take into consideration any relative contribution or overlap (Greenberg et al., 1999; Szatmari et al., 1994). There is now an increasing awareness that the processes linking socio-economic disadvantage to individual development operate at varying levels of specificity and that there is a need to distinguish between economic disadvantage per se and other associated aspects of environmental adversity (Ackerman et al., 1999; Duncan et al., 1994; McLoyd, 1990; Szatmari et al., 1994). Furthermore Ackerman et al. (1999) have argued that a single multiple risk index aggregates a set of variables that may relate differently to child functioning, or that may function differently for advantaged and disadvantaged families and that it does not distinguish between persistent and transitory experiences. He thus recommends the use of discrete groupings of indicators, narrowing the focus of the variables involved, or isolating specific factors that pose risks for individual adjustment. The usefulness of such an approach has been demonstrated in a number of studies (Ackerman et al., 1999; Deater-Deckard et al., 1998; Schoon et al., 2002; Schoon et al., 2003; Szatmari et al., 1994) and is adopted here. Instead of aggregating various co-factors of socio-economic disadvantage, only indicators of the socio-economic family background will be included to assess the unique effect of socio-economic disadvantage on individual development. The study will draw on indicators of socio-economic family status as well as indicators of living conditions and material resources available to the family. This approach will thus go beyond studies using social status or income as sole indicators of socio-economic risk and reflects more accurately the everyday experiences within the proximal family context.

Modelling strategy

In a first step, the degree of inequality in adult psychological health was assessed, as well as the strengths of the relationship between social risk at birth and adult psychosocial adjustment. The next step investigates the impact of early, current and persistent disadvantage on individual adjustment across the life course, testing the pathways defined by the developmental-contextual model depicted in Figure 4.1. All analyses were carried out using the structural equation modelling programme AMOS 4.01 (Arbuckle, 1999), which is described in more detail in Appendix B. The data was fitted to the model, running separate analyses for each cohort. Only cohort members for whom complete data was collected at birth, i.e. 16994 cohort members for NCDS and 14229 cohort members for BCS70, were included in the analyses. In line with current practice, several criteria were used to assess the model fit (see Appendix B).

Table 4.2. *Distribution of the risk variables (%) in the 1958 National Child Development Study (NCDS) and the 1970 British Cohort Study (BCS70)*

Risk variable	Cohort	
	NCDS (%)	BCS70 (%)
Birth (1958 / 1970)		
Social Class at Birth (% in SOC IV and V)	22	24
Age 7/5 (1964 / 1975)		
Social Class (% in SOC IV and V)	23	19
No Housing Tenure	55	44
Overcrowding (1+ person per room)	66	40
Shared use of amenities	19	7
Age 11/10 (1969 / 1980)		
Social Class (% in SOC IV and V)	23	18
No Housing Tenure	54	39
Overcrowding (1+ person per room)	51	30
Shared use of amenities	7	3
Family receives benefits	27	22
Age 16 (1974 / 1986)		
Social Class (% in SOC IV and V)	22	13
No Housing Tenure	50	28
Overcrowding (1+ person per room)	60	17
Shared use of amenities	7	1
Family receives benefits	23	27

Note: SOC = social position.

Prevalence of social risk indicators in both cohorts

The distribution of the risk indicator variables is shown in Table 4.2. Generally, material conditions have improved for the later born BCS70 cohort. In comparison to cohort members born in 1958, more families own their home, there is less overcrowding and fewer households have to share basic amenities such as toilet, bathroom or access to hot water. The percentage of families who are in receipt of state benefits has remained stable. We can also see upward mobility among the parents of cohort members born in 1970, while the social position of parents of the earlier born NCDS cohort remained stable over the years. If one compares the risk prevalence in the older cohort at age sixteen to the ones of the younger cohort at age five, which were assessed at roughly the same time (i.e. 1974 and 1975), it appears that our samples represent well the state of affairs over the historical period covered. The distribution of social status of the parents is comparable in the two samples, as are housing tenure and shared use of amenities. Differences in the rate of overcrowding might be explained by different stages of family formation in the two cohorts.

Inequalities in adjustment

The magnitude of inequalities in attainment, i.e. social variations in individual adjustment, are indicated by the associations between concurrent risk and academic adjustment. The bivariate correlation between adult social status and adult psychological well-being, before any intervening processes were considered, was $r = .23$ in NCDS and $r = .20$ in BCS70 suggesting that inequalities in adult psychological well-being have remained more or less the same for the two cohorts. In NCDS the strengths of the relationship between socio-economic risk at birth and adult social status was of moderate size ($\beta = .32$). The relationship between parental social class and own psychological well-being in adulthood was only small ($\beta = .13$). In BCS70 the relationship between parental social class at birth and adult social status was also of moderate size ($\beta = .39$), and between parental social class at birth and adult well-being it was also only small ($\beta = .16$). These relationships indicate that there were developmental processes to be explored further. Likewise the relationship between adult social status and adult psychological well-being suggests the existence of persisting health inequalities which we aim to explain with the developmental-contextual model.

Pathways linking experiences of socio-economic adversity to individual adjustment

The impact of early, current and persistent socio-economic adversity on individual adjustment across the life course was assessed by testing the pathways depicted in Figure 4.1. In both cohorts the goodness of fit indicators suggest that relations in the data are well described by the model ($\chi^2 = 1625.36$, df = 142; CFI = 0.997; RMSA = 0.025; 90 per cent CI = 0.024–0.026 in NCDS, and $\chi^2 = 946.50$, df = 123; CFI = 0.998; RMSA = 0.022; 90 per cent CI = 0.020–0.023 in BCS70). The results of the SEM model are given in Table 4.3, which shows the standardised parameter estimates of the measurement model for both cohorts. The measurement model defines relations between the observed indicator variables and the unobserved (latent) variables,

Table 4.3. The Measurement Model: Standardised parameter estimates for the National Child Development Study (NCDS) and the 1970 British Cohort Study (BCS70)

	NCDS at 7 Standardised estimate	BCS70 at 5 Standardised estimate	NCDS at 11 Standardised estimate	BCS70 at 10 Standardised estimate	NCDS at 16 Standardised estimate	BCS70 at 16 Standardised estimate	NCDS at 33 Standardised estimate	BCS70 at 30 Standardised estimate
Measurement model								
Social risk								
Risk→ Parental social class	0.79	0.79	0.78	0.76	0.74	0.76		
Risk → Material Deprivation	0.42	0.41	0.53	0.50	0.53	0.46		
Academic adjustment (ACA)								
ACA→ Copy Test	0.48	0.61						
ACA→ Draw-a-Man	0.50	0.34						
ACA → Reading	0.80	0.56	0.85	0.82				
ACA→ Maths	0.66		0.88	0.81				
ACA → Exam score					0.69	0.85		
ACA → Highest Qualification at age 16					0.61	0.62		
Adult psychological well-being								
Well-being → Malaise							-0.57	-0.61
Well-being → Control							0.51	0.44
Well-being → Satisfaction							0.51	0.60
Adult social status								
Social Status → RGSC							-0.88	-0.74
Social Status → Cambridge Score							0.95	0.65

i.e. it specifies the loading of the different measure on a particular latent factor.

The causal processes under study are represented by a series of structural, or regression equations which are modelled pictorially to enable a clearer conceptualisation of the postulated pathways under study. The structural model, depicted in Figures 4.2 and 4.3, describes relations among the unobserved (latent) variables for each of the cohorts. Figures 4.2 and 4.3 show the pathways between the latent or unobserved variables, which represent continuities and interactions of social risk and academic adjustment and give the standardised coefficients for the structural model, fitted separately for both cohorts. Several covariances between the error terms for the observed variables were included *a priori* to account for the autocorrelations over time. Parental social class and material deprivation were hypothesised to covary for the measurement points at consequent ages, as were the academic attainment scores. The hypothesised pathways were supported by the data, with the parameter estimates all being significantly different from zero (p < .005) and in the predicted direction. The variables shown are all latent or unobserved variables.

Continuities in risk and adjustment

In both cohorts there is strong evidence of continuities in both social risk and individual adjustment across time, as indicated by 'c' paths in Figure 4.1. There is a strong continuity of social risk effects, which is of similar strength for both cohorts. Risk experiences are not randomly distributed in a population, and being born into a relatively disadvantaged family increases the probability of accumulating risks associated with that disadvantage, setting the child off onto a risk trajectory (Rutter, 1990). The experience of socio-economic risk at an earlier time point was carried forward to the next and increased the probability that risk was also encountered at a later time point. The strength of the association can be explained by the fact that in addition to indicators of material disadvantage indicators of socio-economic status had also been used, which denote relative position in society. Despite improved material conditions and the experience and upward social mobility among parents of the BCS70 cohort, the relative social position has remained remarkably stable.

The experience of social risk at birth also influenced the level of later academic attainment. In both cohorts parental social class has a moderate influence on academic adjustment, yet the influence of parental social class at birth on academic attainment is greater for cohort

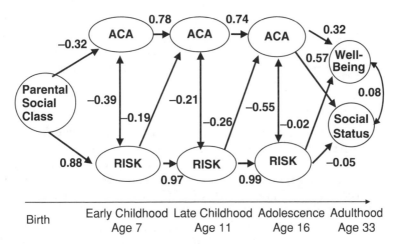

Figure 4.2. The developmental-contextual model of psychosocial adjustment in the 1958 National Child Development Study (NCDS).

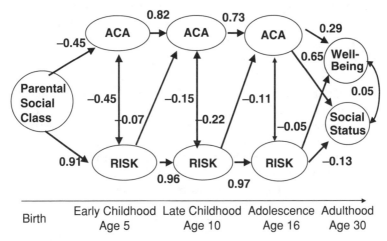

Figure 4.3. The developmental-contextual model of psychosocial adjustment in the 1970 British Birth Cohort (BCS70).

members born in 1970 than for those born in 1958 ($\beta = -.45$ in BCS70 versus $\beta = -.32$ in NCDS). There are strong continuities in academic attainment over time (though not as strong as the continuities in social risk). Academic attainment at one time point is a significant predictor of academic attainment at a later time point. The detrimental effect of experiencing disadvantage at one measurement point was carried forward into the future via decreased levels of academic adjustment. Continuities occur because current adjustment encompasses previous adjustment as well as earlier structural and functional change.

Cumulative risk effects

The paths from current risk to later individual adjustment indicated the cumulative risk effects added at each time point. In addition to the initial influence of parental social class at birth there were also significant associations between social risk and individual adjustment at subsequent time points. These 'time-lagged' risk effects ('b' paths) indicate the added negative influence of social risk on subsequent attainment not accounted for by the risk carried forward in time. In both cohorts the time-lagged risk effects are greatest at the transition from late childhood to adolescence, when important decisions about future educational and occupational careers are made. The added risk effects were only of small size in both cohorts, yet they were significant ($p < .05$) and in the predicted direction. The data thus provided support for the assumption of *cumulative continuities* as well as for the assumption of *social causation*.

Concurrent risk effects

The association between *concurrent* social risk and individual adjustment (paths 'a' in Figure 4.1) varied for the different life stages. Among cohort members born in 1958 the influence of concurrent social risk was highest during early childhood at age seven and especially during adolescence, at age sixteen. Among cohort members born in 1970 we find a moderate effect of concurrent risk on individual adjustment at age five, while at later ages the associations are only small. These differences in timing of risk effects might be explained by changes in the socio-historical context as discussed in the following.

Period effects: Coming of age in times of an economic crisis

Cohort members turned sixteen in 1974 and 1986 respectively. While the cohort members born in 1958 entered the labour market at the beginning of an economic crisis, the later born cohort completed their compulsory education at the height of the recession. In consequence to the virtual disappearance of the youth labour market that occurred between 1979 and 1986, the later born cohort encountered more complex and varied education, training and employment choices. While in the 1970s the predominant pattern was to leave school at the minimum age and to move directly into a job, by the 1990s most young people continued in full-time education after the age of sixteen (Bynner et al., 2000; Bynner et al., 1999). Cohort members born in 1970 are under increasing pressure to acquire formal qualifications, while most young people born in 1958 could expect to obtain employment regardless of their educational attainment (Bynner, Joshi & Tsatsas, 2000). Thus while parents of cohort members born in 1958, especially less privileged parents, might not have pushed their children to obtain good grades and rather might have encouraged their children to leave school early in order to earn a wage, parents in the later born BCS70 cohort might have generally put more emphasis on achieving good academic results. It could also be that among cohort members born in 1970 other factors, such as support from the school environment or contact with peers which are not captured in the model, might play a more important role in influencing academic achievement at age sixteen than in the earlier born 1958 cohort.

Transition from adolescence to adulthood

In both cohorts the direct influence of social risk experienced at age sixteen on adult psychosocial adjustment is only small. However, the influence of social risk on adult social status has nearly trebled for the later born cohort ($\beta = -0.05$ in NCDS versus $\beta = -0.13$ in BCS70). It has also to be kept in mind that the experience of social risk does have additional indirect effects on social status operating through the child's academic adjustment.

The influence of academic attainment on adult psychosocial adjustment was highly significant in both cohorts, confirming the crucial role of educational resilience in determining adult outcomes. The influence of academic attainment at age sixteen on adult psychological well-being was of comparable moderate effect size in NCDS and BCS70, indicating continuities in psychosocial adjustment in both cohorts.

The pathway linking academic attainment at age sixteen to adult social class (path 'd' in Figure 4.1) shows the extent to which *selection effects* may be regarded as operating in the data. Academic attainment has been considered as an indicator of 'developmental health', which is likely to be related to both adult social position and adult psychological well-being. The relationship between academic attainment during adolescence and adult social status can be regarded as showing evidence for indirect selection effects. Differences in the risk of later psychological maladjustment between more and less socially advantaged individuals could result in part from the movement of individuals with academic adjustment problems into less privileged social circumstances. On the other hand, there is considerable continuity in individual adjustment, regardless of family socio-economic circumstances.

The continuous experience of social risk, however, plays a vital role in the persistence of adjustment problems throughout childhood and adolescence. These cumulative continuities form a major part of the explanation of social variations in adjustment. The effect of academic attainment on adult outcomes must be interpreted in the light of the contribution of earlier social risk on adjustment throughout childhood and adolescence. The degree of continuity in social risk and its contribution to adjustment problems throughout childhood suggests that the pathways model offers a comprehensive and integrative approach for understanding the links between individual and environment over time.

Conclusion

Despite improving material conditions, there are persistent, or even increasing inequalities in academic attainment as well as adult psychological well-being. Those individuals born in 1970 who were experiencing socio-economic adversity, appear to be more disadvantaged relative to other children in the same cohort than similarly affected children born in 1958. For example, the influence of parental social class at birth on academic attainment is greater for cohort members born in 1970 than for those born in 1958. The direct influence of social risk experienced in adolescence on adult social status has nearly trebled for the later born BCS70 cohort. These findings suggest that for cohort members born in 1970 contextual factors have to some extent become more important in shaping academic adjustment and in influencing adult outcomes than for cohort members born in 1958. Material conditions have improved, yet socio-economic disadvantage and material hardship continues to be a barrier for individual achievements.

The approach adopted here begins to give us an understanding of the ways in which constellations of social risk and individual adjustment emerge early in the life course and how they interrelate over time. The findings suggest that pervasive social inequalities exist which influence academic attainment during childhood, and which are consequently reflected in adult achievements. Experience of early social risk influences the level of academic adjustment, which in turn influences adult attainment. Early deficits in skill acquisition are especially important because such deficits are carried forward in time. They can enlarge with grade and thus constrain possible future (academic) trajectories, irrespective of persistent or concurrent experiences of adversity. Early achievement promotes later attainment across multiple areas, and the early family environment is crucial in shaping subsequent development. Yet, one also has to consider intervening processes occurring at later ages to obtain a better understanding of adult outcomes. The whole life path is important in shaping individual development, not just the early years.

The findings lend support to the proposition made by Bronfenbrenner and Ceci (1994) that individual adaptation across the life span is a joint function of the characteristics of the developing person and the context in which development takes place. The experience of early disadvantage weakens individual adjustment and this detrimental effect is then carried forward into the future. Subsequent experiences of adversity add to the deterioration of already reduced adjustment. A general premise of life-course studies postulates that adaptations to change are influenced by what people bring to the new situation (Ferner, 1991). If individual adjustment is already weakened at a very early age, it becomes more and more difficult to fully develop one's potential. This negative chain effect undermines consequent academic adjustment of the young person and ultimately shapes attainments in adulthood. Generally the results imply that cumulative adversity has effects beyond those associated with current or early adversity (Ackerman et al., 1999; Bolger et al., 1995; Duncan et al., 1994; Pungello et al., 1996). As suggested by Sroufe et al. (1990), adjustment problems possibly do not lie with the individual per se but in the persistent adjustment of the individual to adverse conditions over time.

The findings have shown that constellations of social risk and academic adjustment vary by age, context and duration of the experiences, suggesting that different factors and processes might be important at different developmental stages, in different contexts and for different developmental outcomes. The developmental-contextual perspective offers a useful framework that allows us to move to a fuller understanding of the processes linking social disadvantage to individual development. The findings have confirmed the vital role of contextual experiences on individual adjustment, and thus underline the importance of an ecological approach within developmental psychology.

5   Protective factors and processes

> The first duty of a state is to see that every child born therein shall be
> well housed, clothed, fed, and educated, till it attain years of discretion.
> John Ruskin, 1867

Although there is a strong relationship between exposure to cumulative
adversity and developmental outcomes, the relationship is by no means
deterministic. There is considerable diversity in the way in which individuals respond to adversity or hardship, and many young people growing up in socio-economically disadvantaged families go on to lead
rewarding and well-adjusted lives (Garmezy, 1991; Werner & Smith,
1992; Werner & Smith, 2001). The identification of individuals who
are able to transcend exposure to adversity and who appear to avoid
developing later adjustment problems, raises important issues regarding
the factors and processes that lead to this resilience. The study of resilience not only entails the identification of individuals who succeed in the
face of adversity but also the search for potential antecedents of such
varying pathways, the protective factors and processes that mitigate,
exacerbate or mediate the risk associated with adverse socio-economic
conditions. The aim of this chapter is to identify protective factors and
processes facilitating academic resilience in early childhood, as levels of
early academic attainment are especially important in shaping later
academic trajectories.

Studies have taken a variety of approaches in their attempt to identify
factors associated with positive adjustment in the face of adversity and
then to understand the process that underlay positive adjustment. Initially the search for protective factors focused on personal attributes,
such as high IQ, that were associated with manifestations of competence
in children exposed to stressful events (Garmezy et al., 1984). Yet, not
only personal attributes but also factors in the social context are vital for
developing and maintaining positive adjustment in the face of adversity
(Bronfenbrenner & Crouter, 1983; Luthar, 1999; Sameroff et al., 1998).
As already stated in Chapter 1, previous research has identified three

broad sets of variables operating as resource factors that may impede or halt the impact of adverse experiences and promote academic resilience in the face of socio-economic adversity. These factors include characteristics of the individual, as well as factors that are external to the individual such as the family environment or the wider social context (Masten et al., 1990; Rutter, 1987; Werner & Smith, 1992).

Models of resilience

How do the different factors operate in changing the negative trajectory associated with risk? Previous research has identified three models of resilience: the protective, the cumulative and the challenge model, each describing possible links between risk, resource factors and adjustment. The protection model of resilience assumes that the resource factors interact with the risk factor in reducing the effect of a risk on an outcome (Rutter, 1985). This model is therefore also referred to as an interaction effect model. The cumulative effect model assumes a direct effect of the resource factors on an outcome, which can be independent from the risk factor. This model is also referred to as a compensatory model because the resource factors are supposed to counteract the risk factors (Masten et al., 1990b). A third model is the challenge model where the association between a risk factor and an outcome is curvilinear (Garmezy et al., 1984).

The challenge model

The challenge model of resilience suggests that low levels of risk exposure may have beneficial or steeling effects, providing a chance to practise problem-solving skills and to mobilise resources (Garmezy et al., 1984; Masten, 1999; Rutter, 1987). The risk exposure must be challenging enough to stimulate a response, yet must not be overpowering. In this model, moderate levels of risk are associated with less negative outcomes, in contrast to high levels of a risk experience, that are associated with negative outcomes. The crux of the challenge model is that moderate levels of risk exposure open up the opportunity to learn how to overcome adversity. From a developmental perspective, the challenge model can also be considered as a model of inoculation, preparing the developing person to overcome significant risks in the future (Rutter, 1987). In the challenge or inoculation model the risk or protective effect depends on the level of risk exposure.

Cumulative effect models

In the cumulative effect model, the risk or protective effect depends on the availability of psychosocial resources. The joint influence of different assets and resource factors on outcomes has been specified in terms of a main effects model, which describes the cumulative effects of these factors, which combine additively to compensate or counteract the effects of adversity (Fergusson & Horwood, 2003; Luthar et al., 2000; Masten, 1999; Masten, 2001; Sameroff et al., 1998). According to such a cumulative or main effect model, resource factors can have an equally beneficial effect for those exposed and those not exposed to adversity. And indeed, most of the well-established resource factors, such as parenting skills or self esteem show their effect in general (low-adversity) conditions as well as high-risk conditions. According to a cumulative effect model (sometimes also referred to as main effects or additive effects model) the cumulation of assets or resources will outweigh the risks. Increasing the protective resources in quality or number could theoretically offset the negative effects of risk or adversity, or improve positive adjustment in general.

Interaction effect model

The term 'protective factors' has originally only been used to describe beneficial effects in the presence of risk conditions, but not in their absence (Garmezy et al., 1984; Rutter, 1985, 1987). It has been argued by Rutter (1999) that in order to be meaningful, protective factors have to be defined by an interactive process in which exposure to the protective factor modifies the effects of the risk factor on the outcome. The exposure to a protective factor should have beneficial effects on those exposed to the risk factor, but should not benefit those not exposed to the risk factor, i.e. there should be an interactive relationship between the protective factor, the risk exposure and the outcome. In such an interactive model, the influence of adversity on outcomes is moderated by the protective factors.

Protective and vulnerability factors

Protective factors associated with positive adjustment, such as a supportive family environment can, however, be the opposite of those associated with poor adjustment – so-called vulnerability factors. For example, in a study of ten-year-old children Osborn & Milbank (1987) could show that children whose parents showed little or no interest in their education achieved a lower than average mean score on a reading test, whereas those whose parents showed a lot of interest had higher than average scores. Protective factors can lead to the amelioration or protection against risk factors, or in their reversal to some form of intensification or increased vulnerability (Garmezy, 1991; Rutter, 1987; Werner & Smith, 1982).

There has been some debate about the identification of risk and protective factors with bipolar variables, where risk or protectiveness may occur along the negative and positive poles of a continuum. While some authors have argued that there is no principled distinction between risk and vulnerability factors (Stouthamer-Loeber et al., 1993), others disagree. For example, Rutter (1990, p. 188) has emphasised that there is a crucial difference between vulnerability and protection processes on the one hand and risk mechanisms on the other. While the latter lead directly to disorder or maladjustment, the former operate indirectly, with their effects apparent only by virtue of their interactions with the risk variable. Either the vulnerability/protective factor has no effect in low-risk conditions or its effect is magnified in the presence of the risk variable. This interactive component of protection has to be put to empirical test, since without its presence there is no point in differentiating risk mechanisms from vulnerability processes (Rutter, 1990).

Interaction effects   Interaction effects are usually small in magnitude and are thus difficult to detect in variable-based analysis (Rutter, 1990; Owens & Shaw, 2003). The statistical significance of an interaction effect is dependent on the number of individuals for whom the modifying factor and risk variable co-occur. It is, for example, possible to have a strong interactive effect, which is non-significant because it applies to only a small proportion of the sample (Rutter, 1990). It has also been noted that the absence of interaction effects can be an artefact of the research design, where close matching of the groups involved is necessary to rule out confounding factors (Owens & Shaw, 2003). While the importance of interaction effects is widely acknowledged, there is some debate whether statistical interaction effects are necessary to infer specificity of processes (Luthar et al., 2000), i.e. whether predictors of positive adaptation in the face of adversity are synonymous with predictors of general positive adaptation occurring in high- or low-risk conditions.

Classification of protective effects

In an attempt to reach consensus and consistency in the description of protective factors and processes, Luthar et al. (2000) have suggested using the term protective in a broader, colloquial sense, referring to all links involving at-risk groups and offering more elaborated terms for interaction effects. They distinguish four different attributes of protection.

1 'General protective' factors have direct ameliorative effects, operating in both high- and low-risk conditions.
2 'Protective-stabilising' factors confer stability in competence despite increasing risk.
3 'Protective-enhancing' factors allow individuals to engage with stress, such that their competence is raised with increasing risk.
4 'Protective but reactive' factors generally confer advantages but less so when risk levels are high.
(Luthar et al., 2000, p. 547).

Comparable attributes should be used for the description of vulnerability effects.

Even this more elaborated classification of protective effects can be problematic, as the colloquial use of the term protection implies a barrier or shield that insulates from risk (Luthar & Zelazo, 2003). In order to differentiate more clearly between 'protective enhancing factors' that interact with a risk variable and other more general factors associated with desirable outcomes independently of the occurrence of disadvantage or adversity, some authors have suggested using terms such as promotive factors (Sameroff, 1999), resource factors (Conrad & Hammen, 1993; Pulkkinen & Caspi, 2002) or compensatory factors (Garmezy et al., 1984; Masten et al., 1988) to distinctly identify factors that have a beneficial effect in both high- and low-risk populations.

Non-universality of protective factors and processes

What constitutes an effective protective factor or process can vary both with the level and form of risk, the outcome under consideration, and the developmental stage of the individual. Children experiencing the divorce of their parents need different forms of protection or support than children growing up with mentally ill parents, or young people facing socio-economic adversity. Likewise, children responding to adversity with behavioural maladjustment or conduct problems have most likely different needs than children who in response to adversity are failing to develop their academic potential. In addition it has been argued that positive adjustment among very young children (infants and toddlers) experiencing socio-economic adversity is more likely to be influenced by the child's own characteristics and characteristics of the family environment than by extrafamilial factors such as peer relationships, relationships with adults outside the family, or community resources which become more influential as the child grows older (Luthar & Cushing, 1999; Owens & Shaw, 2003).

Focus on academic attainment in early childhood

Most research on resilience has focused on middle childhood and adolescence, while early childhood is a less researched period. There are relatively few studies focusing on positive adjustment among young children growing up in disadvantaged circumstances. Yet, the early years are generally considered as a critical time for acquiring many of the basic skills, attitude and values that tend to remain over the life span (Duncan et al., 1998; Smith et al., 1997; Werner & Smith, 1992). Young children may also be the best candidates for interventions that result from increased understanding of the processes that lead to positive outcomes under conditions of risk. Early experiences have a vital influence on later adaptation and an early history of positive adjustment is an important source of enduring influence on a child's future development (Rutter, 1990). This chapter focuses on the protective factors and processes that enable young children who have just started their school education to develop their academic potential, despite the experience of socioeconomic adversity. Previous research in this area has suggested a range of individual, family and contextual factors that may bestow academic resilience to children growing up in high-risk conditions. These are discussed below.

Characteristics of the child Individual characteristics associated with educational attainment during early childhood include temperament and behaviour as well as gender. Several studies involving children growing up in poverty have shown that during the early childhood years, girls are less affected by family socio-economic hardship than boys. For example, girls experiencing family socio-economic adversity tend to perform better in standardised achievement tests than their male counterparts (Eckenrode et al., 1995; Luthar, 1995). Developmental studies of children living in socio-economic adversity have found that girls show more resilience than boys (Werner & Smith, 1982). It has been suggested that being female is a protective factor, that young girls are less susceptible to the risks associated with socio-economic disadvantage than boys (Butler et al., 1986; Rutter et al., 1970), or that boys react emotionally and behaviourally in more negative ways than girls to negative family situations (Bolger et al., 1995).

There has also been some evidence to suggest that temperamental and behaviour factors are associated with resilience to adversity (Werner & Smith, 1992; Wyman et al., 1991). Previous investigations have established that school failure is associated with behavioural maladjustment (Cairns et al., 1989; Carlson et al., 1999; Masten & Coatsworth, 1995; Rutter, 1989). School attainment and behaviour adjustment in turn are associated with the socio-economic family background. It has been shown that multiple problem children come from multiple problem home environments characterised by social and material disadvantage and impaired parenting (Fergusson et al., 1990; McCulloch et al., 2000). Children who are perceived as good-natured, however, tend to be among those children who show positive adjustment despite the experience of multiple socio-demographic disadvantages (Moffitt & Caspi, 2001; Werner & Smith, 1992; Wyman et al., 1991).

Family characteristics   It has been suggested that the effects of socio-economic family background are mediated through the socialisation experiences within the family environment. For example, Elder's studies on families during the Great Depression (Elder, 1974/1999; Elder, 1985) indicated that parental characteristics seem to mediate at least some of the effects of poverty on children's adjustment. The role of family functioning as mediator of the effects of poverty on child functioning has been confirmed in a variety of contexts (Conger et al., 1992; Dodge et al., 1994; Felner et al., 1995; Masten, 2001; McLoyd, 1998; Sampson & Laub, 1994). Using data from the British Cohort studies, for example, Schoon & Parsons (2002b) could show that a stable and supportive family environment is beneficial for developing individual resources despite the experience of socio-economic adversity.

Family factors associated with educational resilience include parenting styles, parent–child interactions and parental involvement in the child's education (Clark, 1983; Coleman, 1988; Eccles & Harold, 1993; Epstein, 1990; Lee & Croninger, 1994; Masten, 2001; McLeod & Shanahan, 1993; Pilling, 1990). Parents influence the development of educational achievement through direct involvement with schools (Steinberg et al., 1996), or by encouraging their children to succeed academically (Reynolds & Walberg, 1991). A number of studies have confirmed that the family plays an important role in offering emotional support and socialising their children to do the best they can academically (McLoyd, 1998; Osborn, 1990; Pilling, 1990; Steinberg et al., 1989).

Social integration   Informal support systems within the community can play a vital role in helping disadvantaged children and their parents to cope with ongoing stressors of life in poverty. Social integration describes the embeddedness in the community, the social relationships and involvement with various groups within the community of which the family is part, including contact with relatives and friends (Coleman, 1988). There is consistent evidence of the benefits of social integration for parental functioning and parenting behaviour (Belsky, 1980; Brown & Harris, 1978; Burchinal et al., 1996; McLoyd, 1994). Social relationships within the community have also been conceptualised in terms of family social capital, which can play an important role in a child's educational development (Coleman, 1988). There is furthermore evidence that children's relationships to other children, or friendships among children can act as a protective factor, promoting children's competence and self-esteem (Bolger et al., 1995; Werner & Smith, 1992).

Modelling socio-economic risk and protective processes

To assess to what extent the characteristics of the child, the family and the social context described above are associated with academic attainment of young children facing socio-economic hardship, a series of regression models were run to examine the relative influence of the different resource factors on academic resilience in early childhood and to gauge whether the effects of these factors are additive (main effects) or protective (interactive). Using hierarchical regression analysis allows us to investigate the importance of different resource factors in moderating the impact of socio-economic risk experiences on academic attainment. The analysis draws on data gathered at age five for the BCS70 cohort (in 1975) and at age seven in the NCDS cohort (in 1964). Key issues to be addressed are:

- To what extent is exposure to socio-economic adversity associated with academic attainment during early childhood in both cohorts?
- Can the influence of socio-economic adversity on academic adjustment be moderated by characteristics of the child, the family and the wider social context?
- Are the psychosocial resources under investigation beneficial to those exposed to high risk but have no benefit (or less benefit) to those not exposed to high risk, i.e. are there genuine protective processes?, or do psychosocial resources have an equally beneficial effect on those

exposed to high risk and those not exposed to risk (low risk), i.e. are there promotive or compensatory processes?

A social risk index of childhood adversity

Individual risk factors do not exert their effect in isolation, but in inter-action with other influences. It is their number and their combined effect that shape development (Sameroff et al., 1993; Rutter et al., 1979). Using the same indicators of socio-economic adversity as described in Chapter 4, a composite 'social risk index' was created to assess early childhood disadvantage. The social risk index brings together into a single scale five items associated with socio-economic adversity in early childhood (age five in BCS70 and age seven in NCDS). It includes parental social status (per cent in social class IV and V), home owner-ship, overcrowding and access to amenities (see Table 4.2). In addition, the mothers' education was included as a risk factor (in NCDS 75 per cent of mothers had left school at fifteen and in BCS70 66 per cent).

A simple unweighted summary score of socio-economic adversity was created to assess the overall exposure to childhood adversity. Each of the five adversity conditions has been dichotomised to indicate the presence (1) or absense (0) of risk. The resultant scores were then added to obtain the social risk index, which ranges from 0 to 5 with a mean of 2.58 (std. 1.02) in NCDS and a mean of 2.38 (std. 1.05) in BCS70. A low score indicates a privileged family background or low risk and a high score, high socio-economic disadvantage or high social risk.

The variables included in the social risk index were all positively correlated, reflecting the tendency for family socio-economic adversities to co-occur. Table 5.1 shows that in comparison to cohort members born in 1958, more children born in 1970 had experienced low risk

Table 5.1. *Rates of low, medium or high social risk experiences in NCDS and BCS70 during early childhood*

	NCDS		BCS70	
	n	%	n	%
Low risk (0 or 1 risk factor)	2044	16%	1872	21%
Medium risk (2 or 3 risk factors)	8184	65%	5600	62%
High risk (4 and more risk factors)	2341	19%	1542	17%
Total N	12569	100	9014	100

(none or only one social risk factor). The proportion of children experiencing two or three risk factors (medium risk) is slightly higher in NCDS and slightly more children born in 1958 had experienced four or more adversities (high risk) when compared to children born in 1970.

Measures of academic adjustment

Academic attainment during early childhood was assessed by a measure of the child's reading ability. Reading ability of seven-year-olds in the NCDS cohort was measured with the Southgate Reading Test (Southgate, 1962). In BCS70, a British adaptation of the Peabody Picture Vocabulary Test (Brimer & Dunn, 1962) was used to assess reading ability of the five-year-olds. Both tests measure reading comprehension and vocabulary and are a good indicator of school readiness (see Appendix C for a more detailed description). The test scores were z-standardised, with a mean of zero and a standard deviation of 1.

Measurement of protective factors

Protective and vulnerability factors included in this analysis cover characteristics of the individual (gender and behaviour adjustment), of their families (parent–child interaction and parental involvement with child's education), as well as aspects of the wider social context (social integration).

Behaviour Behavioural adjustment was measured using a modified version of the Rutter 'A' Scale (Rutter et al., 1970) based on parental report. (See Appendix C.) Three subscales were used, indicating emotional problems, conduct problems and hyperactivity. For further analysis the subscales were recoded so that a high score in the different subscales indicates emotional stability (i.e. no emotional problems), self-regulation (i.e. no conduct problems) and no hyperactivity problems.

Family characteristics Family characteristics that can mediate some of the effects of social disadvantage on children's academic attainment include parent–child interaction and parental involvement in their child's education. Here parent–child interaction was assessed with the parents being asked whether they read to their child on a regular basis. Parental involvement in the child's education was assessed on the basis of whether the parents of the cohort member have been up to the school to talk to the teacher about the progress of their child. Both questions are described in Appendix C.

Social integration   Two measures of social integration or em-beddness in the community were used: the number of family moves since birth and whether the child has regular contact with other children (see Appendix C). It has been suggested by Coleman (1988) that a proximate indicator of social capital outside the family is the number of times that the family has moved. The social relations that constitute embeddedness of the family in the community are broken at each move. Here we have recoded the number of family moves so that a high score indicates continuous residence in the same place, i.e. no moves.

Distribution of resources by level of social risk

A profile of academic adjustment, as well as the different resources by the level of socio-economic adversity is given in Table 5.2. In comparison to children experiencing low or moderate risk, children experiencing high levels of social risk (four or more risk indicators) do less well academically and have generally lower-level psychosocial resources. In NCDS, 37 per cent of the seven-year-old children show good academic attainment (above the median) despite the experience of four or more risk factors – in comparison to 33 per cent of five-year-olds in BCS70. There are no great differences in emotional adjustment between high- and low-risk children in both cohorts, although high-risk children show more conduct problems and more hyperactivity than low-risk children. In both cohorts, parents of high-risk children are less likely to read to their child or to meet the school teacher than parents of low-risk children, although parents of BCS70 cohort members are generally more likely to read to their child or to visit the school teacher than parents of NCDS cohort members. While in NCDS a similar proportion of high- and low-risk children have never moved house since birth, in BCS70 high-risk children are more likely to move than low-risk children. On the other hand, while in NCDS children in high-risk conditions are more likely to meet other children than their more privileged peers, in BCS70 there are no great differences in the child's contact with other children between high- and low-risk children[1].

Modelling resilience processes

A series of hierarchical regression analyses were run to assess the impact of socio-economic adversity on academic attainment in early childhood

---

[1] It has to be kept in mind, however, that these variables are assessed differently in the two cohorts.

Table 5.2. *Characteristics of the child, the parents and the social context according to the level of social risk (%)*

	Social Risk Index		
	Low Risk (0,1)	Medium Risk (2,3)	High Risk (4+)
Academic attainment above median			
NCDS	69	48	37
BCS70	65	49	33
No emotional problems			
NCDS	59	60	61
BCS70	70	70	69
No conduct problems			
NCDS	59	54	47
BCS70	68	58	47
No hyperactivity			
NCDS	52	45	42
BCS70	49	44	38
Parents read to child			
NCDS	68	56	49
BCS70	81	68	60
Parents meet teacher			
NCDS	72	57	49
BCS70	88	84	81
No family moves since birth			
NCDS	38	37	35
BCS70	50	46	32
Child meets other children			
NCDS	72	80	81
BCS70	91	89	87

and to test whether the resource factors can counter-balance the influence of social risk on academic adjustment. To check possible effects of non-response on the variables under investigation two correlation matrices were compared: one using pairwise and one using listwise deletion of cases with missing values. In addition, linear regression analyses were run using the FIML approach offered in the AMOS 4.01 programme (see Appendix B for a more detailed description). All models were run separately for each cohort. Similar results from the three different estimation procedures suggest that there is little systematic sample bias related to differing rates of non-response.

In the first step a main-effect model was run with the full sample in each cohort (i.e. cohort members with complete data on the social index indicators and the reading test at age five in BCS70 and age seven in NCDS) involving 12,569 cohort members from NCDS and 9,014 from BCS70. The variables assumed to moderate the effect of socio-economic adversity on academic attainment were entered into the analysis based on their proximity to the individual, starting with individual characteristics (or personal resources), followed by characteristics of the family (or family resources) and then by characteristics of the social context (social resources). The results of the hierarchical multiple regression analyses predicting reading ability in early childhood are given in Table 5.3, which gives the unstandardised regression coefficients, as well as the 95 per cent confidence interval for the unstandardised regression estimates for the different predictor variables.

In Model 1 (Wave 1) the link between socio-economic adversity and academic attainment was estimated for each cohort separately. Consistent with previous research the regression coefficient is negative and significant, indicating that socio-economic adversity is a significant risk factor, undermining academic achievement in early childhood. In both cohorts socio-economic adversity alone predicts about 6 per cent of the variation in reading ability in early childhood (at age seven in NCDS and age five in BCS70).

Table 5.3. *Hierarchical multiple regression analysis predicting reading ability in early childhood. Unstandardised estimates, 95% confidence interval for B and ΔR^2*

	NCDS at age 7			BCS70 at age 5		
	B	95% CI for B	ΔR^2	B	95% CI for B	ΔR^2
Social Index	−.19**	(−.22−−.18)	.06	−.19**	(−.21−−.17)	.06
Child Indices			.04			.01
Gender	.15**	(.13−.17)		.00	(−.05−.02)	
Emotional Stability	−.03*	(−.04−−.01)		.01	(−.01−.03)	
No conduct problems	.08**	(.06−.10)		.05**	(.03−.07)	
No hyperactivity	.09**	(.07−.10)		.04**	(.02−.07)	
Family Indices			.01			.01
Parents read to child	.04**	(.02−.08)		.19**	(.15−.24)	
Parents meet teacher	.19**	(.17−.24)		.07*	(.01−.13)	
Social Integration			.00			.01
No family moves	.01	(−.02−.03)		.07**	(.04−.09)	
Child meets other children	.00	(−.05−.04)		.20**	(.13−.26)	
Total R²			.11			.09

Note: gender: boys = 1; girls = 2; ** p <.000; * p < .005.

Wave 2 adds the first set of resource factors to the equation, i.e. the child's gender and behavioural adjustment. In both cohorts the addition of these factors significantly increases the amount of explained variance, although in BCS70 the difference in R^2 is only one per cent. In NCDS, being female has a significant beneficial effect, while in BCS70, gender shows no significant effect on early reading ability in addition and above the experience of socio-economic adversity. In NCDS, emotional adjustment is negatively correlated with academic attainment at age seven, while in BCS70, emotional attainment has no significant association with academic attaintment. In both cohorts self-regulation and lack of hyperactivity are significantly associated with good reading ability.

Wave 3 adds to the equation the characteristics of parents in their interaction with the child as well as their involvement with the child's education. Both variables are significantly and positively associated with academic attainment, yet to a different extent. In NCDS, parental contact with the teacher shows a stronger association with academic attainment of the child than parental reading to the child. In BCS70 parental reading is more important for the child's academic attainment than parental contact with the school teacher.

Wave 4 adds the variables indicating social integration of parents and child in the community. While in BCS70 the number of family moves and the amount of contact of the child with other children are significantly related to academic attainment, in NCDS these two variables are not significantly associated with academic attainment, independently and in addition to socio-economic risk, characteristics of the child or the parents.

After including all the protective factors into the main-effect model the impact of social adversity on academic attainment has reduced from $-.24$ to $-.21$ in NCDS and from $-.24$ to $-.20$ in BCS70. In NCDS all factors together predict about eleven per cent of the variation of academic attainment in early childhood, and in BCS70 an overall nine per cent of variation in reading ability can be explained. In NCDS the most significant beneficial factors for good academic attainment at age seven are being female, parental contact with the school teacher, and behavioural adjustment (no or low conduct or hyperactivity problems). In BCS70, academic attainment at age five is best predicted by parent–child interactions, i.e. by parents reading regularly to their child, social integration followed by self-regulation.

In order to determine the specificity of the protective processes additional regression analyses were run separately among children experiencing high social risk (four and more risk factors) and those exposed to low-risk conditions (none or one risk factor). Separate analyses per group are considered preferable to using interaction terms in regression, as interaction effects tend to be small in magnitude and highly unstable (Luthar et al., 2003; Owens & Shaw, 2003).

Table 5.4 gives the regression coefficients predicting reading ability in early childhood, as well as the 95 per cent confidence interval for the unstandardised regression estimates. Among low-risk children in NCDS significant predictors of reading ability at age seven are gender, low hyperactivity, self-regulation, parent's involvement with the child's education and contact of the child with other children. In BCS70, the most important predictors of academic attainment among low-risk children are parent–child interactions and parental involvement with their child's education, the child's low hyperactivity and self-regulation. Among high-risk children in NCDS all resource factors, except for child's contact with other children, show a significant association with academic attainment – all in the predicted direction, except for emotional attainment, which shows a negative association with academic adjustment. Among high-risk children in BCS70 significant predictors of academic attainment are whether the parents read to the child, the number of family moves and low hyperactivity of the child.

Among high-risk children in both cohorts the combination of the resource factors explains a higher proportion of variation in academic attainment than among low-risk children. There are a number of protective enhancing factors that operate more strongly among high-risk children than among children experiencing low risk. In NCDS these include negative emotional adjustment, self-regulation, parents reading to the child, whether the parents have met the teacher and no family moves since birth. In BCS70, differences between high- and low-risk children are less strong. Protective factors for high-risk children are if their family does not move house, parents reading to the child and no hyperactivity.

Conclusion

In this chapter, data collected in both cohorts during early childhood has been used to examine the relationship between early social risk, academic attainment and psychosocial resources which are assumed to moderate the influence of socio-economic adversity on individual adjustment. A social risk index measure was created using a range of indicators, all reflecting the socio-economic resources available to the family. For the assessment of academic attainment standardised and validated test instruments assessing reading ability have been used. A range of psychosocial resources that may influence academic resilience

Table 5.4. *Hierarchical regression predicting academic attainment in early childhood*

	NCDS age 7 low risk			NCDS age 7 high risk			BCS70 age 5 low risk			BCS70 age 5 high risk		
	B	95% CI for B	ΔR^2	B	95% CI for B	ΔR^2	B	95% CI for B	ΔR^2	B	95% CI for B	ΔR^2
Child Indices			.05			.07			.01			.01
Gender	.16**	(.10–.30)		.15**	(.12–.42)		.01	(-.10–.07)		.00	(-.11–.11)	
Emotional stability	-.03	(-.04–.10)		-.06**	(-.12—.04)		.02	(-.02–.05)		.03	(-.02–.07)	
No conduct problems	.05#	(.00–.07)		.13**	(.08–.17)		.05#	(.01–.09)		.03	(-.02–.07)	
No hyperactivity	.07**	(.04–.12)		.09**	(.04–.13)		.08*	(.07–.10)		.07*	(.01–.11)	
Family Indices			.01			0.1			.01			0.2
Parents read to child	.02	(-.04–.07)		.05*	(.01–.15)		.13*	(.04–.25)		.22**	(.10–.33)	
Parents meet teacher	.07*	(.03–18)		.20**	(.12–.32)		.19**	(.06–.31)		.01	(-.15–.13)	
Social Integration			.00			.01			.00			.01
No family moves	.02	(-.02–.07)		.08*	(.03–.15)		.00	(-.06–.06)		.11**	(.07–.20)	
Child meets other children	.08#	(.00–.15)		.07	(-.06–.19)		.16	(-.03–.27)		.15	(-.01–.30)	
Total R²			.06			.09			.02			.04

Note: gender: boys = 1; girls= 2; ** p <.000; * p <.005; # p <.05.

in the face of socio-economic adversity have also been considered in the analysis. Unfortunately as is often the case with large-scale surveys, the data collected for the two cohort studies were originally not intended to be used for the investigation of resilience in the face of adversity, limiting the choice of available indicator variables. It is possible that a number of factors not included in the analysis might have advanced a better understanding of the protective factors and processes under investigation. Furthermore, a number of the moderating variables included in the analysis could only be measured dichotomously. By reporting the 95 per cent confidence interval for the unstandardised regression estimates, the variability in the mediating variables can be better appreciated. The combination of risk and protective factors explains only about ten per cent of the variation in the reading ability during early childhood. The results correspond to findings reported by Smith et al. (1997) in their examination of the consequences of income poverty, family structure and home environment on the reading ability of five- and seven-year-old children in the National Longitudinal Study of Youth (NLSY). It has been argued by Duncan (2002) that some measures of psychosocial factors prove to be more powerful in differentiating individuals according to their attainments in the long term, rather than in the short term and that only longitudinal studies enable the appreciation of long-term influence of risk factors experienced in early life.

The present analysis confirms that socio-economic adversity is a risk factor for academic attainment in early childhood. In agreement with previous research, there was evidence that with increasing exposure to socio-economic adversity there was a corresponding decrease in academic attainment. Despite improved material conditions experienced by the later born cohort, the negative influence of socio-economic adversity on early academic attainment has remained more or less the same in both cohorts. The impact of socio-economic risk factors was, however, moderated by the psychosocial resources included in the analysis, i.e. by characteristics of the individual, the family and the social context. The influence of the psychosocial resources varies for the two birth cohorts, and for different risk conditions, i.e. for high- versus low-risk environments.

The results suggest the existence of both compensatory and protective processes. The regression models run separately for the full sample of each cohort provide evidence in support of the main effect model, suggesting that the psychosocial resources included in the analysis are compensating to some extent for early socio-economic adversity. The model was then tested within extreme groups of children exposed to either high or low social risk, to examine possible interaction effects. In both cohorts we find a combination of protective and promotive processes.

In NCDS a number of protective factors could be identified which showed a greater beneficial impact on academic attainment among children experiencing high social risk than among low-risk children. These protective factors were parents' involvement with the child's education, emotional adjustment, self-regulation of the child, as well as social integration (no family moves). General promotive factors which show a similar beneficial effect under low- and high-risk conditions include gender and low hyperactivity. In BCS70 the experience of no family moves since birth is confirmed as a protective factor among high-risk children, indicating the importance of social integration for children experiencing socio-economic adversity. Parents reading to the child appears also as a protective factor highlighting the role of parent–child interaction for positive development. Low hyperactivity, on the other hand, appears to be a general promotive factor.

The findings suggest that academic resilience depends on age and context-specific factors that provide protection against specific risks for children in specific life contexts. The observed variations could be due to developmental fluctuations, as children in the NCDS cohort are two years older than the children in the BCS70 cohort at the time of assessment. On the other hand, the observed variations could suggest the existence of period or cohort effects, since some factors show their impact only for the earlier born NCDS cohort, but not for the later born BCS70 cohort. For example, gender appeared as a cohort-specific resource factor. In NCDS the findings indicate that young boys are more susceptible to the risks associated with socio-economic disadvantage than girls, confirming findings from previous studies (Butler et al., 1986; Rutter et al., 1970). In the BCS70 cohort, however, gender differences have disappeared. The same result emerged in a study by (Osborn, 1990) on resilient ten-year old children in the BCS70 cohort. Osborn argued that gender differences in vulnerability and competence depend on the types of stressors and outcomes involved, but also on the child's age when the assessment is made. Furthermore, the present study suggests that gender differences depend on the overall socio-historical context that dictates new opportunities and obstacles. It is possible that with the growing importance of school achievements and qualifications during the 1970s as well as decreasing gender inequalities, academic achievements were equally encouraged among boys and girls in high- and low-risk conditions.

There are furthermore cohort-specific differences in the effect of behaviour in moderating the influence of socio-economic adversity on academic attainment. In NCDS emotional stability appears to be a vulnerability factor, while in BCS70 it has no significant effect. Low hyperactivity, on the other hand, is a general promotive factor in both cohorts, showing its beneficial effect in both high- and low-risk conditions. While the beneficial effects of behaviour adjustment are well documented in the research literature (Cairns et al., 1989; Carlson et al., 1999; Masten & Coatsworth, 1995; Rutter, 1989; Werner & Smith, 1992; Wyman et al., 1991), the increased risk of academic maladjustment among high-risk children who show no emotional adjustment problems is something of a surprise. It might, however, be possible that high-risk children who are perceived as anxious by their parents are performing better academically than their more emotionally stable peers. This interaction is, however, only apparent in one cohort and cannot therefore be generalised. Possibly in the wake of newly emerging anti-authoritarian parenting styles the demonstration of emotional distress among children was more likely to be tolerated and did not call for special attention.

Parental involvement with the child's education, i.e. whether the parents have been to the school to discuss their child's progress with the teacher is a protective factor for high-risk children in NCDS. In BCS70, on the other hand, parental involvement shows a beneficial effect among both low- and high-risk children. This finding could indicate either an age or a period effect. In the NCDS cohort the seven-year-old children have already completed their first year of schooling, while the five-year-old BCS70 children are just starting. Parental involvement in their child's education might thus be more important for high-risk children who are already immersed in the education process and less so for children just about to start their education.

Parent–child interaction, as manifested in parents regularly reading to the child is an important resource factor in both cohorts, confirming the vital role of parent–child interactions in stimulating children to achieve academically (Clark, 1983; Eccles & Harold, 1993; Epstein, 1990; Lee & Croninger, 1994; Masten, 2001; McLeod & Shanahan, 1993; Pilling, 1990; Reynolds & Walberg, 1991).

The number of family moves since birth, which has been used as a proximate indicator for social relationships in the community (Coleman, 1988), is associated with academic attainment among high-risk children in both cohorts. Children in disadvantaged families who do not have to move perform better academically than their peers in similar circumstances who have to move often. These findings suggest that families and their children experiencing residential continuity, possibly being embedded in a stable network of social relationships in the community, are better equipped to deal with the effects of socio-economic adversity than isolated families and children who are constantly uprooted.

In summary, in both cohorts we find a combination of compensatory and protective processes. Not only characteristics of the child, but also of the family environment and the wider social context play a role in influencing academic attainment when facing socio-economic risk. However, the observed protective processes appear to be more effective among the earlier born cohort, suggesting that despite the generally improved material circumstances and the greater emphasis on and importance of academic achievement, children born in 1970 who were experiencing socio-economic hardship were relatively more disadvantaged than similarly afflicted children born twelve years earlier. While characteristics of the child seem to have become less important in explaining academic attainment when facing socio-economic adversity during early childhood, parent–child interactions seem to have become more important, especially among high-risk children.

The findings have implications for interventions which should aim to reduce adversity, work with families to strengthen parent–child interaction and parental involvement with the education of the child, provide treatment for children with behaviour problems and aim to improve social integration. While some of these measures would benefit all individuals, as for example, the treatment of behaviour problems among children, or the improvement of parenting skills, there are measures that would specifically help young children experiencing socio-economic adversity. Such measures include improvement of housing conditions and the strengthening of social cohesion.

6   Stability of early adjustment over time

I am 25 so I do not have to live with Mum and Dad anymore. If I stay at their house I would pay for my keep and clothing, etc. At first I would go to university and take drama, music and English (art would be a hobby). I would try and get a degree so I could apply for any job. . . . When I came home I would be helpful to Mum and Dad if I lived with them, if not, I would buy a record player and go round with long haired boys! I should try to live a quiet, peaceful life and would wear decent, smart clothes and would buy a small homely flat that I could share with my colleagues. . . .

Response by an 11 year-old female NCDS cohort member to the question:
'Imagine that you are now 25 years old. Write about the life you are leading,
your interests, your home life and your work at the age of 25'.

The questions addressed in this chapter concern the stability of early adjustment over time and across domains. Is there continuity of positive adjustment across the life span? Do patterns of adjustment persist as individuals move from childhood into adolescence and into adult life? If there are continuities in adjustment in one domain, such as academic attainment, does this suggest adjustment across other domains as well? Following the lives of individuals from birth into adulthood the onto-genetic stability of resilience is examined, mapping educational attainment and behavioural adjustment during childhood and adolescence. Subsequent transitions into adult roles as worker, partner and parent are described, as well as the psychological well-being of cohort members in their early thirties. Adopting a person-centred approach, individuals are grouped according to early constellations of risk and academic adjustment. Continuity and changes in adjustment across domains are assessed for different subgroups of individuals in both cohorts. Furthermore, interdependencies of life-course adjustments and life-course transitions are illustrated with case stories. The findings are discussed in terms of their relevance for life-course theory.

Resilience: a dynamic state

There is evidence to suggest stability in adjustment levels among at-risk children followed over time (Cowen et al., 1997; Egeland et al., 1993; Masten et al., 1999; Werner & Smith, 1992). Yet, some researchers argue that although some at-risk individuals show positive adjustment at a particular point in time, many falter subsequently (Coie et al., 1993; Kaplan, 1999). It has also been shown that competence over time can be displayed within but not necessarily across distinct groups of behaviour (Luthar, 1997). There are, however, only a few studies linking early adjustment during childhood to adult outcomes and still fewer comparing how young people with different exposure to socio-economic adversity fare across the transition from school to adult life. It is generally acknowledged that resilience is not a static state (Cicchetti et al., 1993; Coie et al., 1993; Egeland et al., 1993), yet only long-term longitudinal studies can provide evidence of the dynamic nature of resilience.

Continuity and change in transitions and adjustment over time

The process of development necessarily involves a complex mix of both continuities and change (Lerner, 1984). It has been argued that out-comes following early adversity are quite diverse, with long-term effects depending on the nature of subsequent life experiences (Clarke & Clarke, 2000; 2003; Rutter, 1989). The life course is marked by life transitions when roles are transformed, refined or left behind for new roles (Bronfenbrenner, 1979). Starting school, transferring from primary to secondary school, ending full-time education, finding a first job, leaving home, starting a long-term relationship, having a child – each of these transitions happens in a particular sequence which has been described by Elder (1985) as the *principle of timing* in life states. Individuals do 'not march in concert across major events of the life course' as there are variations in the pace and sequencing of these transitions (Elder & Shanahan, 2006). Especially in times of recent social changes life-course transitions have become more varied and individualised (Shanahan, 2000).

The developmental impact of a life transition is contingent on when it occurs in a person's life. An event such as getting a first job, or having a baby, will have different meanings and consequences if it occurs before or after completion of education. Furthermore, life transitions have to be considered both as end products of past processes as well as instigators of future ones (Luthar, 2003; Rutter, 1989).

Following an 'early timing hypothesis' one could expect that early academic resilience has beneficial long-term consequences through its effects on subsequent transitions. It might be possible that early resources, such as academic capabilities, can shape the life chances and choices of individuals and influence the timing of important life course transitions such as leaving school, leaving home, first partnerships and family formation. Yet, lives are lived interdependently. According to the principle of 'linked lives', we could expect that children growing up in relatively disadvantaged circumstances have fewer opportunities and resources to help them develop and maintain their early academic attainments (as discussed in Chapter 4). Considering the principle of historical time, we also have to assume that socio-historical changes, such as the onset of a major recession in the early 1980s, can influence the timing and sequence of transitions. According to the principle of human agency we would furthermore expect heterogeneity in individual response to adversity across time.

A person-centred approach to identify early academic resilience

The influence of context, timing and duration of risk experiences on individual adjustment has already been examined in Chapter 4. The Structural Equation Models illustrated the effect of cumulative disadvantage and showed how constellations of risk and individual adjustment develop over time. In the following a person-orientated approach is adopted, going beyond the variable-based approach that examines main effect models or interaction effects (Cairns et al., 1998; Luthar et al., 2000). In contrast to variable-centred approaches, the person-centred approach considers how variables combine in individuals when conceptualising the connection between conditions of social risk and manifest competence. Individuals are categorised on the basis of selected criteria, reflecting patterns of resilience as they occur naturally (Masten, 2001; Masten & Coatsworth, 1998; Pulkkinen, 1996).

Here four groups describing different patterns of early academic adjustment were identified on the basis of experiences of socio-economic adversity and concurrent reading ability. Socio-economic adversity was defined by the social risk index developed in Chapter 5, and academic adjustment was measured by early reading ability assessed at age five in BCS70 and age seven in NCDS (using the same measures as in Chapter 5). Children who showed good reading ability (above the median) in early childhood despite experiencing high socio-economic risk (four or more risk indicators) were identified as educationally resilient. Children with low reading ability (at or below the median) in similar circumstances were identified as vulnerable. The experiences of these two socially disadvantaged groups were compared and contrasted to a control group of individuals who grew up in circumstances characterised by low socio-economic risk (none or one risk factor). Among these privileged children a differentiation was made between individuals with reading ability above or below the median. The first group was defined as the 'multiple-advantaged', the latter had been labelled as 'under-achievers'. The categorisation of sample members into four groups aimed at identifying high- and low-risk children with high or low levels of educational adjustment. Comparisons between the groups allows for person by situation interactions to be explored more fully (Hinde, 1998).

Figure 6.1 shows the distribution of resilient and vulnerable individuals, as well as of multiple-advantaged and underachieving children in the two cohorts. In NCDS, 69 per cent of cohort members exposed to low social risk showed above average reading skill, in comparison to 37 per cent of cohort members facing high socio-economic adversity. In BCS70, 65 per cent of low-risk individuals showed good early reading skills, compared to 32 per cent of children growing up in high social risk conditions.

Long-term academic adjustment

What are the long-term academic attainments of the four different groups? Figure 6.2 shows the mean z-scores, standardised for the whole sample (males and females), for educational attainment of NCDS cohort members at ages seven, eleven and sixteen years and BCS70 cohort members at ages five, ten and sixteen. The lines differentiate between performances of children classified as multiple-advantaged, advantaged underachievers, resilient and vulnerable, at seven (NCDS) and at five (BCS70) respectively.

In NCDS, resilient and multiple-advantaged children had similarly strong reading abilities at seven, while the low-achieving children from privileged backgrounds were performing better than vulnerable seven-year-olds from relatively disadvantaged families. In the transition from childhood to adolescence the multiple-advantaged showed consistently above average attainments, although there was a slight drop at sixteen. The educational attainment of resilient seven-year-olds fell by eleven, yet they maintained above average performance. At sixteen they showed average exam performance, but had fallen behind in their attainment when compared to the advantaged early low-achievers, who were catching up. The advantaged early low-achievers increased their educational

Educational resilience NCDS

Reading at age 7	Socio-economic risk	
	Low-risk (none or 1 risk factor)	High-risk (4 or more risk factors)
Above median	Multiple-advantaged (n=1412)	Resilient (n=867)
At or below median	Under-achievers (n=632)	Vulnerable (n=1474)
Total	n=2044	n=2341

Educational resilience BCS70

Reading at age 5	Socio-economic risk	
	Low-risk (none or 1 risk factor)	High-risk (4 or more risk factors)
Above median	Multiple-advantaged (n=1218)	Resilient (n=498)
At or below median	Under-achievers (n=654)	Vulnerable (n=1044)
Total	n=1872	n=1542

Figure 6.1. Identification of resilience based on risk and adjustment status.

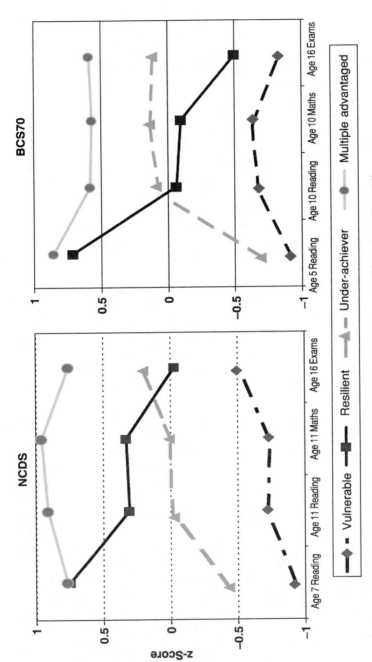

Figure 6.2. Educational attainment in NCDS (ages 7 to 16) and BCS70 (ages 5 to 16).

performance over time. They obtained average maths and reading scores at eleven, and at sixteen they showed above average exam performance. Educational attainment of vulnerable children increased at eleven and at sixteen, although their exam performance was consistently below average.

In BCS70 the multiple-advantaged showed consistently above average educational attainment across their childhood years, although their performance fell slightly by eleven. The educational performance of resilient children dropped dramatically at eleven, and at sixteen they had exam scores half a standard deviation below the average. The advantaged early low-achievers, on the other hand, considerably improved their performance by eleven and maintained above average performance at sixteen. Vulnerable children with low reading ability at five showed the lowest attainment across all assessments, with a slight increase at ten, followed by a drop at sixteen. Among the four extreme groups there were similiar patterns of educational attainment throughout childhood for both girls and boys in both cohorts, following the trends reported above.

The findings suggest that early academic resilience is to some extent maintained throughout childhood and adolescence, confirming an early timing assumption, especially in the NCDS cohort. Yet, children from relatively disadvantaged family backgrounds who demonstrated good reading skills during early childhood did not maintain their performance to the same level as their more advantaged peers. In both cohorts there was a drop in their attainment by eleven, which marks the transition from primary to secondary school. Another hurdle at which early resilient children stumble is the exam at sixteen. While advantaged early under-achievers in both cohorts were able to improve their academic attainments at both these transition points, early resilient children were falling behind, leading to an increasing divide between children from privileged and less privileged backgrounds, especially in the later born BCS70 cohort.

It is possible that the changes in test scores among the selected extreme groups merely represent a regression towards the mean. Yet, there were not only changes in level, but also in position. The improved performance of advantaged early underachievers as well as that of vulnerable individuals at eleven and sixteen could possibly also be explained by increased attention and support aimed at and provided for low achievers in general, and the socially advantaged in particular. Young people from disadvantaged backgrounds who appear to be getting by in school, however, receive less attention and support (Iacovou & Berthoud, 2001), which might explain the steep decline in educational attainment among the resilient group during adolescence.

Academic accomplishments in early adulthood

After the age of sixteen early resilient young people in both cohorts were more likely than vulnerable individuals to continue with full-time education and to obtain degree-level qualifications. They were also less likely to leave school without qualifications. Yet, in both cohorts, early educationally resilient individuals were not achieving to the same level as their more privileged peers. We have seen in Chapter 3 that among the thirty-three-year-old cohort members in NCDS, 29 per cent of men and 26 per cent of women had obtained degree-level qualifications, compared to 34 per cent of men and 35 per cent of women among the thirty-year-old cohort members in BCS70. In NCDS, 7 per cent of the vulnerable young men and women succeeded in gaining degree-level qualifications, in comparison to 20 per cent of the early resilient cohort members, 38 per cent of the advantaged early underachievers and 60 per cent of the multiple-advantaged. In BCS70, 11 per cent of the vulnerable individuals gained degree-level qualifications, compared to 21 per cent of resilient, 45 per cent of advantaged early underachievers and 57 per cent of multiple-advantaged cohort members.

Early academic resilience showed some degree of stability throughout the transition from childhood to adulthood. Furthermore, it appears to be associated with continued participation in further education. Yet, manifest early academic resilience did not enable young people to completely overcome the adversity of disadvantage. Privileged underachievers who showed below average reading ability in early childhood were clearly outperforming their less privileged peers who demonstrated above average early reading skills. The findings suggest a persistent and growing gap in educational attainment between individuals experiencing high versus low socio-economic risk during childhood, indicating the continuous polarisation between privileged individuals and children from less advantaged backgrounds, despite the increasing rates of young people participating in further education.

Long-term behavioural adjustment

Behavioural adjustment in both cohorts was measured with the same modified version of the Rutter 'A' Scale (Rutter et al., 1970) already used in Chapter 5. The scale differentiates three subscales indicating conduct, hyperactivity and emotional adjustment problems (see Appendix C) as assessed by parental report. The scores in each of the subscales were z-standardised for the whole sample (males and females). Here a high score indicates behaviour problems.

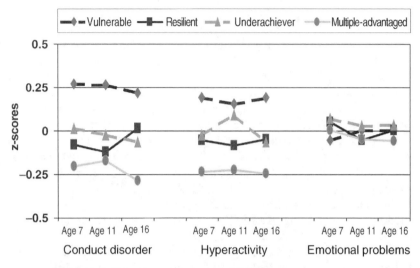

Figure 6.3. Behaviour adjustment (NCDS).

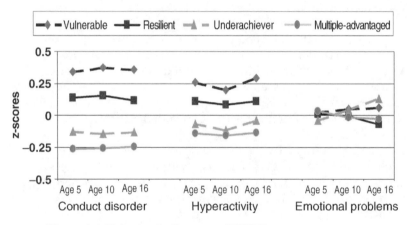

Figure 6.4. Behaviour adjustment (BCS70).

Figures 6.3–6.4 show the mean z-scores for behavioural adjustment of NCDS cohort members at ages seven, eleven and sixteen and BCS70 cohort members at ages five, ten and sixteen. The lines in each figure differentiate between performances of children classified as multiple-advantaged, advantaged, early underachievers, resilient and vulnerable, at five (BCS70) or seven (NCDS). In both cohorts vulnerable children showed more conduct and hyperactivity problems at all measurement points than the other groups. The multiple-advantaged children showed the least adjustment problems in these two subscales.

In NCDS, privileged underachievers presented slightly more conduct problems than resilient individuals at ages seven and eleven, but their conduct improved at age sixteen, while resilient individuals showed an increase in conduct problems at age sixteen. Parents of both early under-achievers and resilient individuals reported average levels of hyperactivity at seven and sixteen, although at eleven, early underachievers showed nearly as high levels of hyperactivity as the vulnerable group. There are less distinct differences for emotional adjustment and the four groups show comparable levels of emotional distress.

In BCS70 children experiencing high socio-economic adversity pre-sented higher levels of conduct and hyperactivity problems than children exposed to low social risk. This finding might indicate that in BCS70, behaviour problems were more prevalent among children experiencing socio-economic adversity. As in NCDS emotional problems showed the least differentiation between the four groups, suggesting that in both cohorts emotional problems were not as important for good academic adjustment as conduct problems and hyperactivity.

It is also noteworthy, that in both cohorts there are significant gender differences in behavioural adjustment. At all ages boys showed signifi-cantly more conduct problems and hyperactivity than girls. Girls on the other hand, showed more emotional problems. The differences were greatest for conduct problems during early and mid-childhood, and were less marked for emotional problems. These findings confirm other studies, including cross-national comparisons, which report that boys show more conduct problems than girls (Crijnen et al., 1997; Meltzer et al., 2000), that girls show more emotional problems than boys (Bebbington, 1996; Emslie et al., 1999), and that sex differences in conduct problems narrow in middle adolescence (Moffitt et al., 2001; Zoccolillo, 1993).

Despite these gender differences, early educational resilience was associated in both cohorts with behavioural adjustment among boys and girls, especially in early and mid-childhood. There were clear links between early educational resilience and conduct problems as well as hyperactivity. Boys and girls showing early academic resilience were less likely to present conduct problems or hyperactivity than vulnerable children from disadvantaged backgrounds with below average reading skills. Emotional problems, on the other hand, appeared not to be associated with differences in academic adjustment, suggesting that academic adaptation can occur at the cost of emotional disturbance.

The findings here suggest differences in adjustment based on the effect of relative disadvantage. In NCDS, early academic resilience seemed to be associated with positive behaviour adjustment through-out childhood (although conduct problems increased in adolescence), while in BCS70, academically resilient boys and girls showed fewer conduct problems and hyperactivity than vulnerable boys and girls, but higher levels when compared to both advantaged underachievers or the multiple-advantaged. In BCS70, there seemed to be a stronger association between early social disadvantage and behaviour problems than in NCDS, confirming previous findings (Schoon et al., 2003). The effect of early socio-economic stress on consequent behavioural adjustment was found to be twice as strong in BCS70 as in NCDS, suggesting that those suffering adversity in BCS70 were a more extreme group relative to their peers than similarly affected children in the NCDS and that this increased relative disadvantage showed its impact very early on. If behavioural adjustment is already undermined at an early age, it becomes more difficult for the young person to fully adjust. This negative chain effect can hinder the psychosocial adjust-ment of the young person and ultimately impede adult psychosocial functioning.

Adult psychosocial adjustment

Are cohort members demonstrating early educational resilience less likely to develop adjustment problems as adults when compared to their peers showing below average attainment in early childhood? Table 6.1 gives the percentages of men and women in both cohorts reporting signs of psychological distress in their early thirties as well as an indication of how satisfied cohort members are with their lives and how much they feel in control of their lives.

Psychological distress

Levels of psychological distress were measured with the twenty-four-item Malaise Inventory (Rutter et al., 1970) described in Appendix C. Cohort members with a score greater than seven were identified as showing high levels of psychological distress or depression (Rodgers et al., 1999). Women reported generally higher levels of psychological distress than men, yet rates of depression had generally increased for the later born cohort, especially among men. In NCDS about 3 per cent of men from privileged backgrounds as well as men from disadvantaged backgrounds showing early academic resilience expressed signs of psychological distress, compared to 8 per cent of men from disadvantaged backgrounds with below average reading skills. In BCS70, the rates of depression among men from privileged family backgrounds had increased to 8 per cent for multiple-advantaged men and 9 per cent for privileged early underachievers. Twelve per cent of men from disadvantaged family backgrounds showing early academic resilience reported high levels of psychological distress, compared to 16 per cent of vulnerable men with below average educational capabilities. It appears that early academic resilience had been protective especially for men in NCDS. In BCS70, men from disadvantaged family backgrounds demonstrating early academic resilience reported less psychological distress than vulnerable men with below average academic capabilities, but were not doing as well as their more privileged peers. For women in both cohorts a similar picture emerges: women showing early academic resilience were less distressed than their more vulnerable peers, yet women growing up in disadvantage reported higher levels of depression than women born into privileged circumstances regardless of early academic attainment.

Life satisfaction

Levels of life satisfaction in both cohorts were measured with a ten-point rating scale item: 'All things considered how satisfied are you with your life?' Cohort members with a score of eight and higher were identified as being very satisfied with their lives. We have already seen in Chapter 3 that cohort members born in 1958 were slightly more satisfied with their lives in their early thirties than cohort members born in 1970, and that women were generally more satisfied with their lives than men. Comparing levels of life satisfaction in the four extreme groups (see Table 6.1), it appears that in both cohorts multiple-advantaged and early academically resilient men from disadvantaged family background were more satisfied with their lives than men showing below average academic ability in early childhood, suggesting that early academic resilience was a beneficial factor for later life satisfaction among men. For women the picture was less clear cut. In NCDS, multiple-advantaged women showed the highest levels of life satisfaction, followed by, early underachievers and then early academically resilient women. In BCS70, early underachievers expressed similar levels of life satisfaction as multiple-advantaged or early academically resilient women. Women from disadvantaged family backgrounds with low academic capability showed the lowest levels of life satisfaction.

Table 6.1. *Outcomes in adulthood: Psychological well-being during early thirties by early academic adjustment (in %)*

	NCDS				BCS70			
	Multiple-advantaged	Underachievers	Resilient	Vulnerable	Multiple-advantaged	Underachievers	Resilient	Vulnerable
Psychological distress								
Men	2.6	3.1	3.3	8.2	8.3	9.0	12.4	16.1
Women	4.3	6.7	8.2	11.4	10.1	11.7	17.1	21.6
Very satisfied with life (8+)								
Men	56.0	50.6	53.8	48.0	55.7	43.9	46.7	40.0
Women	59.4	56.6	54.6	47.7	59.0	60.1	56.5	47.1
Feeling in control								
Men	77.7	77.4	70.8	57.6	81.5	70.1	67.9	57.6
Women	80.8	78.0	71.2	65.2	85.3	80.5	74.8	67.3

Feeling in control

Another indicator of positive adjustment in early adulthood assesses feelings of being in control of one's life (described in Appendix C). As shown in Table 6.1, multiple-advantaged cohort members born in 1970 appeared to feel more in control of their lives than cohort members born in 1958. Women seemed to feel more in control than men, especially in the later born BCS70 cohort. Furthermore, in both cohorts, men and women showing early academic resilience appeared to feel more in control of their lives than vulnerable individuals. Yet, men and women in both cohorts growing up in privileged circumstances reported generally higher levels of control than men and women growing up in disadvantaged circumstances, regardless of early academic attainments.

These findings indicate cohort as well as gender differences in adult adjustment. The increasing participation of women in the labour market might be associated with an increasing assertiveness and independence among women. Yet, individuals born in the emerging 'Crisis Decades' of the 1970s, characterised by increasing instability and uncertainty, experienced more distress in their everyday lives than the cohort born twelve years earlier, at the end of the 'Golden Age'. On the other hand, especially privileged cohort members born in 1970 felt more in control of their lives than those born in 1958. This finding might be indicative of the dawn of the new era of 'individualisation' (Beck, 1992; Giddens, 1991) with a new impetus for personal control, choice and decision making for some. There is research evidence to suggest that young people are increasingly considering that their own choices, decisions and actions are influencing the course of events and that their lives are not solely the outcome of general social pressures and trends (Evans, 2002). Nevertheless, social inequalities remain and young people growing up in disadvantaged circumstances were feeling less in control of their lives, were more depressed and less satisfied with their lives than their more privileged peers. Early academic resilience showed some beneficial effect in increasing levels of psychological well-being among the most disadvantaged, yet it did not enable young people to completely overcome the effect of early adversity.

Adult employment status

Educational attainment is considered as protective against adverse adult psychosocial outcomes in high-risk individuals, mainly because it is associated with stable career lines and well-paid employment (Pulkkinen et al., 2002). Thus the association between early educational attainment and adult employment experience will be assessed next. Table 6.2 shows the employment status of cohort members in their early thirties differentiated by the four groups of early educational resilience.

In both cohorts multiple-advantaged men were least likely to experience unemployment. In NCDS men who showed early academic resilience were less likely to experience unemployment in their early thirties than vulnerable men, as well as privileged early underachievers. In BCS70 men showing early academic resilience were less likely to experience unemployment in their early thirties than vulnerable young men, yet had a greater risk of unemployment when compared to their more privileged peers.

Women were generally more likely to be out of the labour market than men, although female participation in the labour market had increased considerably for the later born BCS70 cohort. In NCDS, 27 per cent of women in their thirties were at home looking after the family, compared to 19 per cent of thirty-year-old women in BCS70. In NCDS the major difference between the four groups was that the multiple-advantaged women were least likely to stay at home when compared to the other three groups. In BCS70 women who had no experience of socio-economic adversity in early childhood were generally less likely to stay at home in their thirties than women who were less privileged.

Regarding occupational status, academically vulnerable men and women from disadvantaged family background were generally less likely to be in prestigious occupations than their more advantaged peers and were more likely to be in manual and semi/unskilled jobs. Individuals showing early academic resilience were generally climbing higher on the occupational ladder than their vulnerable peers, but did not achieve the same level as their more privileged peers. In comparison to the multiple-advantaged and the advantaged early underachievers, they were less likely in professional or managerial positions and more likely in semi- or unskilled jobs.

Partnership and family formation

Table 6.3 shows the partnership and family status of cohort members in their early thirties. Women generally made the step into partnership and parenthood earlier than men. In comparison to cohort members born in 1958 fewer men and women born in 1970 had made the step into parenthood and family formation by their early thirties, yet in both cohorts young men and women from socially disadvantaged families were more likely than their more advantaged peers to have started

Table 6.2. *Outcomes in adulthood: Employment status in early thirties by early academic adjustment (in %)*

	NCDS				BCS70			
	Multiple-advantaged	Underachievers	Resilient	Vulnerable	Multiple-advantaged	Underachievers	Resilient	Vulnerable
Employment status								
Men (unemployed)	3.4	4.5	3.9	9.8	3.6	3.9	7.0	11.4
Women (homecare)	21.7	27.0	27.2	29.1	13.3	13.0	22.7	19.5
Occupational status								
Prof/Managerial	61.6	53.5	33.0	18.4	58.0	44.8	26.6	14.9
Skilled non-manual	19.2	15.8	25.9	17.7	24.8	29.9	26.3	23.8
Skilled manual	9.2	18.2	18.3	30.1	10.3	13.0	26.8	27.6
Semi/unskilled	9.9	12.5	23.8	33.8	6.9	12.3	20.3	33.7

Table 6.3. *Outcomes in adulthood: Partnership and family status during early thirties by early academic adjustment (in %)*

	NCDS				BCS70			
	Multiple-advantaged	Underachievers	Resilient	Vulnerable	Multiple-advantaged	Underachievers	Resilient	Vulnerable
Single								
Men	20.8	27.3	16.0	22.5	33.9	42.8	32.0	37.2
Women	20.6	21.5	19.8	19.9	27.9	32.6	21.2	28.1
Cohabiting								
Men	9.3	9.5	10.7	11.3	26.3	15.5	29.0	25.7
Women	11.6	9.0	7.4	8.6	23.6	20.4	23.2	26.4
Married								
Men	69.9	63.3	73.4	66.2	39.9	31.7	39.1	37.2
Women	67.8	69.5	72.7	71.6	48.5	47.0	55.6	45.5
Parenthood								
Men	57.9	53.6	63.5	66.1	28.4	27.7	43.6	49.5
Women	63.2	75.1	76.0	82.4	39.9	46.1	68.2	71.9

their family formation. Young men and women from privileged back-grounds, in contrast, were more likely to delay the step into family commitments.

There were interesting differences between the groups regarding part-nership status and parenthood. In both cohorts vulnerable men and women were most likely to have had children by their early thirties. Disadvantaged individuals who demonstrated early academic resilience were most likely to be married and least likely to be single when com-pared to the other three groups. Possibly one long-term outcome of early academic resilience is the ability to find and to commit to a partner, indicating good interpersonal skills. Another explanation for the earlier step into parenthood and family formation among young people who had experienced early disadvantage might be different preferences and values regarding attainable goals and life styles in comparison to the more privileged cohort members who are delaying the assumption of traditional adult roles.

Individual life stories

So far we have seen outcomes of early academic resilience in different domains. Yet, the outcomes under study refer to interlinked transitions, where the outcome in one domain influences the outcome in another. For many an extended period of further education leads to a delayed entry into the labour market, which in turn leads to a delayed step into marriage and parenthood. In an attempt to gain a better understanding of how the lives of individual cohort members are evolving, individual case stories have been selected to illustrate the delicate balancing act of how individuals combine different and changing social roles in the transition to adulthood. The following are anonymised portraits, not using real names.

Jackie

Jackie was born in March 1958 as the fourth of five children to married parents. Jackie's parents had both left education at minimum school leaving age. Jackie's father had a partly skilled manual job at her birth, but remained in unskilled work later on. Throughout her childhood the family lived in their own home, yet in overcrowded conditions. The family did not claim benefits, but the children received free school meals. Jackie's mother did not work before Jackie went to school, but then she started to work in the evenings (as a packer in a factory). The mother rated her father as very helpful both with the children and around the house at each survey point. Her parents were very interested in Jackie's education and wanted her to continue with full-time education or training after the age of sixteen. Jackie showed early academic resilience and performed well in all academic tests and in her examinations at sixteen. She showed no behaviour problems. Her teacher rated her performance as 'average and above' in all subjects. Jackie thought of herself as someone with quite good academic abilities. She had a positive view on school and schooling, but wanted to leave education at sixteen to get married and start a family. She wanted to work with children as a career, but expected to work in a bank and to work her way up into management.

Jackie left full-time education at sixteen. At seventeen she was working full-time at a bank. By eighteen Jackie had left the family home. She married and became a mother before she was twenty. She had two more children with her husband. They bought a house in 1983, but lost it in the recession during 1987 and the family had to move into rented accommodation, where they remained until 1991. At age twenty-six she worked part-time in a bank again. She then started an access course and studied for four years to obtain a degree. By thirty-three, she had completed her degree and was working as a primary school teacher. She and her husband had bought another house with a mortgage. She was very happy in her relationship and with her husband and was satisfied with how her life had turned out.

This case study illustrates that there are no straight pathways in the transition from school to work and into independent living. Jackie's life is characterised by ups and downs and she had to make major choices about which direction to take in her life. She decided against an academic career, despite her good academic performance, and instead wanted to start her own family as soon as possible. Jackie returned to further education later on and studied to become a primary school teacher. Her case can be considered as illustrating the principle of human agency and life planning. She succeeded in combining her aspirations regarding family and work. She had chosen a supportive husband and was content with what she had achieved. Her life was, however, not plain sailing and she encountered major upheavals, such as losing their family home during the recession in the late 1980s. Nonetheless she fell back on her feet and succeeded in the face of adversity.

Jackie's case demonstrates that long-term resilience depends on the availability of support and opportunities, as well as on the ways in which individual resources and social resources are used to escape from disadvantage. Jackie grew up in a stable and caring family environment. Her academic capabilities were recognised and supported by both her parents and her teachers, who wanted her to continue with further education. She entered into a wise marriage and was supported in her endeavours by her husband. The findings illustrate the principle of linked lives, which actually extends beyond the family context of origin.

When Jackie was sixteen, she attended a relatively good school, a girls-only grammar school, where 65 per cent of her class were expected to pass the exams. Jackie was in a high ability group class. She enjoyed school, and was described by her teachers as a well-behaved and pleasant girl. It has been argued by Quinton & Rutter (1988) that positive school experiences make it more likely for young people to develop a tendency to show planning in relation to major life decisions, such as marriage or occupational careers. Success in one area of life can increase self-esteem and belief in oneself and makes it more likely that the individual feels more confident to handle new challenges and then acts accordingly. For disadvantaged young people in particular, positive school experiences can be vitally important, especially during the transition from school to work (Schoon et al., 2004).

Luke

Luke's case is another example of a cohort member born in March 1958, showing early academic resilience. Luke was born as the second of seven children to married parents, who both had left school after completing compulsory full-time education at fifteen. His father worked in an un-skilled manual job. By age seven, Luke had three younger siblings and the family lived in rented, overcrowded accommodation throughout his childhood. Luke's mother did not work and rated her husband as very helpful both with the children and around the house. Luke was read to regularly by his parents and had daily contact with other children, although he did not attend nursery before going to school. Luke's parents were interested in his education and wanted him to continue full-time education after the age of sixteen. He performed well in all ability tests and showed no behaviour problems until the age of eleven, when his parents reported conduct problems at home, but they ceased when he was sixteen. In his school only 30 per cent of the students were expected to pass exams at sixteen, and just 10 per cent were studying for O-levels. Nonetheless, Luke held a fairly positive view on school. His teacher rated him as 'average and above' in all subjects, although Luke was slightly more modest in his self appraisal. He did not get outstanding examination results at sixteen, yet he performed well in the maths and reading tests. He had aspirations of entering a professional or managerial job later on in life, aiming for a well paid job with good prospects, involving variety and allowing him to be in charge. His career plans were informed by his teacher.

Luke completed his A-levels and left home at eighteen to attend university. He remained in full-time education until the age of twenty-one. After completion of his studies he immediately started continuous full-time employment and became a university lecturer at twenty-six. He was in a permanent relationship by the age of twenty-four and he and his partner bought a house in 1986. By thirty-three he was married to the same partner and they had one child, born in 1997. Luke got on very well with his wife and they shared the household chores equally. He was very satisfied with how his life had turned out and described himself as happy and in control of his life.

Though lacking self-confidence about his abilities, Luke was encouraged by his teacher to pursue further education and to strive for a professional job. Both Luke and Jackie had supportive teachers and parents who were very interested in their education and who wanted them to succeed in life. Unlike Jackie, Luke remained in full-time education until the completion of his university degree, following the recommendation of his teacher. Jackie, in contrast, took a second chance and returned to further education after her children were born.

The two cases illustrate that social transitions can become turning points that may have major life-course consequences. Elder (1985) differentiates between universal turning points which apply to virtually everyone that experiences them, and conditional turning points that bring different effects for different people. Because of the importance of socio-historical factors as well as biographical contexts, the meaning and consequences of many, if not most life transitions are conditional. Yet, not every major life experience signifies a turning point. Only events or transitions that change the net probability of life-course destinations permanently, without further interventions, should be defined as turning points (Rutter, 1996). Most life events or transitions, such as entry into further education, marriage or parenthood generally promote continuity and stability, rather than discontinuity and change. Elder & Caspi (1988) have described the continuity in direction as the 'accentuation principle', emphasising that life events tend to accentuate or exaggerate existing features and characteristics and thus increase continuity. Turning points occur when events alter a person's life, opening up opportunities that make a difference, changing the direction of previous life trajectories or pathways.

In Luke's case encouragement from his teacher led him to stay on in further education, to complete a university degree and to pursue a professional career. In Jackie's case the circumstances of her life-course transitions constitute an important aspect that need to be taken into consideration. She left school at minimum age, married and became a teenage mother. Yet, instead of experiencing an increased risk of marital breakdown generally associated with teenage marriage, Jackie's transitions were based on careful planning for the future. She accomplished at least three of her key ambitions: she found the right husband, led a happy family life and even succeeded in fulfilling her occupational hopes. Her case shows that turning points can occur at any stage in the life course and that positive adjustment in the face of adversity can be at least partly explained by the principle of human agency.

It has been argued by Clausen (1993) that planful competence, the ability to make strategic choices, emerges during adolescence and can shape the direction that the life course will take across different major transitions. Luke and Jackie both showed a realistic appreciation of their abilities and preferences and they knew what they wanted to achieve in life. It can be argued that in both cases, careful planning appears to have influenced the direction that their life has taken. Another case, illustrating the importance of human agency and persistence in pursuing a life plan can be found in Mike's story.

Mike

Mike, the younger of two children was born in April 1970. His mother was twenty-two when she had her first child and was twenty-five when Mike was born. Neither parent had experienced further education after the age of fifteen. His father worked in a partly skilled manual trade, and his mother in the service industry. At age five, Mike's family lived in rented, overcrowded accommodation, but by age ten, they had moved into a new council home and were no longer overcrowded. Mike's mother had started work and his father was helpful around the house. Mike showed early academic resilience and performed well in all ability tests throughout his childhood and adolescence. He had no behaviour problems. Both parents were interested in his education and wanted post-sixteen education for him.

At sixteen Mike's family experienced financial difficulties and had to draw benefits (income support and free school meals for Mike). Mike attained three grade 1 CSEs and four lower grade CSEs. His teacher rated his ability as above average and wanted him to continue with further education, but Mike left school at sixteen to start full-time employment. Nonetheless he had aspirations to get a professional job. He left home at nineteen and participated in further education, taking a number of courses, leading to a HE Diploma and a degree-level qualification (NVQ4). Mike moved jobs a number of times, working as a glazier and as an office clerk in different companies. He only experienced one spell of unemployment.

By thirty he was employed as an architectural and town planning technician on a full-time basis, working 40 hours per week. At thirty Mike was not married, but has been living with his current partner since 1995. They have no children. He and his partner were both working full-time, earning about £475 per week as a joint income. Mike is very happy in his relationship as well as in his job. He is in good health, is very satisfied with how his life has turned out, and feels in control.

Mike's case illustrates that life-course transitions have become more varied and complex for the later born cohort. Mike did not pursue continuous further full-time education after the age of sixteen, but combined full-time work with part-time studies leading to degree-level qualification. At sixteen his family was hit by financial hardship, which is possibly one of the reasons why he did not continue in further full-time education, illustrating the principle of linked lives, where hardship affects all members in the family. Mike had to juggle different courses and different jobs and experienced a spell of unemployment. Possibly the support and encouragement he had received from his parents and teacher in his school years helped him to sustain his motivation and positive self-image to persevere in gaining the qualifications necessary for the professional career he had in mind. Mike not only succeeded in achieving a professional career, he also found a stable relationship. By the age of thirty he had not made the step into marriage and family formation, illustrating the tendency towards delayed assumption of adult roles (Arnett, 2000), especially among young men and women with degree-level qualifications in the later born cohort.

Lucy

Lucy's case is another example of a cohort member born in April 1970. Lucy was born as the youngest of three children. Neither of her parents had extended education beyond minimum school leaving age. Her father worked in a partly skilled manual trade and her mother in the service industry. At age five, Lucy's family lived in rented, overcrowded accommodation. Lucy's mother worked part-time and her father helped with the household chores. Lucy showed early academic resilience and scored well on all the performance tests. At age ten, her parents were buying their own home and the family no longer had to live in overcrowded accommodation or share access to amenities. Her parents showed interest in Lucy's education and wanted her to continue in further education.

Lucy attended school where about a third of her peers were rated as below average or of low ability level by their teachers. She maintained above-average school performance and gained three grade 1 CSEs and three lower grade CSEs at sixteen. Her occupational aspiration was to become a designer. She left school at eighteen, after completing her A-levels to start full-time employment. She continued to participate in further education until she was twenty-five, attaining a HE Diploma. She had three part-time and two full-time jobs as well as a three-month spell of unemployment before setting up her own business as an industrial designer at twenty-five.

At twenty-five, she still lived with her parents in the family home, although she was in a relationship. By the age of twenty-seven she had left the parental home and had bought her own property. At thirty she was still working as an industrial designer, putting in 65 hours a week, earning about £ 300 per week net. She was still in the same relationship, but was not very happy with her partner. They had no children. Lucy is in excellent health, drinks wine or beer once or twice a week and has never smoked. She feels in control of her life and is satisfied with the way her life has turned out.

Lucy's case illustrates the increasing diversity and uncertainty in pathways leading to a career, as well as the increasing uncertainty of personal relationships. It seems that Lucy is paying a high price for her accomplishments in the face of adversity. Like Mike she had experienced a chequered job history as well as a short spell of unemployment. Unlike Mike, who found full-time employment, she set up her own business, and is putting 65 hours per week into her work. Her case reflects the fact that working hours in the UK are relatively high in comparison to the European average (Gallie, 2000) – although Lucy's workload is exceptionally high, possibly due to her self-employed status. Among cohort members in their early thirties who are in full-time employment, the average working hours in the NCDS cohort are 44 hours per week for men and 39 hours per week for women. In the later born BCS70 cohort the average working hours for men in full-time employment have increased to 48 hours per week, and for women to 42 hours per week. Although Lucy is showing no signs of depression and feels satisfied with her life, it may well be that the long working hours are related to the problems she is experiencing in her relationship.

Conclusions

In this chapter a person-centred approach was used to investigate the long-term outcomes of early academic resilience. The findings suggest that there is both continuity and discontinuity in adjustment across the life span. Patterns of early direction persist to some extent in the transition from childhood to adulthood and are maintained across domains. In both cohorts individuals demonstrating early academic resilience are more likely to maintain above average educational attainment, they show fewer behaviour problems, and are less likely to leave school without qualifications than vulnerable individuals. They are more likely to acquire A-levels or higher qualifications, and during adulthood they are more likely to be in full-time employment. They show fewer signs of psychological distress, are more satisfied with their lives and feel more in control. Yet early resilient individuals, especially in the later born BCS70 cohort, do not succeed to the same level as young people from privileged backgrounds, particularly regarding educational and occupational attainments. The fact that young people with above average competences lose out against their more privileged peers suggests a tragic loss of potential.

The person-centred approach adopted here offers a promising strategy for the study of resilience in the face of adversity. Types of individuals are identified on the basis of particular configurations of attributes providing a bridge between purely nomothethic research, emphasising general principles and ideographic research focusing on unique patterning of characteristics. The person-centred approach offers a more holistic view of individual development and functioning, illustrating the dynamic interdependency of individual and context (Magnusson & Bergman, 1988). Case studies have been used to offer insights about patterns of adjustment across different domains, although their generalisability is limited (Masten, 2003). However, the case stories illustrate that resilience is a dynamic process, reflecting patterns of functioning in response to circumstances that may change because of individual response, changing circumstances, or the interaction between both.

There is considerable heterogeneity in response to adversity and for most cohort members, life course transitions are far from a straight continuation in one direction. Instead of conceptualising the life course in terms of trajectories, which imply a mathematical model in which angle and velocity of projection determine the flight path and endpoint, it has been suggested that it is better to refer to metaphors such as navigation to indicate that transitions are dependent on individual skills and capabilities as well as changing external risks and the ability to evaluate them (Rutter, 1990; Evans & Furlong, 1997). In order to gain a better understanding of the long-term consequences of early adjustment patterns, we have to consider the dynamic interactions of a changing individual in a changing socio-historical context.

The findings suggest that early academic resilience has long-term benefits in both cohorts, confirming the *early timing hypothesis* and high-lighting the importance of early interventions aiming to raise the level of educational attainment for all children. Yet, the findings also illustrate the powerful influence of the socio-historical context on the lives of the cohort members. Not only are children from relatively disadvantaged family background less likely to develop and maintain their early aca-demic resources than their more privileged peers, there also appear to be cohort differences in life-course development.

The findings clearly illustrate the *principle of historical time and place*. Young people born in 1958, who experienced the onset of economic depression after they had completed their education and at a later stage in their lives appear to have more opportunities for developing and realising their potential than cohort members born in 1970 who com-pleted their education and entered the labour market at the height of the economic recession. There has been a persistent and even increasing polarisation of life chances, as reflected in the diverse outcomes for socially advantaged and disadvantaged individuals regarding academic attainments, psycho-social adjustment, occupational accomplishments and patterns of partnership and family formation, even for those men and women from disadvantaged backgrounds who demonstrated good early academic capabilities.

Moreover, socio-historical changes have influenced the *timing and sequence of transitions*. Until the 1970s, the standard sequence of life-course transitions for white males in Western society was to leave school at minimum age, start work, leave the parental home, get married and have children. Women typically left school, left home, got married and had children. Labour force participation of women was exceptional at all ages (Modell et al., 1976; Shanahan, 2000). Since then a shake-up of these trends has became apparent: transitions became more variable and the assumption of adult roles regarding work, marriage and parent-hood was generally delayed until later in the life course, particularly for men and women participating in further education (Arnett, 2000; Ferri & Smith, 2003a; Shanahan, 2000).

The findings presented here suggest a close relationship between individual development and societal progress. Individual development is influenced by social, cultural and historical determinants (Elder, 1985; Elder, 1974/1999; Bynner et al., 1997; Silbereisen, 2005). There is an increasing variety of pathways to achieve economic, emotional and social independence and maturity. Yet, the transitions themselves, like all social phenomena, have histories. They do not suddenly emerge at the threshold to adulthood, but are cumulative, building upon earlier experiences and earlier transitions.

It has been argued that there is an increasing individualisation of life choices and greater freedom to make one's own decisions (Beck, 1992; Giddens, 1991), suggesting an increased importance of *the principle of human agency*. The data reported here support the assumption of heterogeneity in individual response to adversity and the individual case stories have underlined the role of individual action and life planning in influencing future direction of the life course. Yet, life chances and opportunities remain dependent on structural forces, and are shaped by social origin, gender and family roles, as well as the wider sociohistorical context (Evans & Furlong, 1997; Heinz, 2002; Schoon et al., 2001; Shanahan, 2000). The reorganisation of the life course with the addition of the new phase of 'emerging adulthood' (Arnett, 2000) favours those who have the advantage of being able to spend more time acquiring marketable skills and knowledge and who are able to build up their 'human capital' or individual resources, usually the more privileged cohort members.

In the long run, even resilient children are still at least in part handicapped by the experience of early social disadvantage, illustrating the not-so-positive effects of the *principle of linked lives*. The findings suggest that the experience of early social disadvantage has life-long consequences and that young people from relatively disadvantaged family backgrounds who showed early academic resilience are not able to completely overcome the impact of early socio-economic disadvantage. On the other hand, the principle of linked lives can also bring advantages through the reciprocal interactions between the developing individuals and significant others in their immediate environment. During early childhood the direct family environment is of vital importance (as shown in Chapter 5), while in later life the principle of linked lives extends to teachers, friends, employers and family of destination.

The findings suggest that young people from socially disadvantaged families are starting the transition into partnerships and parenthood earlier than their more privileged contemporaries. Although early resilient cohort members show generally a delayed assumption of parenting roles when compared to the vulnerable groups, they are nonetheless more likely than their more privileged peers to have made the step into family formation by their early thirties. As we have seen in Jackie's case, young motherhood is not necessarily a step into a downward negative cycle. Major life transitions such as marriage or parenthood can be instigators of turning points (Rutter, 1996) and the meaning of transition events has to be understood within the context of individual biographies.

The findings demonstrate the power of longitudinal data, which provide a better understanding of life-course development extending over time. People's lives often change and involve turns that cannot be predicted from earlier events. If the data collection for NCDS had stopped in 1981 when Jackie was twenty-three, a different and more pessimistic impression regarding Jackie's life would have emerged, losing sight of later achievements.

Generally the findings suggest that positive adaptation is a dynamic process, responding to time-varying contexts and events. Resilience is a dynamic state depending on the transaction between a developing individual and the socio-historical context experienced by the individual. Adopting a developmental-contextual perspective allows us to recognise that development takes place across multiple, interlinked transitions in different domains. Transitions can provide opportunities or obstacles for the continuation of behaviour patterns and can have life-changing potential. Changes in one sphere of life can bring about significant changes in other overlapping spheres, a phenomenon that has been described as 'cascading effects' by Masten (2001). Trying to understand how individuals navigate developmental transitions is vitally important for gaining a better understanding of risk and resilience across the life course. Over the entire life span, humans are repeatedly confronted with events and changes that challenge or jeopardise adaptive development (e.g. transition into new social roles, changes in living circumstances, or loss of loved ones). These experiences may be temporary or lasting, modifiable or unchangeable, expected or unexpected, beneficial or hindering and often adjustments to new situations are made at high personal costs.

7   Personal goals and life plans

> 'If I had talked with a middle class accent I could have maybe got
> there. . . Yes, I want an education. . . yes, I want a degree. . . I want to
> travel abroad.. . . I want a lot of money, I want success, self-achieve-
> ment. I want not a problem free life but a worthwhile life, I want to
> think that I have lived my life to its full. . . potential. I want to be self-
> reliant, I want to have self-respect, a good self-esteem and good confi-
> dence. I want good friends, want a happy family, I want the best for my
> children. . .'
>
> (Eighteen-year old female quoted in Monica Barry (2001))

The aim of this chapter is to investigate the role of future-orientated
aspirations in moderating the link between early socio-economic adversity, academic attainment during adolescence and adult social status.
The specific focus lies on constellations of educational and career aspirations, which can also be understood as achievement orientations. This
chapter assesses whether aspirations have changed for the two birth
cohorts, whether teenage aspirations are associated with educational
attainment despite the experience of adversity and whether teenage
aspirations are predictive of adult attainment among both high- and
low-risk individuals. The relative importance of parental support and
involvement in shaping adolescent adjustment will also be examined.

Adolescence is a crucial phase or period in the life course when a
young person becomes ready to assume adult responsibilities. It marks
the transition from dependent childhood to independent adulthood.
During this life stage young people develop aspirations for the future,
which come together as a life plan directing and guiding the transition
from the present to the future (Bühler, 1933/1959; Erikson, 1959;
Ginzberg et al., 1951; Heckhausen, 1999; Little, 1983; Nurmi, 1993).
There is consistent research evidence to suggest that educational and
career aspirations developed during adolescence can have life-long
significance, influencing consequent educational and occupational attainment (Clausen, 1993; Elder, 1968; 1999; Holland et al., 1990;
Schneider & Stevenson, 1999; Scott, 2004). It has been argued that

from adolescence onward planful competence affects the direction of the life course and helps to maintain individual adjustment in different domains (Clausen, 1993). One of the most important indicators of upward social mobility is for example, how much schooling an adolescent expects to obtain (Kerckhoff, 1974; Schneider & Stevenson, 1999). There is also evidence that men from socially disadvantaged families who show high vocational ambition are achieving slightly higher status in their adult occupational attainment than their less ambitious peers (Elder, 1974/1999; McClelland, 1961). Drawing on data from the National Child Development Study, Pilling (1990) reported that young people who overcame early social disadvantage identified determination to succeed and hard work as the main reasons for their achievements. Thus, teenage ambitions can be considered as a long-term protective factor, moderating the impact of early socio-economic adversity on consequent attainments.

There are, however, very few longitudinal studies investigating the antecedents of teenage aspirations as well as their role in shaping adult occupational attainment (Clausen, 1993; Schneider & Stevenson, 1999). Still fewer longitudinal studies have studied occupational development in a changing socio-historical context (Elder, 1999; Schoon & Parsons, 2002a).

Changing life plans and aspirations

Life experiences of young people in modern industrialised societies have generally changed quite dramatically over the last three decades. It has been argued that in response to changes in labour market opportunities, the patterns of youth transitions have become more protracted and complex (Arnett, 2000; Blossfeld & Shavit, 1993; Bynner & Silbereisen, 2000; Larson, 2002; Schneider & Stevenson, 1999; Schoon et al., 2001). Many have argued that children born in the 1970s have experienced a major shift in life expectations across the generations. While twenty years ago young people were able to formulate relatively clear ideas about their likely destination in the labour market, today they have to face more uncertainties about the possible outcomes (Lightfoot, 1997). The prospect of achieving employment directly after leaving school and maintaining a continuing career are increasingly in question, especially for young people without qualifications (Bynner, 1998; Roberts, 1995; Schoon et al., 2001; Surridge & Raffe, 1995).

There have been concerns about lack of ambition among young people coming of age in the late 1980s and 1990s, facing increasing economic uncertainty and family instabilities (Holtz, 1995). Despite negative views about school and the curriculum, young people nonetheless appreciate the link between completing their studies, better qualifications and the increased likelihood of finding a job (Furnham & Gunter, 1989; Poole, 1983; 1990). It has been argued that in response to technological transformation and the changing nature of labour market opportunities, young people are under increasing pressure to continue full-time education beyond the age of sixteen and to acquire formal qualifications (Blossfeld & Shavit, 1993; Shanahan, 2000). Poor academic achievement, which presented no significant barrier to employment in the past, now predicts real difficulties in finding employment, and ultimately exclusion from the labour market (Bynner et al., 2000). While most of the cohort members born in 1958 left school at sixteen to move directly into full-time employment, a larger number of the 1970 cohort remained in full-time education after the age of sixteen (Bynner & Parsons, 1997; Furlong, 1992). Educational opportunities have been expanding for young people all over the world (Fussell & Greene, 2002; Shanahan et al., 2002), and there is consistent research evidence to suggest that the educational and occupational aspirations of young people have generally increased.

In a longitudinal study of youth, comparing aspirations of a cohort born between 1945 and 1955 with aspirations of their children born between 1978 and 1983, Bengston and colleagues (Bengston et al., 2002), for example, could show that the younger generation displayed higher achievement orientations than their parents. Especially young women outpaced their mothers and were more ambitious than their male counterparts. Findings from the more recent Sloan Study of Youth and Social Development (four waves since 1992) also suggest that there has been a significant rise in the aspirations of American adolescents since the 1970s (Schneider & Stevenson, 1999).

Achievement orientations among British teenagers born in 1958 and 1970

Young men and women born in the UK in 1970 are more likely to obtain A-level as well as degree-level qualifications than cohort members born in 1958 (see Chapter 3). There has generally been an increase in the proportion of young men and women staying on in full-time education. Not only is the participation in secondary education increasing, there are also rising rates of tertiary education, as demands for professional and technical skills in the labour market rise. So it comes as no surprise that

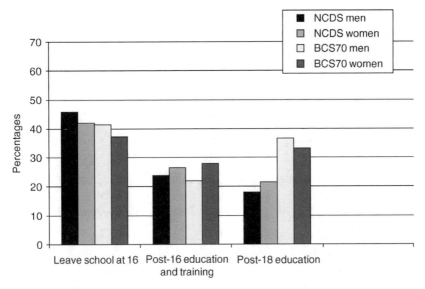

Figure 7.1. Teenage educational aspirations in NCDS and BCS70.

the educational aspirations among sixteen-year-olds in the later born cohort have generally increased.

Educational aspirations

At sixteen, all cohort members were asked about their educational plans, whether they wanted to continue in full-time education or leave school at minimum school leaving age (questions are described in Appendix C). Figure 7.1 shows the educational aspirations of the two cohorts separated by gender. In comparison to cohort members born in 1958 a larger number of young people born in 1970 aim for further education beyond eighteen. Only about one-fifth of young people born in 1958 aspired to an academic career, compared to about one-third in the later born cohort. Among the 1958 cohort 46 per cent of sixteen-year-old boys and 42 per cent of girls want to leave school at the age of sixteen, in comparison to 41 per cent of boys and 37 per cent of girls born in 1970. About a fourth of young people in each cohort wanted to continue with further education or training after leaving school at sixteen, especially young women. In both cohorts girls are generally more ambitious in their

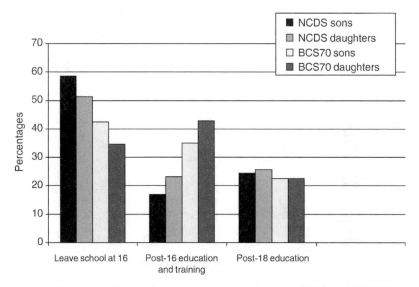

Figure 7.2. Parental educational aspirations in NCDS and BCS70.

educational aspirations than boys. Fewer girls than boys want to leave school at minimum age, and more want further education and training, beyond sixteen. Regarding tertiary education, girls in NCDS are more ambitious than boys, while in BCS70 boys aim higher than girls.

Parental educational aspirations for their children

It is not just the young people who have become more ambitious: so have their parents. In both cohorts parents were asked about their expectations for their child regarding school leaving age and further education when the child was sixteen (questions described in Appendix C). Figure 7.2 shows parental educational aspirations separated by the gender of their child.

In comparison to parents of children born in 1958, parents of the later born cohort have generally higher educational aspirations for their children. Compared to parents of NCDS cohort members, fewer parents of BCS70 cohort members want their child to leave school at the minimum school leaving age and more parents expect their child to continue further education, particularly regarding post-sixteen education and training. Parental aspirations are generally higher for their daughters than for their sons, yet regarding post-eighteen education,

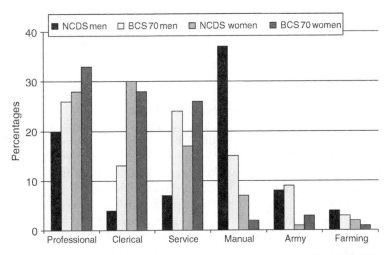

Figure 7.3. Teenage occupational aspirations in NCDS and BCS70.

gender differences are more or less levelled. Furthermore, it appears that parents of BCS70 cohort members are more in favour of post-sixteen education and training than their children are. The teenagers are themselves more likely than their parents to opt for post-eighteen education, especially boys in BCS70.

Teenage job preferences

What jobs do the sixteen-year-old teenagers aspire to? Figure 7.3 illustrates a shift in occupational aspirations and shows that the later born cohort has generally become more ambitious in its career planning. In comparison to cohort members born in 1958 more young people born in 1970 want a professional job that requires degree-level qualifications, especially young girls. Moreover, there is a shift in the kind of aspirations young people have. There has been a dramatic increase in young men aiming for an occupation involving clerical and administrative office work. Furthermore, distinctly more sixteen-year-old boys aim for a career in the service industries, while the rate of aspirants for manual jobs, the preferred option among young men in the 1958 cohort, has dropped considerably. There is a slight increase among men and women aspiring to a career in the army. Farming, on the other hand, has seen a decline in aspirants. These findings reflect the changes in labour market opportunities, suggesting that young people have adjusted their aspirations for future careers in response to a changing socio-economic context.

The aspiration gradient

Educational and occupational aspirations as well as academic and occupational attainments are associated with social background factors (Erikson & Jonsson, 1996; Heinz, 2002; Schoon & Parsons, 2002a; Shavit & Müller, 1998; Trice & Knapp, 1992). As already discussed in Chapter 3, the increasing participation in education since the 1980s did not lead to a process of equalisation between social groups. In both cohorts young people from disadvantaged family backgrounds are more likely than their more privileged peers to leave school at minimum leaving age and are less likely to obtain further or higher qualifications (Bynner & Parsons, 1997; Halsey et al., 1980; Kerckhoff, 1993; Schoon & Parsons, 2002a; Shavit & Müller, 1998). Furthermore, aspirations among young people from relatively privileged socio-economic backgrounds are generally higher than among children experiencing less favourable conditions.

Figure 7.4 shows the educational and occupational aspirations of sixteen-year-old teenagers in both cohorts in relation to the experience of socio-economic adversity during early childhood. There is a persisting aspiration gap based on the experience of early socio-economic adversity (see Chapter 5 for a description of the social index assessed at age five in BCS70 and age seven in NCDS). Nearly three out of five young people (55 per cent in NCDS and 58 per cent in BCS70) who experienced low social risk during early childhood want to continue in further education after the age of eighteen. This rate compares to about one in ten of young people experiencing high social risk expressing interest in participating in further education (9 per cent in NCDS and 15 per cent in BCS70). Figure 7.4 also indicates that in both cohorts 43 per cent of young people experiencing low early social risk have aspirations for a professional career, in contrast to only 14 per cent of young people with high-risk experiences in NCDS and 20 per cent of high-risk young people in BCS70.

The aspiration gradient has been explained on the basis of different opportunities and socialisation processes that exist across socio-economic status levels (Bourdieu & Passeron, 1977; Elder, 1974/1999; Vondracek et al., 1986). Individuals from more privileged homes have greater access to financial resources when they are needed (i.e. to pay for books, computers, or higher education), more educational

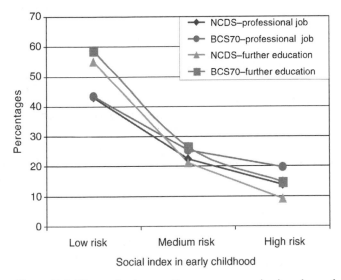

Figure 7.4. The aspiration gradient: teenage aspirations by early social risk.

opportunities, role models, occupational knowledge and informal/ kinship networks. There is evidence to suggest that socio-economic adversity affects parental involvement with and aspirations for their children (Sacker et al., 2002), and that parental aspirations mediate the influence of social disadvantage on individual attainment and aspirations (Bengston et al., 2002; Ginzberg et al., 1951; Vondracek et al., 1986; Schoon & Parsons, 2002a; Schulenberg et al., 1984). Gottfredson (1981), for example, has argued that young people develop ideas about the appropriateness of certain occupations and consider the relationship between opportunities and ability that affect their plans regarding education and employment. In their consideration of which occupations are acceptable or tolerable, young people orient to social class reference groups and are guided by their parents' aspirations for them. It has been suggested that parents have, and youngsters adopt, different views about what is an acceptable job depending on their social class and ability level (Ginzberg et al., 1951; Gottfredson, 1981). Yet, there is also research evidence to suggest that high levels of parental aspirations are positively associated with the child's aspirations and achievement, regardless of social class factors (Catsambis, 2001; Zellman & Waterman, 1998), and that parental aspirations have a powerful influence on their children's achievement, even after controlling for prior achievement (Singh et al., 1995).

Moderating influence of achievement orientations

It has been shown that children's and parents' performance expectations have a considerable influence on children's achievement in maths and reading (Entwistle & Haydeck, 1982). Thus, in the following, the influence of parental aspirations and involvement in their child's education on achievement will be examined in conjunction with the aspirations of the teenagers themselves. The relationship between motivation and behaviour is generally reciprocal and not causal, with motivation influencing achievement and vice versa. Yet, in most instances the exam performance of cohort members has been collected after the actual interviews had taken place. Furthermore, data on adult occupational status have been collected when the cohort members were in their early thirties. Thus, the timing of the assessments in both cohorts allows us to assess the influence of achievement orientations on educational attainment during adolescence as well as adult outcomes.

Predicting exam performance at sixteen

In the following analyses the experience of early socio-economic disadvantage is linked to exam performance at sixteen, which in turn is considered as a predictor of adult outcomes, in this case adult social status. In a first step a series of hierarchical regression analyses are run to assess the influence of early socio-economic adversity on later academic attainment, as well as the role of family and individual characteristics in moderating the impact of early social risk on academic adjustment, controlling for earlier academic attainment:

- To what extent is exposure to socio-economic adversity during early childhood associated with academic attainment at sixteen in both cohorts?
- Can the influence of early socio-economic adversity on academic adjustment in adolescence be moderated by characteristics of the child and his or her parents?
- To what extent do educational and occupational aspirations shape developmental outcomes independently from parental characteristics and socio-economic background factors?

Table 7.1. *Hierarchical multiple regression analysis predicting academic attainment at sixteen (controlling for early reading ability), unstandardised estimates, 95% confidence interval for B, and ΔR^2*

	NCDS			BCS70		
	B	95% CI for B	ΔR^2	B	95% CI for B	ΔR^2
1. Social index	−.10*	(−.12 −−.07)	**.17**	−.21*	(−.23−−.16)	**.20**
2. Parental support			**.09**			**.07**
Parents want further education for child	.15*	(.11−.18)		.15*	(.08−.23)	
Parents meet teacher	.16*	(.11−.21)		.04	(−.14−.06)	
3. Teenage characteristics			**.05**			**.10**
Gender	.01	(−.06−.03)		.02	(−.08−.11)	
Educational aspirations	.32*	(.28−.36)		.32*	(.25−.39)	
Occupational aspirations	.14*	(.08−.21)		.33*	(.22−.44)	
Total R^2			**.31**			**.37**

Note: gender: boys = 1; girls = 2;
* p <.000;
ΔR change values associated with the block/wave.

The following analysis is based on 12,569 NCDS cohort members for whom we have complete data on the Social Risk Index collected at seven and 9,014 cohort members in BCS70 for whom the Social Risk Index was assessed at age five (see Chapter 5). To check possible effects of non-response when linking data collected in early childhood to assessments made at sixteen, the results from analyses using pairwise and listwise deletion of cases with missing values were compared. Furthermore, results were checked against estimates from linear regression analyses using the FIML approach provided by the AMOS 4.01 programme (see Appendix B for a more detailed description). Similar results from the three different estimation procedures suggest that there is little systematic sample bias related to differing rates of non-response. For the analysis the overall exam scores have been z-standardised. The results of the hierarchical multiple regression analyses predicting exam performance at sixteen are given in Table 7.1. Due to the measurement level of the data, unstandardised estimates are reported as well as the 95 per cent confidence interval for B.

In Wave 1 the link between early socio-economic adversity and later academic attainment was estimated for each cohort separately, controlling for earlier reading ability (assessed at age five in BCS70 and age seven in NCDS). In both cohorts early socio-economic adversity is a significant risk factor, undermining academic achievement at sixteen, even after controlling for early reading ability. In NCDS the experience of early socio-economic adversity explains 17 per cent of the variation in exam performance at sixteen, and 20 per cent in BCS70.

Wave 2 adds the parental educational aspirations for the child as well as parental involvement with the child's education, covering both aspirations and behaviour of the parents (see Appendix C). In both cohorts the addition of parental aspirations and involvement significantly increases the amount of explained variance ($\Delta R^2 = .09$ in NCDS and $\Delta R^2 = .07$ in BCS70).

Wave 3 adds three characteristics of the teenagers themselves to the equation: their gender, educational aspirations and occupational aspirations. In both cohorts the addition of these variables significantly increases the amount of explained variance, in NCDS the difference in R^2 is 5 per cent, while in BCS70 it is 10 per cent. In both cohorts gender shows no significant effect on exam performance at sixteen over and above the other variables in the equation. Educational aspirations are a significant resource factor in both cohorts. Occupational aspirations also show a significant and independent association with exam performance at sixteen especially in BCS70.

After including all the resource factors in the main-effect model the impact of early social adversity on exam performance at sixteen has reduced from −.24 to −.10 in NCDS and from −.36 to −.21 in BCS70. In NCDS, all factors together predict 31 per cent of the variation of academic attainment at sixteen, and in BCS70, 37 per cent of variation in exam performance can be explained. In NCDS the most significant resource factors for good academic attainment are parental aspiration and involvement as well as individual aspirations. In BCS70, exam performance at sixteen is associated with parental aspirations and the aspirations of the teenagers themselves.

Academic resilience in the face of social risk: specificity of effects

The findings suggest that in the later born cohort teenage aspirations show a greater effect in moderating the impact of early social adversity on exam performance at sixteen than among cohort members born twelve years earlier. The next question to be examined is whether the same applies for high- and low-risk groups of individuals in both cohorts. High- and low-risk individuals were identified on the basis of the Social Risk Index introduced in Chapter 5. Individuals who experienced four or more risk indicators in early childhood are classified as high-risk individuals, while cohort members experiencing none or only one risk factor are identified as low-risk individuals. In order to assess the specific effect of the resource factors on exam performance at sixteen, a path analytic model was run for high- and low-risk groups separately, controlling for earlier academic attainment (i.e. reading ability at age five in BCS70 and age seven in NCDS).

Path analysis is an extension of multiple regression analysis, which assumes that relationships between observed variables are linear, additive and asymmetric (Loehlin, 1998). Path analysis requires that each dependent variable is completely determined by variables within the system. A residual factor, assumed to be uncorrelated with the antecedent variables or with other residuals, must be introduced to account for the unexplained variance. Path coefficients (or partial beta weights) represent estimates of the main or direct effects of independent variables on the dependent variable. The path analyses were carried out separately for high- and low-risk individuals in each cohort using the programme AMOS 4.01. As men and women generally differ in their transition into adult roles separate analyses were also run for men and women within each of these groups.

The path models link experiences in childhood and adolescence to the exam performance at sixteen, which in turn predicts adult social position at thirty in BCS70 and thirty three in NCDS. Multigroup analysis was performed to test for differences between socially disadvantaged and the socially advantaged individuals. The χ^2 differences for models run without parameter restrictions and for the model with constrained parameters (equal regression weights for advantaged and disadvantaged groups) suggest that there are significant differences between the two groups. Because of the measurement level of the variables unstandardised estimates are reported. Results of the analysis are given in Table 7.2.

In both cohorts there are significant associations between the predictor variables. The combination of resource factors explains a higher proportion of variation in exam performance among low- than among high-risk individuals ($R^2 = .26$ for low-risk individuals in NCDS and .40 in BCS70; for high-risk individuals $R^2 = .22$ in NCDS and .23 in BCS70). In both cohorts good predictors of exam performance at sixteen are teenage educational aspirations. This applies to both high- and low-risk individuals. Individual job aspirations are only significant predictors of exam performance among low-risk individuals in BCS70. In NCDS there are significant effects for parental aspiration and involvement among high- and low-risk individuals. In BCS70 only parental aspirations are a significant predictor of exam performance at sixteen, as are individual educational aspirations, especially so among low-risk individuals.

An analysis of gender differences (results not shown) indicates that for high- and low-risk girls in the NCDS cohort the effect of parental educational aspirations on exam performance is greater and the effect of own aspirations is less strong than among boys, suggesting that exam performance of girls at sixteen is more strongly influenced by parental aspirations and support, while boys are more strongly guided by their own aspirations. In BCS70 the effect of teenage aspirations on exam performance is also greater for boys than for girls. For both high- and low-risk males and females, teenage educational aspirations are good predictors of exam performance.

Predicting adult social status

In a last step the long-term influences of teenage aspirations for adult occupational attainment are investigated. In particular the question of whether teenage aspirations are moderating the influence of early social risk on own adult social status is examined. Adult social status was assessed with the Registrar General's Social Class (RGSC) classification (see Appendix C). For ease of interpretation the coding was reversed, so that a high score indicates a high social position.

It has been argued by Elder that the desire to excel is the most important source of achievement among men of lower-status origins: the 'desire to excel is less restricted than IQ to achievement through education, as one would expect, and exerts a stronger direct effect on occupational attainment than either mental ability or family status' (Elder, 1999, p. 175). Assuming that the desire to achieve is predictive of occupational achievements, especially for disadvantaged individuals, it can be expected that the association between individual aspirations and adult occupational status is higher for high-risk than low-risk individuals.

The results from the path analysis are shown in Table 7.2. Among low-risk individuals in NCDS the best predictor of adult social status are individual educational aspirations, followed by individual occupational aspirations and exam results at sixteen. For high-risk individuals, individual educational aspirations as well as exam performance at sixteen are important predictors' of adult social status. In BCS70, exam performance at sixteen is the most important predictor of adult social status, especially for high-risk individuals. In both cohorts the effect of exam

Table 7.2. *Unstandardised parameter estimates for prediction of exam score at sixteen and adult social status among socially advantaged and disadvantaged cohort members in both cohorts (controlling for early reading ability)*

	NCDS				BCS70			
	Low Risk (n = 2044)		High Risk (n = 2341)		Low Risk (n = 1872)		High Risk (n = 1542)	
	Unstandardised estimate	S.E.	Unstandardised estimate	S.E.	Unstandardised estimate	S.E.	Unstandardised estimate	S.E.
Age 16: Predicting exam score								
Parental involvement → Exam	.24**	.06	.20**	.04	.12	.07	.04	.08
Parental aspiration → Exam	.16**	.06	.18**	.04	.27**	.05	.20**	.08
Own job aspirations → Exam	.09	.06	.04	.06	.39**	.06	.09	.10
Own educational aspiration → Exam	.44**	.06	.22**	.04	.32**	.05	.18*	.08
Adulthood: Predicting social status								
Own job aspirations → Adult Status	.16**	.05	.19	.12	.19**	.06	.25*	.12
Own educational aspirations → Adult Status	.36**	.05	.34**	.07	.15**	.04	.15*	.07
Exam → Adult Status	.18**	.04	.34**	.05	.28**	.03	.60**	.07
Model Fit								
χ^2 (df)	19.7(2)		13.54(2)		5.10(2)		2.59(2)	
CFI	0.992		0.993		0.998		0.998	
RMSEA (95% confidence interval)	0.065 (0.041–0.092)		0.049 (0.027–0.075)		0.024 (0.000–0.051)		0.013 (0.000–0.050)	

Note: ** $p < 0.000$; * $p < 0.005$.

performance on adult social status is stronger for high- than for low-risk individuals.

The analysis of gender differences in pathways leading to adult social status suggests that among low-risk men in NCDS teenage aspirations are more strongly associated with adult social status than among low-risk women. For low-risk women, on the other hand, exam performance at sixteen is the most important predictor of adult social status. Among high-risk individuals the pattern is reversed and teenage educational aspirations are more important for high-risk women, while exam performance at sixteen is the best predictor of adult social status among high-risk men. In the BCS70 cohort exam performance is the best predictor of adult social status both for high- and low-risk men and women. The combination of teenage aspirations and exam performance is generally a better predictor of adult social status among men than among women.

Conclusions

The later born BCS70 cohort has become more ambitious in their expectations for the future, especially regarding plans for education beyond minimum school leaving age. For teenagers born in 1958 the predominant pattern was to leave school at the minimum age and to move directly into a job. Most young people born in 1958 who left school in 1974 could expect to obtain employment regardless of their educational attainment, whereas for young people born in 1970 poor educational attainment meant considerable difficulty in gaining entry to employment (Bynner, 1998). Young people born in 1970 seem to have responded to the changing nature of labour market opportunities by adjusting their aspirations. In comparison to the earlier born cohort, more young people born in 1970 want to continue in further education beyond eighteen and aspire to jobs that require degree-level qualification. Yet, it is not just professional occupations that are attracting more young people, there is also an increase in aspirants for jobs involving clerical and administrative office work or jobs in the service industries. Interest in manual jobs or a career in the army has declined.

Most young people who left school during the mid-1970s did so to find a job that paid full wages. To forgo this generally available opportunity to gain relatively secure employment with a living wage, and to continue further education instead was a relatively rare step to take, especially for young people from disadvantaged family backgrounds. The findings suggest that ambitions are generally raised – both among teenagers and their parents – although social differences in aspirations have remained. Aspirations for further education and a professional career among less privileged young people are rather more ambitious than those expressed by their more privileged peers and also might involve more risks.

What role do teenage and parental achievement orientations play in moderating the link between the experience of early socio-economic adversity and later educational and occupational attainment? The experience of early disadvantage is a significant predictor of individual attainment, even after controlling for earlier academic attainment. The fact that the early experience of disadvantage shows a greater impact on individual attainment at sixteen than during early childhood (see Chapter 5) confirms the assumption of cumulative and possibly time-lagged risk effects. We have already seen in Chapter 4 that the experience of early adversity can undermine individual attainment and that this detrimental effect is then carried forward into the future.

The negative effect of early social risk experiences on academic attainment at sixteen can, however, be moderated by positive orientations to the future. In both cohorts aspirations of the teenagers and their parents can reduce the detrimental influence of early social adversity on exam performance at sixteen. In NCDS, parental involvement with their child's education as well as educational aspirations of the parents and the teenagers themselves appear to be general resource factors, showing their beneficial effect both among high- and low-risk children. In BCS70, parental and individual educational aspirations are also important resource factors for academic attainment.

In the long term, teenage aspirations for the future, especially educational aspirations, are an important source of achievement, predicting adult occupational attainment (Elder, 1999; Ginzberg et al., 1951; Heckhausen, 1999; Schoon & Parsons, 2002a). In both cohorts, and for both high- and low-risk individuals, educational aspirations are predictive of adult social status. Among high-risk individuals in NCDS, teenage educational aspirations and exam performance at sixteen are the best predictors of adult social status, while in BCS70 the most important predictor of adult social status for high-risk individuals is exam performance at sixteen.

These finding suggests that young people in the earlier born cohort had better opportunities for career development that were less dependent on their academic attainment, while for the later born cohort, academic attainment became more important in order to succeed, especially for the most disadvantaged (Bynner et al., 2000; Schoon & Parsons, 2002b). While the importance of academic attainment for occupational success has generally increased, young people from relatively dis-advantaged backgrounds seem to have to bring that little extra, and do especially well in their exams in order to achieve.

Given the limitations of the study, the findings suggest that future-orientated aspirations can moderate the detrimental impact of early social risk and are an important resource factor for young men and women to overcome the negative cycle of socio-economic disadvantage. Teenage aspirations, especially educational aspirations, in combination with academic attainment are an important predictor of adult social status. Yet, aspirations themselves are to be explained in terms of the context in which they arise. For the later born BCS70 cohort, the stakes were raised against them, as more young people continued with further education and obtained degree-level qualifications. While the earlier born cohort seemed to have more opportunity to succeed, young people in the later born cohort are generally under more pressure to continue with further education to secure their place on the occupational ladder. The study of achievement orientation in the broader context of socio-historical influences and opportunities might thus provide vital clues for a better understanding of positive adaptation in the face of adversity.

8   Conclusions and outlook

> In the little world in which children have their existence, whosoever brings them up, there is nothing so finely perceived and so finely felt, as injustice.
>
> Charles Dickens, *Great Expectations* (1861)

The research presented in this book has focused on academic resilience in the face of socio-economic adversity, spanning the transition from dependent child to independent adult in two birth cohorts born twelve years apart. Comparing adjustment patterns of the two cohorts over time made it possible to investigate the long-term influence of socio-economic adversity on individual adjustment as well as the context dependency of resilient adaptations. In the following a critical appraisal of the main themes running through the findings is provided, delineating conceptual and methodological issues, and outlining directions for future research.

The findings indicate persistence of deprivation and social inequality in our society despite general economic growth. There is a great deal of common structure and most of the linkages between adversity and adjustment apply in both cohorts and for men and women (see also (Hobcraft et al., 2004). Even though overall participation in further and higher education has expanded, social inequality of educational opportunity has remained. While the overall level of qualifications has increased, young people with good academic ability from disadvantaged family backgrounds are losing out against their more privileged peers. Cycles of disadvantage exist, yet they do not inevitably occur and some individuals demonstrate positive adaptation in the face of adversity. What have we learned regarding the risk factors and processes undermining individual adjustment, and what are the protective factors and processes enabling young people to beat the odds?

Risk and risk processes

The study of resilience is dependent on the presence of a risk factor. Individuals must have been exposed to some risk or risk factors that increase the likelihood of a negative outcome to instigate the study of resilience. The definition of risk, however, is not a trivial matter. The risk under investigation must be a potential cause or precursor of a specified outcome in question, although the same risk factor may affect multiple outcomes. There are furthermore variations in response to adversity and the experience of the same adverse condition may differ across individuals. While for some individuals the risk exposure may not have a great impact, for others it might be a traumatic and highly stressful event. Some risk exposure may have immediate or acute effects, which may dissipate relatively quickly, while the effects of other risk exposures may be chronic and lasting.

The experience of socio-economic adversity, which has been assessed here in relative and not absolute terms, has shown itself to be a powerful risk factor undermining adjustment across domains and over time. It could be demonstrated that being born into a relatively disadvantaged family increases the probability of accumulating risks associated with that disadvantage, which then influences later development. Probabilities are, however, not certainties, and future studies may wish to include assessments of how individuals have experienced the exposure to socio-economic adversity or any other risk factor under investigation, to gain a better understanding of individual variations in response to risk exposure. Even when an exposure is universally experienced as a risk, the level of adversity may differ. Here composite measures of risk have been used, and a Social Risk Index was developed to assess the relative level of risk exposure. Serious risk generally emanates from the accumulation of risk factors over time. It is usually not a particular single risk factor but the combination and number of risk factors that influence developmental functioning (Garmezy & Masten, 1994; Rutter et al., 1979; Rutter, 1990; Sameroff & Chandler, 1975; Sameroff et al., 1993; Szatmari et al., 1994).

Multiple risk factors

The use of multiple risk models is generally considered as the most comprehensive assessment of risk, reflecting multiple and coexisting psychosocial stressors (Ackerman et al., 1999; Rutter, 1987; Sameroff, 1999). Not only the number and intensity of risk factors, but also their nature and how they affect individual functioning inform the definition of resilience. Here, a distinction has been made between distal and proximal risk processes (Bronfenbrenner, 1979), whereby cultural and social value systems associated with social disadvantage are mediated by the more proximal family context. Socio-economic adversity at the family level was associated with a number of co-factors, such as poor living conditions, overcrowding, or lack of household amenities, which are directly experienced by the developing child. These multiple indicators of adversity were included in a multiple risk index to assess the unique effect of socio-economic disadvantage on academic attainment (Ackerman et al., 1999; Deater-Deckard et al., 1998; McLoyd, 1990; Szatmari et al., 1994). Using a multiple, focused risk index of socio-economic adversity goes beyond studies using social status or income as sole indicators of socio-economic risk and reflects more accurately the everyday experiences within the proximal family context. Furthermore, the adopted approach of narrowing the focus on socio-economic disadvantage per se and selecting only specific risk factors goes beyond studies using more diverse indicators of socio-economic adversity such as family structure, parenting factors, or family climate. These factors were, however, included in the analyses presented here in order to investigate specific proximal family processes moderating the impact of socio-economic risk on individual functioning.

Cumulative risk processes

In addition to specifying the risk factors under investigation as well as the level of risk exposure, a clear identification of the operative risk mechanisms is necessary for a better understanding of resilient adaptations. Risk can have a direct effect on an outcome, or its effect can be indirect, operating via mediating factors and processes. Furthermore risk effects can vary across time, context and domain as well as the developmental stage of the individual. For example, individuals have different 'sensitive periods' during which they are particularly vulnerable to the experience of adversity, as for example, in early childhood or during major transition periods. The whole life course is important in shaping individual development, not just the early years, and the study has demonstrated cumulative risk effects beyond those associated with current or early adversity. Risk processes have to be viewed in dynamic terms, taking into account that risk factors can have concurrent, intermittent or persistent effects and that they can accumulate over the life course.

The study has illustrated cumulative processes, which involve the triggering of chains of interrelated events, which in turn influence later outcomes and transitions (Rutter, 1987). The consequences of growing up in a disadvantaged family environment can continue into adulthood, or even into the next generation, as one risk factor reinforces another, leading to increasingly restricted outcomes or possible transition pathways in later life (Duncan & Brooks-Gunn, 1997; Gregg & Machin, 1997;

Rutter & Madge, 1976; Rutter, 1990). Pathways into adulthood begin in early childhood and are shaped by the socio-economic background of parents.

Experiences accumulate over time and result in differences in achievement and prospects. For example, at each stage of schooling differences in academic attainments were magnified, with the transitions from primary to secondary school producing an increased deflection. Transitions and pathways commence at a young age and lead to diverging patterns, with adult attainments reflecting the cumulative structural influences originating in early life.

Historical context

The study has shown that risk effects and resulting adaptations can change in a changing socio-historical context, underlining that individuals afflicted by particular negative life circumstances cannot be treated as homogeneous groups. For example, young people born in 1970 appear to be relatively more affected by the experience of growing up in conditions of disadvantage than cohort members born in 1958. The links between economic deprivation and individual attainment have strengthened for the later born cohort, suggesting increasing polarisation. In times of generally improved material circumstances the lack of basic household amenities or overcrowding in the family home appears to have a relatively greater negative impact, suggesting situational variability in the influence of risk conditions. Variability in relative risk levels emphasises the need to consider risk effects not only with regard to individual variations but also in their socio-historical context.

The same risk factors can have a different impact in a changing socio-cultural context, and what appeared as a surmountable risk in one context can become a defeating obstacle in another. For example, young people from a relatively disadvantaged family background are generally less likely to participate in further education than their more privileged peers (Blossfeld & Shavit, 1993; Bynner et al., 2000c). Yet, while in the mid-1970s the predominant pattern was to leave school at the minimum age and move directly into a job, by the 1990s most young people continued in full-time education after the age of sixteen to meet the increasing demands of employers for a highly skilled workforce (Bynner, 1998). While low educational attainment or lack of qualifications presented no significant barrier to employment in the past, changes in the labour market meant that young people from disadvantaged family background without, or with only relatively low, qualifications were finding it increasingly difficult to secure a place on the occupational ladder. It has to be considered that young people born in 1958 reached the end of their minimum schooling just at the beginning of a deepening recession, while the later born cohort entered the labour market at the height of the recession, encountering greater difficulties in establishing a career immediately after leaving school.

Changing labour market opportunities are furthermore reflected in changing aspirations regarding educational and occupational plans for the future. Teenage aspirations have been shown to influence later occupational attainments and career pathways (Clausen, 1993; Elder, 1974/1999; Pilling, 1990; Schneider & Stevenson, 1999; Schoon & Parsons, 2002a). The later born cohort generally showed raised ambitions with more young people aiming for further education and a professional career. Yet, aspirations and life plans are socially acquired skills and the findings suggest a persisting aspirational gap, with young people from disadvantaged backgrounds being less ambitious than their more privileged peers, even when controlling for ability level. Furthermore, aspirations for further education and a professional career among less privileged young people are relatively more ambitious than the same desire expressed by their more privileged peers and also might involve more risks, underlining again the context-dependency of resilience.

For a better understanding of individual response to adversity the context dependency of risk experiences has to be considered. Risk factors may show different effects in a changed socio-historical context, for different groups of individuals (i.e. high versus low socio-economic status or for men and women), for different age groups, or may function in different ways for the same individual at different life stages. Individuals afflicted by particular negative life circumstances cannot be treated as homogeneous groups, as there are variations in the degree to which their lives are shaped by the risk processes. Furthermore, experience of socio-economic adversity does not necessarily set an individual off onto a trajectory of maladjustment and low achievement. There are rather multiple life pathways if possible. Although children reared in disadvantaged or deprived circumstances are at an increased risk of adverse developmental outcomes, some children exposed to adverse conditions appear to avoid consequent adjustment problems and thus provide vital information about factors and processes enabling positive adjustment in the face of adversity.

Adjustment as development in context

A major criticism concerning the conceptualisation of resilience is that the identification of positive adjustment is based on subjective judgments of what is a successful or desired outcome. Here the identification of positive adaptation was not based on outstanding achievements. Positive adaptation was defined through academic attainments within or above the average performance on a standardised achievement test used in a general population sample. Conceptualising resilience as 'ordinary magic' (Masten, 2001) defeats the notion that resilience is a special quality or characteristic, only to be found in exceptional individuals who are capable of overcoming adversity. Yet, on the other hand it raises expectations that everyone can make it, if they try only hard enough. When comparing achievements for high-risk groups and low-risk controls over time (see Chapter 6), it emerged that high-risk individuals who showed above average academic attainment in early childhood did better than their more vulnerable peers, but were not able to maintain their adjustment levels to the same extent as their more privileged peers. Their academic performance decreased with the transitions from primary to secondary school and in subsequent adult attainments. The attainment gap has been attributed in part to a lack of psychosocial resources, as individuals from disadvantaged backgrounds have generally fewer resources to draw on than their more privileged peers.

Resilience processes

At least three different mechanisms have been identified that may lead to positive adaptation. Firstly, there are protective processes in which the availability of resource factors is beneficial to those experiencing risk or adversity, but has no or less benefit among those not exposed to risk. Secondly, there are promotive or compensatory processes in which a promotive or resource factor has an equally beneficial effect on those exposed and those not exposed to adversity. The essential difference between these two processes lies in the characteristic of the relationship between risk factors, protective factors and the outcome, which is either interactive or additive. While protection is defined by a modification of the risk effect (involving interaction between risk, protective factors and outcome), compensatory processes are defined by the cumulation of resource factors. The third type of process is the so-called challenge model where the protective effect depends on the level of risk exposure (Garmezy et al., 1984).

The findings presented here provide evidence for both compensatory processes involving cumulative resource factors, and protective processes such as supportive family processes and social integration that enabled at-risk individuals to beat the odds. It has been argued by Rutter (1990; Rutter et al., 1998) that there are specific types of protective experiences that are especially important in shaping the development of high-risk individuals over time. These specific protective mechanisms lead to a reduction either of risk impact or in sensitivity to risk. They reduce negative chain reactions, or increase positive chain reactions. They promote the establishment and maintenance of self-esteem and self-efficacy, open up opportunities, or are associated with a positive orientation towards life as reflected, for example, in planful competence.

The findings presented here suggest that the experience of a stable and supportive family environment can reduce the impact of socio-economic adversity and consequently reduce negative chain reactions by influencing the level of early academic adjustment, and by shaping outlook and planning for the future. The study furthermore indicates a vital role for social ties and embeddedness in the community in providing a safety net and support system facilitating positive development. The experience of successful coping with challenges might reduce the sensitivity to later risk. Positive response from significant others, such as parents or teachers, can increase the chance of positive chain reactions or open up positive opportunities. Affirmative school experiences can promote feelings of self-esteem and self-efficacy, which in turn might stimulate the individual to persevere in difficult circumstances and to maintain a positive outlook on life. It has, however, to be noted that the evidence in support of these suggestions is still jagged and more research of the interactive processes that foster and promote positive adjustment in the face of adversity is needed.

The role of these factors and processes varied with the context and the developmental stage under investigation, highlighting the importance of considering the context dependency of resilience and the changing needs at different developmental stages and transition periods when designing intervention programmes. There are content- and context-specific variations in response to adversity and young people who demonstrate resilience in the face of one type of risk may not be able to overcome other types of risk. Some children may be resilient against the negative effects of poverty because they have supportive families, but the same children may be less successful in overcoming the effects of attending underfunded schools or living in violent neighbourhoods. It is also the case that different resource factors may be associated with different risks and outcomes, or with the same risk and outcome at different life stages. Although all individuals have the same basic needs, there are concerns regarding any asset lists postulating similar effects for all groups of individuals, in all contexts and for all outcomes (Fergus & Zimmerman, 2005). Findings from one context or population may not apply in another, as assets and resources are not equally distributed.

Context dependency of adjustment

The findings presented here illustrate the dynamics and heterogeneity of individual response to adversity. Good adjustment relative to others does not necessarily mean high competence in absolute terms. The criteria used to identify 'average' achievements are themselves culturally determined, reflecting biases grounded in the internalisation of values within the predominant culture we are participating in (Masten, 2001; Ogbu, 1981; Ungar, 2004; Walsh, 1998). Educational attainment is vitally important in our culture, and today it matters more than ever before in laying the foundations for future careers. Yet, academic achievement is not necessarily the most important indicator of high competence or mastery among all disadvantaged young people, as some might be more concerned about coping with violence, drug abuse, sexual activities, peer pressure, marginalisation and disrespect (Coie et al., 1993; Griffin, 1993; Ungar, 2004; Willis, 1977). High-risk individuals have to choose their pathways to resilience from within the economically, socially, geographically and even physically constrained choices available to them.

For example, in both cohorts the majority of low-risk individuals with good academic attainment pursued higher education leading to degree-level qualifications, while only one in five of the high-risk individuals with good academic attainment gained degree-level qualifications. Furthermore, high-risk individuals showing early academic resilience are less likely to enter a professional career than their more privileged peers. They are, however, more likely to obtain further qualifications and to climb the social ladder when compared to high-risk individuals with below average academic attainment. But, does entry into further education or the pursuit of a professional career indeed mean the same to individuals from different backgrounds? The findings presented here suggest that there might be different preferences regarding attainable goals and life styles. Resilient high-risk individuals, for example, were more likely to be married during their early thirties when compared to their more privileged peers or high-risk individuals with low academic attainment, suggesting a potential preference for intimate relationships and family life.

There has been a growing concern to further contextualise the study of resilience in order to get a better understanding of the competences and coping processes of individuals exposed to different forms of adversity and to study the pathways leading to effective adjustment despite adversity in different socio-historical circumstances (Coll et al., 1996; Glantz & Sloboda, 1999; Moen et al., 1995; Silbereisen & Eye, 1999; Ungar, 2004). With the increasing number of cross-cultural studies across and within nations, the question of who decides the criteria of positive adaptation is becoming even more pressing (Master, 1999).

Multidimensionality of adjustment

Furthermore, individual adjustment can vary depending upon the domain under consideration (Luthar, 1993). Resilience is a multidimensional phenomenon, and even when identified in an individual in one aspect of his or her life, it might not exist in a different domain. For example, the findings presented here suggest that academic resilience is associated with behavioural adjustment, but not necessarily with emotional stability, implying that good academic attainment might be achieved at the cost of emotional disturbance. Adjustment in one domain should be considered in relationship to adjustment in others to gain a better understanding of adjustment patterns across multiple domains and to avoid overly narrow definitions. There is evidence to suggest the existence of 'cascading effects', whereby changes in one sphere of life can bring about changes in other, overlapping, spheres (Masten, 2001). This would, for example, be the case where conduct problems undermine academic achievement, which then in turn appears to undermine later psychosocial adjustment and well-being.

Developmental perspective

Developmental processes involve the age-dependent sequencing of emerging capacities and competences within and across domains. The emergence of certain competences is based on changing manifestations of a capacity with developmental transformations and reorganisations being the rule. Early patterns of adjustment evolve to later patterns of adaptation. In Chapter 4 we saw that the experience of early disadvantage weakens individual adaptation and this detrimental effect is then carried forward into the future. Subsequent experiences of adversity add to the deterioration of the already reduced adjustment. If individual adjustment is already weakened at a very early age, it becomes more and more difficult for the young person to fully develop their potential. This negative chain effect undermines the positive adjustment of the young person, erodes individual potential and increases the likelihood of negative outcomes in adulthood.

The notion that there is coherence to the course of each individual's development is, however, not incompatible with the notions of discontinuity (Rutter, 1987; Lerner, 1991). It has been argued that the formation of new capacities or a change in trajectory is based on prior adaptations across domains of adjustment and maturational change, as well as subsequent environmental challenges and self-directed action (Sroufe & Rutter, 1984). Changes in adjustments do not simply spring forth without connection to previous quality of adaptation, without changing support, or challenges from the organism or the environment.

Early experiences of adversity influence later outcomes. The experience of socio-economic disadvantage does not always have an immediate impact and vulnerabilities may emerge only later in life. Early experience of adversity may be overcome, but leave the individual potentially more vulnerable to any risk experienced at a later age (Anthony, 1987; Cicchetti & Tucker, 1994). Repeated exposure to adversity may either thwart, amplify or accentuate initial adjustment (Elder & Caspi, 1988), implying that there is a multiplicity of pathways across the life course and great diversity of endpoints. Although the impact of repeated adversity may vary for different outcomes and for different domains of adversity, the research presented here suggests that persistent socio-economic disadvantage has stronger effects than intermittent adversity on academic attainment and that chronically stressful environments hinder the development of the personal adjustment needed for successful adaptation.

Dynamic state versus stable trait

Examining intra-individual change over time has raised the awareness of turning points in human development representing lasting changes in psychological functioning, and affecting the future course of development (Elder & Shanahan, 2006; Laub & Sampson, 2003; Rutter, 1996). For example, in Chapter 6 we saw that turning points can happen at any stage in the life course, illustrating the plasticity of human development. There is a wide range of experiences associated with these turning points, including both those over which the individual has no control, such as the occurrence of an economic boom or recession, and those reflecting individual choice and action. Resilience is not of a fixed nature. It may occur at one stage of the life course, but might not be a lasting quality.

The study of resilience as an individualistic phenomenon is misleading. If circumstances change, the risk alters, as does the response of the individual. The findings presented here generally underline that resilience is not some mysterious trait or characteristic of the individual, but a dynamic and interactive process. Individual attributes may contribute to adaptive functioning, but they themselves are shaped by conditions and circumstances experienced by the individual. Adaptive functioning is embedded in the systems and structures that are implicated in the distribution of resources, life chances and opportunities. The relationship between risk factors and adaptive functioning cannot be attributed to a high or low score on a personality trait. Neither is it helpful to describe resilience merely as a statement of positive status or outcome. Individuals who are not exposed to particularly severe problems or trauma and who have plenty of resources, support or opportunities would usually not be considered to be resilient, no matter how well they are functioning (Rutter, 1990). Individuals who can draw on high levels of personal and social resources or protective factors are generally more likely to do well when experiencing adverse situations than individuals with fewer or lower level resources. Yet, individuals growing up in adversity have generally fewer resources to draw on than their more privileged peers. What is needed is to move beyond resource or asset models of resilience, unless assets and resources are equally distributed or made accessible to everyone. All children need the same basic developmental supports and opportunities, and it is vital to gain a better understanding of the interactive mechanisms and processes in different contexts, enabling young people to develop and maintain these resources, and to function adaptively in the face of adversity.

Methodological considerations

How can assumptions about adaptive development in context be operationalised? What are the measurement strategies available to capture the dynamic resilience processes? There is a vast array of methods applicable for psychosocial studies of resilience, but most of them have been applied in cross-sectional studies. Focusing on the emergence of resilience in time and context, the research strategies adopted here will be appraised, with particular emphasis on the use of longitudinal data and the combination of variable-based and person-based approaches.

Use of longitudinal data

Laboratories are rare in the study of human development. The closest we get to them is when the opportunity arises to compare and contrast experiences in different societies or in different socio-historical contexts. In this study data collected for two national birth cohort studies born twelve years apart has been used for the investigation of individual adjustment in a changing socio-historical context, allowing for the control of age and cohort effects which any single longitudinal study is subject to (Baltes et al., 1988; Giele & Elder, 1998; Rutter, 1988; Schaie, 1965).

The use of longitudinal data is generally recommended in order to gain a better understanding of the dynamic processes involved in the pathways from childhood to adolescence to adulthood. The use of prospective, longitudinal data enables empirical attentiveness to the ontogenetic fluctuations involved in human development, allows the investigation of change and enables the investigator to disentangle association from cause (Cicchetti et al., 1993; Egeland et al., 1993; Elder, 1999; Rutter, 1988; Werner & Smith, 1992, 2001). Long-term patterns of experiences can be mapped, accounting for fluctuations in duration of experiences and cumulative continuities. This study, for example, has revealed cumulative continuities in both risk experiences and individual adjustment (see Chapters 4 and 6). Furthermore, the use of large data sets from general population samples makes it possible to determine differences and variations between individuals or groups who are and who are not exposed to the risk factors in question, as controls are readily available in the sample.

Despite these advantages, the use of longitudinal cohort data is not without problems. Cohort studies suffer from missing data both because of survey loss and of incomplete response, especially in analyses drawing on data from several waves (Menard, 2002; Rutter, 1988; Wolke et al., 1995). There are some indications that the most socially excluded are also most likely to be excluded from analysis, unless 'missingness' is sensitively handled. A crucial precondition of any cohort analysis is the balanced treatment of the impact of missing data both in terms of unit and item non-response. To address these possible effects, a variety of imputation models have been recommended (Little et al., 2000; Menard, 2002; Wothke, 2000). Here maximum likelihood estimations, which are provided as a feature of the structural equation modelling programme AMOS 4.01 (Arbuckle, 1999), have been adopted in combination with pairwise or listwise deletion of cases with missing values (see Appendix B for more details).

Longitudinal data collection is also rather costly in terms of money and investment of time. By drawing on data collected up to forty years ago by different research agencies, the choice of variables is determined and restricted by the theoretical considerations, the research questions and research practice prevalent at that time. In order to use data which has already been collected for a different purpose to answer newly emerging research questions it became necessary to re-cast and recode some of the data, and to render variables eligible for a cross-cohort comparison. This meant that the best had to be made of available measures. To facilitate comparison of data across cohorts, a latent variable modelling approach was used, investigating relationships between latent variables rather than focusing on the relationship between observed variables. Great care was taken to measure the relevant variables in as similar a way as possible. To explicate the effects of a changing socio-historical context more clearly, comparative longitudinal cohort studies need to be planned and coordinated, using a common core of broad measures and adjusting them as necessary to reflect cultural specifics and changes. Ideally the data collection should account for the heterogeneity of different cultural groups to make intergroup comparisons meaningful.

Another issue to be considered is that longitudinal studies based on extreme groups, i.e. high levels of risk exposure, may be affected by the tendency of the selected subsamples to regress towards the mean. Thus resilient adaptation involving improvement over time may be ascribed to the presence of a protective factor, but may be a mere statistical artefact. Longitudinal designs involving extreme groups therefore need to apply an approach that allows them to identify and eliminate regression towards the mean as an explanation of their results.

In the light of these problems it has been emphasised that not only long-term but also short-term longitudinal studies, focusing on changes in specific life-span developmental trajectories, can provide valuable insights into developmental functioning (Garmezy, 1991; Rutter, 1990). Shorter-term longitudinal studies should include at least three measurement points spaced far enough in time to cover specific periods of the life course and should ideally include measurements on all competence domains and influences relevant for a particular developmental stage (Luthar et al., 2000). Short-term studies are however less well suited to map complex chains of continuities and discontinuities over time.

Variable- and person-centred approaches

The link between risk and manifest competence can be analysed using either a variable- or a person-centred approach, each of which has its specific strengths and weaknesses. The variable-based approach focuses on general nomothetic probabilities, examining either main effect models or interaction effects (Luthar et al., 2000; Masten et al., 1988; Rutter, 1987). Variable-based approaches use a variety of multivariate strategies such as hierarchical regression, path analysis or structural equation modelling to identify linkages between risks, resources and adaptive functioning. A major problem with this approach is that it tells us nothing about how many individuals are actually facing high levels of risk or are manifesting high levels of competence (Luthar & Cushing, 1999). Furthermore, interaction effects are notoriously unstable and difficult to establish because they are generally associated with small effect sizes (Rutter, 1990).

The person- or individual-based approach, on the other hand, involves the selection or grouping of specific individuals based on selected
criteria (Block, 1980; Cairns et al., 1998; Magnusson & Bergman, 1988;
Masten, 2001). There are various ways in which categories can be
formed, based on theoretical considerations, classificatory analysis,
empirical grouping or the identification of extreme cases (Hinde,
1998). Empirical grouping techniques, for example, encompass cluster
analysis, latent profile analysis, log linear modelling or configural fre-
quency analysis (Magnusson, 1995). Here the grouping of individuals
was based on extreme cases in order to assess interaction effects of
protective factors in high- and low-risk conditions.

Studies adopting the person-centred approach have varied considerably in their stringency in categorising individuals as resilient. For
example, some researchers used adjustment scores in the top 16 per
cent (+1SD) of the sample distribution (Cicchetti et al., 1993; Luthar,
1991), while others defined adaptive functioning through scores higher
than the average or median within the sample (Egeland & Kreutzer,
1991; Osborn, 1990; Schoon & Parsons, 2002b). Some have used a
global competence index, combining several discrete areas of adjustment
(Cicchetti et al., 1993; Egeland & Kreutzer, 1991), while others focused
only on specified domains (Luthar, 1991; Wyman et al., 1991). Despite
such variation in criteria for identifying high adversity and positive
adjustment, it has been argued that person-based approaches may be
less prone to statistically artefactual insights inherent in variable-based
approaches, because a particular subset of high-risk, high competence
individuals has been identified (Luthar & Cushing, 1999). The study of
resilience through descriptive profiles of individuals can reduce ambigu-
ities sometimes inherent in variable-based approaches. Person-centred
investigations can furthermore bring valuable insights into the dynamic
interdependency of individual and context, offering a more holistic view
of individual development (Magnusson, 1995).

Values and meaning

As discussed before, cultural and group values are crucial to the study of
resilience, as adaptation is based on transactional interactions between
individual characteristics and environmental contingencies. Notions of
resilience or adversity may hold different meanings for different populations or subgroups within a population and subcultural norms may differ
from the majority culture (Masten, 1999). It has been argued that, in
order to determine if and when a person is 'doing alright' in the face
of adversity, the person in question has to be asked about how s/he

is experiencing the situation (Massey et al., 1998; Ungar, 2004; Canvin et al., 2004).

The use of life histories and biographies providing individual stories of perseverance against the odds has long been established as one of the empirical pillars in life-course research (Bateson, 1990; Clausen, 1993; Rossi, 1983; Vaillant, 1977). The identification of positive adaptation should not be concluded without reference to the voices, interpretations and viewpoints of those individuals, families and communities experiencing the adversity. Definitions, meanings and understanding of what constitutes risk as well as success or failure in adjustment should be obtained from the people concerned. This would require the researcher or practitioner involved to be open to and respect the interpretations and choices made by the individuals, instead of labelling them as 'non-compliant' or 'problematic' (Ungar, 2004). Avoiding the participation of those under study, especially when health or welfare professionals working closely with the people concerned are involved, implies that their views are not valued, their difficult choices not respected. Hopefully future studies will aim to address the cultural dependency of resilience in more detail.

It is only on the basis of the accumulated empirical evidence from different sources that we can hope to generalise insights into the processes and mechanisms associated with resilient functioning. The complementary value of quantitative and qualitative data in studying the origins of successful attainment and adaptations over the life span has long been recognised (Cairns et al., 1998; Clarke & Clarke, 2000; Clausen, 1993; Giele & Elder, 1998). Some phenomena are best understood as linearly-related continua, yet especially designed qualitative approaches can help to gain a better understanding of the meaning and interpretation of risk, as well as success or failure in adjustment from the individuals concerned. Qualitative studies which involve listening to the voices of the study participants can generate new insights into how constellations of risk and competence are experienced by the individuals themselves and how these experiences are embedded in the multiple and wider aspects of their lives. These insights are not only important for the empirical study of resilience, but can also be invaluable in guiding the design and planning of effective intervention strategies.

Future directions of research

First and foremost, future research must address variations in definitions and terminology. The term resilience should only be used to refer to the observation of manifest effective adaptation despite the experience of adversity. Any reference to specific personality traits or mere observations of competent functioning in the absence of a significant risk or trauma should be avoided. Luthar et al., for example, recommend that the term resilience should only be used in conjunction with profiles, trajectories or adaptations to emphasise the dual aspects of risk and adjustment inherent in the notion of resilience (Luthar & Cicchetti, 2000).

It is important to differentiate between protective factors and processes (involving interaction effects between risk, protective factor and outcome) and cumulative effect models where promotive or resource factors combine additively to compensate the effects of adversity. While protective factors show their beneficial effect primarily among individuals at risk, promotive factors can have an equally beneficial effect for those individuals experiencing adversity and those who do not.

Clear definitions of the criteria used to operationalise risk and adjustment at different life stages are necessary in order to obtain a consolidation of research evidence across domains and cultures. The choice of criteria should be guided by specified theoretical and conceptual considerations regarding the nature of adversity under investigation and about the risk processes involved in a particular domain and during a particular life stage.

Researchers should avoid an overly-narrow or overly-broad specification of the domain under investigation. Resilience is a multidimensional phenomenon and high-risk individuals may demonstrate competence in one domain, but experience problems in other areas of their lives. To focus on a particular domain of adjustment is essential in order to elucidate the underlying mechanisms and processes within that domain, yet might lead to the wrong conclusion regarding the overall adjustment of individuals across domains. The decision whether to examine multiple domains in combination or separately, or whether to give particular outcome domains priority over others should be guided by theoretical considerations (Luthar et al., 2000).

If only one domain is chosen overgeneralisations should be avoided. This study has focused primarily on the investigation of one domain, i.e. academic resilience. Future studies might home in on the central principles, fine-tuning the different empirical approaches and aggregating findings across several different domains in order to build more integrative, yet parsimonious, theories regarding risk and adjustment and the links between them.

Resilience is a dynamic process. Ideally researchers should aim to investigate continuity and changes in adaptation over time, and to gain a better understanding of the mechanisms and processes underlying stability in adjustment as well as the factors, events and processes leading to discontinuities in adjustment. The pathways linking earlier experiences to later outcomes can be both direct and indirect and the mechanisms are likely to be multiple. A major challenge for future research is to give detailed attention to the analysis of ongoing interactions and transactions between individuals and their environment and to consider the multiple bi-directional influences involved.

The findings presented here suggest age differences in individual response to adversity. Longitudinal studies are vital to assess change over time. Where the use of longitudinal data is not possible, researchers should focus on specified ages and stages of development as well as developmental transitions to elucidate the associated vulnerability and protective processes within and across domains of adjustment.

Most of the recent research on resilience has focused on children and adolescents and considerably less is known about adult adjustment in modern society. Most adults are facing the task of balancing competing demands in their role as worker, lover, parent and home maker. As indicated in Chapter 3 an increasing number of adults may be confronted with the combination of linked problems such as unemployment, low incomes, poor health and family breakdown. Given the importance of family factors and processes in shaping the developmental functioning of their children, more research efforts should concentrate on the study of effective adjustment in adult life.

Another issue to be considered are gender differences in response to adversity. Although the linkages observed between adversity and adjustment apply to both men and women, there is evidence to suggest gender differences in adjustment. It has long been argued that boys are more vulnerable than girls to family stress and socio-economic adversity in early childhood (Moffitt et al., 2001; Rutter, 1970; Werner & Smith, 2001). The findings presented here suggest that gender differences are reducing, especially regarding inequalities in educational and occupational opportunities and attainment. Yet, in the transition to adult roles, women encounter more diverse pathways than men, reflecting the integration of multiple social roles. Future research should aim to gain a better understanding of how gender shapes the individual context interactions across the life course and include family and parenting histories in its scope.

Special attention should also be paid to the role of biology and genetic processes, particularly in the light of new and exciting research evidence in the study of neural, neuroendocrine, cognitive, emotional and immune system functioning in relation to stress reactivity (Caspi et al., 2002; Davidson, 2000; Huttenlocher, 2002; Jausovec & Jausovec, 2000; Nelson, 1999). Biological and genetic processes are an important component of a much larger series of possible explanations for human behaviour. Human behaviour and development is shaped by complex gene–environment interactions, involving for example contextual influences on whether or not a genetic disposition will find expression, or individual variations in sensitivity to specific environmental factors. The contribution of biological variables to the reciprocal and dynamic processes underlying resilient adaptation can only be fully understood in relation to their interactions with psychosocial processes and their embeddedness in a wider socio-cultural environmental context (Bronfenbrenner & Ceci, 1994; Gottlieb et al., 1998; Horowitz, 2000; Rutter, 2003). Taking into consideration the conjoint effect of multiple levels of influence on the phenomenon of resilience there have been calls for increasing interdisciplinary and multidisciplinary research collaboration and training aiming for an integration of insights gained from different disciplines (Elder & Shanahan, 2006; Luthar et al., 2000; Curtis & Cicchetti, 2003).

Human development is shaped by multiple spheres of influence and the findings presented here have illustrated the dynamic and multidimensional nature of adjustment. Comparing individuals in a changing socio-historical context has highlighted the role of social change which involves the transformation of context in which people live their lives. The recognition that individual development does not occur in a social vacuum will hopefully lead to an elaboration of resilience research to include social structures and cultures as constituent elements in developmental processes.

In summary, the individual's experience of adversity and his or her long-term response to it are determined by the dynamic interaction of individual and context, by the interaction of psychosocial resources within the socio-economic structure of society, and the obstacles, opportunities and life chances provided by those structures. The developmental-contextual systems approach adopted in this study enabled the integration of individual, family and wider community factors in the study of resilience and also allowed for the consideration of historical aspects. Conceptualising resilience as development in context enables us to account for both continuity and change in adjustment through the dynamic interactions between a changing individual and a changing context. Conceptualising positive adaptation as a product of person–environment interactions makes it possible to move away from directing blame for maladjustment at individuals and families, shifting the focus from individuals to the wider socio-historical context, the prevailing systems and structures that are implicated in the distribution of life chances, resources and opportunities.

9 Implications of findings for interventions and social policy

> 'The goal, in other words, is not simply to help talented children from poor backgrounds progress up the social ladder, and so have access to a broader range of goods and opportunities than their less-talented peers, but to challenge the very existence of an exclusive and divided society, in which access to public goods such as health and education depends on one's social position.'
>
> (Bamfield, 2004)

In this final chapter the evidence presented here will be evaluated and suggestions and directions for interventions put forward, thereby shifting the focus of concern from basic to applied science. What can be done to facilitate the development of individual potential and to enable individuals to overcome the odds stacked against them? Knowledge about protective factors and processes involved in positive adaptation can bring a new impetus to the development of social policies aiming to promote the well-being of disadvantaged children and populations. The focus of this study has been on the factors and processes most important for the development and maintenance of academic resilience in the face of socio-economic adversity. Given the central importance of both socio-economic risk and educational attainment in our culture, as well as their long-term consequences across domains, the findings will also be helpful for informing our understanding of other domains of adjustment. Yet, it has to be kept in mind that findings from one context or population may not apply to another. Therefore, the aim of this chapter is not to list individual risk modifiers or resource factors but to extract the overarching messages emerging across the findings.

A differentiation is made between a risk and a resilience approach. Risk research is usually focused on outcomes that have a negative valence, such as risk of maladjustment. In contrast, resilience research explicitly encompasses both negative and positive dimensions of both predictors and outcomes (Luthar & Zelazo, 2003a). Issues related to the protective factors and processes that facilitate adaptations in the face of adversity are evaluated, taking into consideration the context and dynamics of adjustment.

157

Why do risk and resilience matter? Stated broadly, policy directed at improving the life chances of children and young people needs to be directed at eliminating the risk factors undermining individual adjustment, or if that is not possible, at reducing the detrimental impact of risk factors and enhancing resilience through ensuring that appropriate protective mechanisms are in place. A risk focus is useful to maximise predictions of outcomes, following the assumption that the probability of maladjustment is heightened, based on the presence of one or more risk factors. Risk factors therefore provide targets for policy aiming to remove obstacles and barriers to the development of individual potential. The focus on risk is also helpful to identify populations at risk – those growing up in adverse circumstances – together with related components of experiences that may be directly susceptible to intervention, e.g. children living in poverty exposed to poor housing, violent neighbourhoods or overcrowded schools. A focus on resilience and resources, on the other hand, aims to understand adaptive development in spite of risk exposure and to maximise wellness even before maladjustment has occurred.

Focus on risk

Being born into a relatively disadvantaged family increases the probability of accumulating risks associated with that disadvantage. Children from a relatively disadvantaged family background are more likely to accumulate risks throughout their life than children born to more privileged families. This accumulation of risk begins early in life and its consequences can continue into adulthood, or even into the next generation. It is usually not a single risk factor that causes difficulties, but the accumulation of adversity that reduces developmental adjustment.

The experience of early hardship weakens individual adaptation and this detrimental effect is then carried forward into the future. Subsequent experiences of adversity add to the deterioration of already reduced adjustment. In Chapter 6 we have seen that young people from relatively disadvantaged family backgrounds who demonstrated early academic resilience did not maintain their performance to the same extent as their more privileged peers. A general premise of life-span developmental psychology is that adaptations to change are influenced by what people bring to the new situation (Lerner, 1984). As shown in Chapter 4, if individual adjustment is already weakened at a very early age, it becomes more and more difficult for the young person to fully develop their potential. This negative chain effect undermines the positive adjustment of the young person, erodes individual potential and increases the likelihood of negative outcomes in adulthood. The findings presented here suggest that cumulative adversity has effects beyond those associated with current or early adversity.

It has been argued that certain risk factors can be viewed as the negative versus positive poles of the same underlying construct, and the same variable may operate both as risk and as a protective factor (Stouthamer-Loeber et al., 1993). Yet some risk factors, such as geographical location, are fixed predisposing conditions that cannot be directly reached or changed by policy interventions. Some factors are merely correlates of risk factors, such as parental consumption patterns that may not play a direct part in the causal processes involved in child development (Bynner, 2001a). Where risk factors are difficult to eliminate, intervention strategies should aim to build up relevant psychosocial resources.

Focus on resources

It has been argued that individuals who can draw on high levels of personal and social resources are better equipped to tackle adverse situations than individuals with fewer or lower level resources. The combined or additive effect of these resources has been conceptualised in terms of a main effects model, which describes the cumulative effects of these factors (Fergusson & Horwood, 2003; Luthar et al., 2000; Masten, 1999; Masten, 2001; Sameroff et al., 1998). Increasing the protective resources in quality or number could theoretically improve positive adjustment in general. Supportive and stable families, good schools and social ties to the wider community can each compensate and ameliorate the influence of socio-economic risk factors and can facilitate the individual's capacity to engage with a changing psychosocial environment. Yet, individuals growing up in adversity have generally less opportunity to draw on or to build up and maintain potential psychosocial resource factors. The research findings suggest that individual capabilities are susceptible to environmental influences, illustrating the dynamic interactions between individual and context as well as the plasticity of human development. Resourcefulness and individual competences are not a guarantee for overcoming high-risk conditions. There is great heterogeneity in responses to adversity which correspond to the contingencies of environments and the risks encountered therein.

The findings have illustrated a variety of protective processes that enable young people to overcome adverse conditions. Besides promotive processes where resource factors show an equally beneficial effect on those exposed and those not exposed to adversity, we could also identify interactive effects where the influence of adversity was moderated by specific protective factors, such as social integration or parental involvement and support for the child's education. The protective factors and processes under investigation did buffer against the effects of adversity, yet they did not extinguish the effects of risk. Young people who showed early academic resilience did not achieve to the same extent as their more privileged peers, and were, at least in part, held back in their attainments by the experience of early disadvantage. Therefore, interventions that target both risk and resource factors simultaneously are the ones most likely to make a difference.

Implications for interventions

With respect to appropriate policy interventions, the resilience framework implies a focus on positive outcomes, not just negative ones (Luthar & Cicchetti, 2000). Of central interest are not problems or failures, which are the traditional focus of research on high-risk groups, but positive adaptational outcomes and their antecedents (Garmezy et al., 1984; Luthar & Cicchetti, 2000; Masten et al., 1990; Pittman et al., 2002). Moving away from a deficit model, the resilience approach recognises and builds on strengths and strategies among high-risk populations for managing their lives and avoiding crises. Instead of pathologising individuals and populations at risk, the resilience approach aims to provide an overarching framework for conceptualising social problems, intervention strategies and practice (Fraser et al., 1999; Lurie & Monahan, 2001; McMillen, 1999). From a policy perspective this implies a shift of emphasis from crisis intervention to primary prevention before serious maladjustment has manifested itself. It would, for example, involve a shift from preventing youth problems to the promotion of youth development and youth engagement in their communities and societies (Pittman et al., 2001). Countering objections to preventive measures on financial and fiscal grounds, Luthar & Cicchetti (2000) have argued that carefully conceived preventive interventions can be more cost effective than attempts to reduce maladjustment after it has become well ingrained. After all, correcting maladjustment once it has occurred is harder than preventing it in the first place.

Emphasis on strengths

The resilience framework entails emphasis not on deficits but on areas of strength, such as academic attainments, school motivation and the hopes and aspirations of less privileged parents for their children's welfare and future development. From a resilience perspective efforts should try to harness notable strengths of 'vulnerable populations' to derive a significant momentum for positive change (Luthar & Cicchetti, 2000). The findings have shown that at-risk individuals as well as their families and communities develop solutions and strategies of how to respond to experiences of adversity. Identifying and building upon the strengths of individuals in adverse circumstances can promote their own feelings of competence and capability and can stimulate enduring positive changes.

It has been argued that the downward pathologising gaze of welfare professions may compound the problems of their clients and undermine their capabilities and resilience (Beresford, 2000). Individuals at risk, as well as significant others in their immediate context, should be consulted and included in designing and implementing interventions, drawing on their experiences in overcoming disadvantage and their understanding of how positive adjustment can be maintained in adverse circumstances. This might imply the identification of adaptation patterns that are congruent with the experiences of marginalised populations. For example, in certain instances it might be the resilient solution to sacrifice or postpone further education in order to find a well-paid job (Bartelt, 1994; Ungar, 2004b). The voices of those afflicted voices need to be heard if we are to understand their experiences of adversity and to identify solutions that fit their constructions of reality (Caputo, 1999; 2000; Ungar, 2004; Canvin et al., 2004). Excluding individuals from taking part in decisions concerning their lives means denying them dignity and self-respect (White & Smith, 1994; Sennett, 2003).

Listening to and respecting individual choices and strategies could trigger alternative forms of interventions aiming to support and foster individual capabilities. Recent government initiatives have endorsed the concept and practice of listening to and acting upon the voices of usually marginalised groups (Department of Health, 2001; Social Exclusion Unit, 2000a), yet caution has to be exercised so that what is heard are not only issues acceptable to the authorities, while unacceptable points remain unheard (ATD Fourth World, 1996).

Systematic investigation of underlying processes

The focus of attention should not rest on outcomes alone, but should also consider the processes and pathways leading to successful adaptation. What has to be done to create communities and institutions within which individuals can flourish? Effective strategies for prevention or remediation need to be developed on the basis of what is known about the influences shaping positive adjustment within and across domains, both in early life and later on. We have seen that there is great heterogeneity in response to adverse circumstances, and that there are complex variations in needs and resources by age, family and community. Often there are multiple needs stretching across domains concerning issues related to teaching and learning, work, housing or health. What is needed is an empirical and theoretical framework guiding the design of interventions aiming to address the multifaceted interactions between individuals and their environmental contexts over time.

When planning interventions, evidence based on the systematic investigation of processes underlying adaptation in different and changing contexts (i.e. the study of high-risk groups at different ages and in different contexts) is of vital importance. The study has shown that different resources and processes are associated with different constellations of risk and outcomes and that protective processes may not operate in the same manner for all groups, all contexts or all outcomes. The findings suggested that it is necessary to assess individual variations in level of risk exposure as well as subjective evaluations of the risk experience.

Context is crucial for resilience

Interventions should not attempt to improve isolated skills or competences with little consideration of the wider context in which they occur (Pianta & Walsh, 1996). Rather they should aim to understand the functional utility of the competencies targeted – that is to say their implications within an ecological system that reinforces and maintains them (Bronfenbrenner, 1977; Luthar & Cicchetti, 2000). There have been changes in transition pathways from childhood to adulthood, as reflected, for example, in the increasing participation in further education and delay in the assumption of adult roles for some. The routes within education and training are, however, not neutral to cultural-structural factors and participation in further education remains premised upon class-related assumptions concerning opportunities and resources. Therefore, intervention or prevention programmes should be integrated into the cultural context, the educational programme and the personal behavioural repertoire of the developing individual (Pianta & Walsh, 1996). They should respond to the needs of individuals for affiliation, value structuring, achievement and experience of mastery (Ungar, 2004). Insights gained from consultation with service users, in addition to rigorous research evidence, are vital in guiding social policies to promote effective adaptation.

The notion that there is one basic mechanism underlying adjustment in different contexts and at different life stages is untenable. Multiple factors are involved in the development of resilience. Policy makers have to recognise and appreciate the increasing diversity of pathways in the transition from school to work and in the assumption of adult roles, as well as the existence of multiple interlocking transitions. There is a great diversity in pathways leading to resilience. What is required are culturally- and developmentally-sensitive prevention strategies. It is vital to gain a better understanding of what is needed and what works for individuals in different circumstances and at different transition points.

Holistic approach

Considering the multidimensional nature of forces that affect individuals, as well as the interactive nature of human development, appropriately designed interventions should operate on multiple levels, spanning both proximal and distal environments. A high degree of differentiation and specialisation in services can be counterproductive for at-risk children who are exposed to co-occurring, multiple or accumulating risks. Interventions should aim for a holistic approach, for community-based interventions and integrated service delivery, involving children and young people as well as their families and communities (Bronfenbrenner, 1977; Luthar & Cicchetti, 2000; Luthar & Zelazo, 2003). It has been argued that the most effective programmes are those that are the most comprehensive and multifaceted, building up resources from inside the community care network and strengthening the social fabric (Brooks-Gunn, 1995; Graham & Barter, 1999; Ungar, 2004).

Increasing the number of protective influences can lead to a greater likelihood of positive developmental outcomes. Ideally interventions should be building on macrolevel policies: community-based partnerships among different service agencies, involving cross-training of staff and integrated service delivery. Services should aim to meet the needs of individuals struggling with multiple disadvantaging factors, experiencing substantive challenges to adaptation across different domains (physical and mental health, housing, child care, etc). An integrated service delivery would imply the integration of devolved financing models, as well as breaking down barriers related to different professional orientations, training and procedures, leading to increased capabilities of staff in responding to individuals and families with multiple needs (Burt et al., 1998).

In the UK, for instance, Communities that Care (CTC), a programme established in 1997 by the Joseph Rowntree Foundation, endeavours to change the way that agencies interact with communities and the way they both plan the delivery of services, breaking down some of the barriers between professionals and researchers. It is based on the idea of risk audits undertaken by local people in vulnerable communities (Catalano & Hawkins, 1996), followed by specific action plans for building the protective resources needed at different life stages: from infancy through primary and secondary school to leaving school, focusing in particular on supporting parents and schools (Utting, 1999).

There are also other recent UK government initiatives adopting a systemic holistic approach directed at enhancing opportunities and minimising risk through each stage of the life course. For example, the major theme of 'neighbourhood renewal' in the government's social exclusion agenda reflects an acknowledgement that risk factors tend to go together with multiplicative effects on child outcomes. Unless we can improve the quality of the social and physical environment in which children grow up, their development may be permanently stunted (Social Exclusion Unit, 2000d).

Developmental focus

Interventions should have a clear developmental focus. Early interventions are of obvious preventive value to safeguard children from social exclusion. The earlier intervention occurs through pre-school provision and then through home–school links, the more opportunity there is to build a positive set of home–school relationships around developmental processes and to remove obstacles to the acquisition of capabilities (Bynner, 2001). In most cases accumulating risk appears to derive less from any irreversible effect in early life than from continuing disadvantaged circumstances reinforcing the social relations identified with the risk. Although early life experiences are vital, there is considerable developmental flexibility after early development. Every stage of the life course is important, not just the early years. To enable young people to fully develop their potential, investments in development need to extend throughout childhood, adolescence and early adulthood. Early life interventions can make a crucial contribution in influencing the level of adjustment, yet development is ongoing. Children have different 'sensitive periods', during which they are particularly responsive to different types of interventions, especially when confronting major transitions such as school entry, leaving school and entry into the workforce. 'Investing in early childhood is necessary but not sufficient, . . . as there is no way to adequately "inoculate" children so that they will be immune to later challenges and developmental tasks' (Pittman et al., 2002, p. 155).

Contrary to some common assumptions about the roots of individual adaptation, protective experiences may occur well past early childhood. For example, by compiling the life histories of criminals, Laub and Sampson (2003) could show that differences in early experiences or temperament were insufficient to predict avoidance of a career in crime. Critical turning points often occur later in life, generally in association with the assumption of adult roles. Likewise, the case stories presented in Chapter 6 have illustrated the occurrence of turning points in adult lives, leading to a change in trajectory.

Research-based evidence of resilience during periods of developmental transitions can help to create unique opportunities for promoting successful adaptation in changing circumstances across the life course. It is never too early and never too late to intervene (Bynner, 2001). Interventions should aim to foster resilient pathways responding to the changing needs at different life stages and in a changing socio-historical context. They should address what is needed at each developmental stage and transition point and facilitate progression.

For example, it has been argued that there is less variance in children's achievement across, rather than within, schools, that differences between schools are small because all schools induce substantial growth in children (Entwistle et al., 2002). There is, however, a shortfall in educational attainment among children from disadvantaged families at the end of the first year in comparison to their more privileged peers. This drop in attainment has been attributed to a lack of home background resources before the disadvantaged children begin the first grade. Therefore, resources need to be directed at families and neighbourhoods to sustain academic engagement and to close the gap between advantaged and disadvantaged children even before they start school (Entwistle et al., 2002).

The findings presented here furthermore demonstrated that constellations of risk and adjustment develop throughout the whole period of schooling, emphasising the need for continuing support for children throughout their school careers as well as in the transition from school to work. UK government programmes such as Sure Start attempt to put such a strategy in place, starting during the pre-school years (Glass, 1999) and continuing until the age of fourteen (up to age sixteen for those with special educational needs). The aim of Sure Start is to support children, families and communities through the integration of early education, childcare, health and family support. Those starting from a position of disadvantage clearly require particular attention. Services such as the Children's Fund offer the opportunity to continue the strategy through the school years. Connexions prepares the child for the range of difficult choices to be made preceding and following the school leaving age of sixteen (Social Exclusion Unit, 1999). Revisions to the fourteen to nineteen school curriculum, although not without their critics (Nuffield, 2002), further exemplify government attempts to enhance life chances by offering children of all 'abilities' appropriate tracks to adult life.

Sustainability of programmes

Without appropriate support, individuals exposed to multiple risks have a greater risk for serious long-term problems. Drawing on findings from the American Head Start and other competence-enhancement and prevention programmes, there is evidence to suggest that longer periods of intervention are more effective than shorter ones (Pianta & Walsh, 1996). Intervention efforts should therefore aim to foster sustainable programmes and services that may eventually become self-maintaining (Luthar & Cicchetti, 2000). The dynamics of development dictate that children who are free of risk at one point in their lives may become 'at risk' later. Similarly, those who are at risk may move out of it as family circumstances change. Continuing protective support therefore needs to be directed at all children.

Targeting

Many interventions are targeted at high-risk groups or high-risk areas, possibly based on the assumption that it is more cost-effective to provide preventive services only for those most in need. Targeted interventions are however not without criticism. Area-based interventions for example, have been described as suffering from the 'ecological fallacy' because if the average level of socio-economic disadvantage is higher in one area than another that does not mean that all families in the high-risk area are equally affected (Bynner, 2001). Many families in high-risk areas are not in need of enhanced provision, while many outside the high-risk areas need more support. The risk of area targeting is that the problems of families and children outside the target area become scattered and therefore invisible to policy makers (Bynner, 2001).

Likewise, targeting individuals most at risk might single out indivi-duals with an increased likelihood of showing maladaptive adjustment, yet it will also include many who will not develop problems, and more importantly, might miss out a considerable number of individuals where no problems are yet apparent. Narrowly targeted interventions might furthermore lead to stigmatisation, labelling particular individuals and subgroups of the population as problematic and not able to cope. Targeting at-risk individuals is often based on assumptions that there are highly visible, easily identifiable problem groups with a great number of shared characteristics. The research evidence, however, suggests a great heterogeneity in characteristics and needs and that at-risk individ-uals share many characteristics with those making successful transitions. Human development is dynamic and changing. Disadvantaged individ-uals can move in and out of extreme situations. Therefore, the narrow focus of targeted policies creates concern about the availability of sup-port for all when needed and for all who could benefit (Catan, 2004; Coles, 2000; Jones, 2002). Access to services should be facilitated for all, aiming to raise the floor for every person, at every age and at every place. Targeting therefore needs to occur at every age and at every stage of development with the targets determined by the research evidence. As a result, the potentially stigmatising and undermining effects of being singled out as a high-risk individual or group would be diminished. Furthermore, universal eligibility could detract from what the public might perceive as rewards for problematic, anti-social or undesirable behaviour (Seccombe, 2002; Canvin et al., 2004).

Creating opportunities for development

It is misleading to conceive resilience completely in individualistic terms. An over-individualised approach fails to take account of other, structural explanations and causes of adjustment. In order to sustain beneficial effects of interventions it is necessary to provide stable and dependable structures and to create opportunities for development. Without endur-ing protective structures and opportunities at each step of the life course, even the most resilient individuals will not be able to maintain their adjustment (Elder, 1974/1999). Supporting children, families and com-munities through the provision of national health insurance, child sup-port, paid parental leave and family tax allowances are fundamental pillars of interventions targeting family hardship during the early years (Seccombe, 2002). Provision of child care facilities, pre-school and school-based interventions are crucial, in combination with measures strengthening parental involvement and aspirations for their children, as for example through the medium of continuing teacher–parent inter-action. Other risk factors point to the need for more direct reinforcement in the classroom itself through additional resources for those children who are falling behind (Bynner, 2001). This argues for smaller class sizes alongside the expanded use of classroom assistants in schools. Even the option of grade achievement which dominates American and many continental systems, might also seriously be considered as a means of ensuring that no child can move through the educational system without achieving the stepping stones that need to be taken from one stage to the next.

In adolescence, the consequences of what has happened earlier in the school career come to the fore. It is then that children's choices, dictated in part by family attitudes, teachers' expectations and general economic circumstances may well add another blow to the child's positive devel-opment. Postponement of differentiation between tracks leading to dif-ferent teenage outcomes seems the obvious solution – including that of leaving education at the first opportunity. There should be opportunity structures for young people to learn about and experience possible pathways to work, recreation or higher education. The introduction of mentoring relationships (which is for example part of the Connexions programme) is believed to be one of the key factors promoting resilient adaptations (Rutter et al., 1979; Rutter, 1990).

Furthermore, employment policies need to address local labour-market opportunities and work experience, as knowledge of local job prospects and the nature of the local labour market may affect school performance. Leaving school without qualifications in a labour market that is relentlessly shrinking for those without them, needs to be resisted (Bynner et al., 2000). The challenge for policy makers lies in making sure that young people will receive the support they need, and that positive outcomes and pathways to greater opportunity are open to every young person and are not monopolised by the privileged few.

Conclusion

Empirical evidence gained from resilience research can inform and guide the development of effective interventions for different at-risk popula-tions, addressing issues related to risk factors and psychosocial re-sources, as well as risk and protective processes. We can differentiate between a risk approach aiming to change or reduce the odds, and an assets approach aiming to foster and maintain psychosocial resources. Where risk factors are difficult to identify and/or to eliminate, interven-tion strategies should aim to increase available psychosocial assets and to build up and strengthen protective processes (Coie et al., 1993). The application of the resilience paradigm in designing and planning intervention strategies and programmes can help to reduce the impact of adverse experiences and to optimise opportunities.

Yet, any application has to be based on explicit clarification and definitions of key concepts. There has to be concern especially regarding misconceptions that resilience is a proxy for innate personality traits or some mysterious property of the person. How individuals respond to risk is a function of person–environment interactions. Positive adaptation does not reside within the person, but in the active interactions between an individual and aspects of the environment s/he experiences. Research has indicated that the effects of policy should not be limited to correcting the effects of maladjustment, that programmes and intervention should target the elimination of critical risk factors as well as the promotion of protective factors and processes at multiple levels of influence before maladjustment has occurred. Interventions should aim to address interlinked problems, plan for the provision of strong and integrated service support and create opportunities for successful pathways to beneficial long-term outcomes. Ultimately for interventions to be successful they should lead to a complete and permanent ecological change, reinforcing diversions in development in the long run through ongoing structural improvements.

Appendix A Two British Birth Cohorts

This book reports on the experiences of two British birth cohorts, allowing a glimpse into how socio-historic change has impacted on individual lives. The UK is rather privileged in that respect, as it has four national birth cohort studies following the lives of individuals born in 1946, 1958, 1970, and most recently in 2000/01 (Dex & Joshi, 2004; Ferri et al., 2003; Wadsworth, 1991). These studies offer the unique opportunity to gain a better understanding of the context dependency of adjustment in changing times, and to assess the impact of social change on individual lives.

The evidence presented here is based on research on data collected for two of the British birth cohorts, the 1958 National Child Development Study (NCDS) and the 1970 British Cohort Study (BCS70). Both cohort studies were launched to investigate antenatal and post-natal service provision, perinatal mortality and morbidity. Both collected information about almost all births occurring nation-wide in a target week in 1958 and in 1970 respectively. The development of over 30,000 individuals was followed at further sweeps of data collection at various ages, spanning the period from birth to mid-adulthood.

The National Child Development Study (NCDS)

NCDS originated as the Perinatal Mortality Survey (PMS), a study of virtually every baby born in England, Scotland and Wales during the week of 3–9 March 1958. Information on 17,415 children was obtained from the mothers by the midwives involved and from medical records. The initial survey was sponsored by the National Birthday Trust Fund and was designed to investigate the obstetric factors associated with stillbirth and death in early infancy (Butler & Bonham, 1963; Butler & Alberman, 1969). In five major follow-up studies data was collected on the physical, psychosocial and educational development of the cohort at ages 7, 11, 16, 23, 33 and 42 (Bynner et al., 2000b; Shepherd, 1995; Ferri et al., 2003). The latest follow-up study at age 46 was conducted in 2004–5.

The sample was furthermore augmented by adding immigrants who came to Britain and who were born in the reference week in 1958. This was done to reflect the nature of the British population since 1958, taking into account the increase in immigration from the former colonies. The number of cohort members from ethnic minorities is, however, rather low at about 2 per cent overall.

In 1965, a re-study of the then seven-year-old children and their families was carried out by the National Children's Bureau (NCB) of London with funding from the Plowden Committee, to provide evidence on children passing through primary school in the early 1960s (Central Advisory Council for Education, 1967). This was the true beginning of the NCDS and it is doubtful whether the 1958 Perinatal Mortality Survey would have transformed into a longitudinal study without this funding (Bynner et al., 1998; Ferri, 1998). Most of the children had been in primary school at that time, having started school two years previously, at age five. Detailed interviews were carried out with one of the child's parents (or parent figure), usually the mother. Information was also collected from each child's head teacher and classroom teacher. Medical examinations were carried out by the school health services, and a battery of tests was administered to the children themselves (Davie et al., 1972).

In 1969, when the children were eleven years old and still in primary school, another set of data was collected from the same kinds of sources (Wedge, 1969). Where possible, identical or very similar measures were used. In addition, further information besides test data was collected from the children themselves. In the UK age eleven is the age at which most children make the transition from primary school to secondary school. The allocation to secondary school at that time was based on parental wishes, the location of the family home and the children's school attainment (Rutter et al., 1979).

The next survey was conducted in 1974, when the cohort members were sixteen, although 30 per cent of cohort members were only fifteen at the time of the interviews (Plewis et al., 2004). In 1973 the minimum school leaving age was raised from fifteen to sixteen, making this the first cohort to continue their compulsory school attendance until the age of sixteen (Fogelman, 1983). More information than at age eleven was collected directly from the children themselves, including measures of educational and occupational goals, as well as expectations regarding marriage and family formation. Further information was also collected from parents, from school personnel and a medical examination was conducted. Data on each individual's secondary school leaving age and their secondary school examination performance was collected in 1978 from school records (Shepherd, 1995).

The first adult follow-up took place in 1981, when the cohort members were twenty-three. The focus of these interviews concentrated on the cohort members' transitions into adult life. All the information collected at this stage was obtained from the cohort members themselves. It covered their transitions into early adult life, including data on their post-secondary educational and training activities, their first labour force experiences, their health, the setting up of independent homes, finding a partner and, for some, becoming parents (Kerckhoff, 1993; Power, 1991).

In 1985, responsibility for the NCDS was transferred from the National Children's Bureau to the Social Statistics Research Unit (SSRU) at City University, London, from where the fifth follow-up of the cohort was conducted in 1991, when the cohort members were thirty-three. While the last survey at age twenty-three represents a time of transition and mobility, age thirty-three is characterised by the settled and stable features of mid adulthood. For most, education and training has been completed, occupational careers have been established, and household and family formation will have taken place (Ferri, 1993).

The fifth NCDS follow-up was the most ambitious, designed to obtain information from the cohort members; any husband, wife, or cohabitee; from the natural or adopted children of one in three cohort families; and from the mother of these children. The data collected in 1991 from personal interviews with the cohort members included information on education and training experiences, employment, income, housing, family formation, physical and mental health, health history, citizenship and participation, as well as self-concept measures (Ferri, 1993). The spouses and partners of the cohort members were asked about their education, occupation and earnings, their relationships and children. The major innovation of this survey, however, was the 'Mother and Child' survey, which included all natural or adopted children of a random one in three sample of the cohort (Ferri, 1998). This part of the study was funded by the US National Institute of Child Health and Development. The mother and child questionnaires are based on instruments used for the US National Longitudinal Survey of Youth. The mother was asked to fill in a self-completion questionnaire for each child of the cohort members. This was divided into age-specific sections covering motor and social development, behavioural problems and temperament. This extension of the NCDS created a three-generation longitudinal study of whole families, comprising the cohort members, their parents and their children (Ferri, 1993).

In 1995, when the cohort members were thirty-seven, the Basic Skills Agency (a UK Government agency) sponsored the survey of a 10 per cent representative sample for a study of basic skills difficulties (Bynner & Parsons, 1997).

In 1998, responsibility for NCDS shifted again. The Social Statistics Research Unit (SSRU) moved from City University, London to the Institute of Education, London and was renamed the Centre for Longitudinal Studies (CLS). There the next sweep of data collection was prepared which took place in 2000 when the cohort members were forty-two (Ferri et al., 2003). This time a joint survey strategy was developed and data was collected from both NCDS and BCS70 cohort members (Bynner et al., 2000a). It was envisaged that such a programme would significantly enhance the research potential of the studies, enabling comparisons to be made between cohorts born at different times, or between different age groups at the same point in time. The joint survey design sought to integrate the timing, design and analysis of future surveys of NCDS and BCS70 (taking into account the sequencing of Britain's third birth cohort study, the 1946 National Survey of Health and Development (NSHD), which is housed at University College London and currently funded by the Medical Research Council (MRC)).[1]

---

[1] The 1946 NSHD took as its sample 5,362 individuals born between 3 and 9 March 1946 (a third of all births in one week). Its aim initially was to provide information about the cost of childbearing, the care of mothers and babies (including the availability of specialist care) at the time of birth, and sought to explain why the national fertility rates had fallen consistently since the mid-nineteenth century. It was commissioned by the Royal Commission on Population and by planners of the National Health Service that began two years later in 1948 (Wadsworth, 1991). Data on health, educational, psychological

The Economic and Social Research Council (ESRC) contributed half the costs of the combined survey, and the rest came from Government departments under the coordination of the Office for National Statistics: the Department for Education and Employment (the major funder), Department of Health, Department of Social Security, the Home Office, the Office of National Statistics (ONS), the Scottish Office and the Basic Skills Agency. Information was gathered from NCDS and BCS70 cohort members by interview and a self-completion questionnaire. The survey instrumentation covered the topics of education and employment, family and housing, parenting, health and life styles, citizenship and social attitudes. It was developed to take into account issues of relevance to the stage of life reached, and aimed to provide continuity and comparability across NCDS and BCS70 as well as with other surveys (as for example, the National Survey of Health and Development (NSHD), the British Household Panel Study (BHPS), the General Household Survey and the US National Longitudinal Survey of Youth).

A major innovation of this joint survey was the use of computer-assisted, rather than paper-based, methods of data collection. CAPI (Computer Assisted Personal Interviewing) serves to improve the quality of the data collected, by simplifying the conduct of the interviews with complex filter structures. It also facilitates rapid production of clean data, because data can be edited on entry. The same method, CASI (Computer Assisted Self-Interviewing), was employed with the self-completion instrument, when the laptop computer was handed over to the cohort members themselves.

In 2002 the Medical Research Council funded a biomedical follow-up survey of the NCDS cohort. The study was designed to obtain objective measures of ill-health and biomedical risk factors involving nurse interviewers taking the biomedical measurements including samples of blood and saliva. Furthermore, a short mental health interview was conducted. Fieldwork started in September 2002 and was completed in March 2004.

Most recently a number of qualitative surveys have been carried out with smaller subsamples of NCDS cohort members, investigating attitudes to money and saving, civic participation, health and family (Shepherd, 2004). Following the joint follow-up forward plan for NCDS and BCS70, follow-up surveys will be undertaken every four years, alternating between face-to-face and telephone/postal surveys. The 2004 follow-up data involved a face-to-face interview of BCS70 and a telephone survey of NCDS cohort members. It will update the information gathered during the last sweep in 1999–2000, and has been deposited with the UK Data Archive during spring 2006.

and socio-demographic information has been collected through childhood, adolescence and adulthood. The cohort was last surveyed in 1989 at age forty-three. At age fifty-three home visits were undertaken by nurses employed by the National Centre for Social Research (NCSR), contracted by NSHD. Most of the information collected in adulthood has been obtained by nurses during home visits and through an annual postal questionnaire study of women's health at ages forty-seven to fifty-three, so far.

The British Cohort Study (BCS70)

The British Cohort Study (BCS70) originated as the British Births Survey (BBS), sponsored by the National Birthday Trust Fund in association with the Royal College of Obstetricians and Gynaecologists. It was launched in 1970 when data was collected about the births of 17,287 babies born in the UK in the week 5 to 11 April of that year. Information was collected by means of a questionnaire that was completed by the midwife present at the birth and supplementary information was obtained from clinical records. As with the NCDS, the birth sweep gave valuable insight into the provision of obstetric and neonatal care in the UK at that time (Chamberlain et al., 1973; Chamberlain et al., 1975).

Consequent data sweeps took place when the cohort members were aged 5, 10, 16, 26 and 30 (Bynner et al., 2000a; Ekinsmyth, 1992; Ferri et al., 2003) and most recently at age 34 is currently still in the field. In addition to the major surveys, a smaller-scale survey was conducted in 1972–3 on three subsamples: twins in the original cohort, low-birth-weight and post-mature births, and a random ten per cent sample of the original cohort. The total subsample came to 3,471 children. Some of the children, of course, belonged to more than one of the above categories. The South-West Region Survey, carried out at that time, included 95 per cent of the cohort members who lived in the south-west of England or Glamorgan, South Wales. These smaller-scale surveys were carried out to bridge the gap in child development between birth and five years of age (Ferri, 1998).

In 1975, at age five, the Department of Child Health, Bristol University carried out the first follow-up survey of the full sample. The original, strictly medical, focus of the survey was broadened to include measures of physical as well as educational development of the child and the study was named the Child Health and Education Study (CHES). Parents of the cohort members were interviewed by health visitors. The cohort members themselves undertook ability tests and the school health service gathered medical information on each child. This was supplemented by information gathered from head and class teachers who completed questionnaires. Since 1970, subjects from Northern Ireland, who had been originally included in the birth survey, were subsequently dropped. The study was, however, augmented by adding immigrants who came to Britain and who were born between 5 and 11 April 1970. This was done in 1975 and in 1980. The total number of cohort members from ethnic minority groups in BCS70 is however only about 4 per cent. Key findings relating to this survey can be found in Butler et al. (1986) and in Osborn et al. (1984).

In 1980, at age ten, the second full sample follow-up study was conducted, again by the Department of Child Health, Bristol University. The study was then still named the Child Health and Education Study (CHES). Information was gathered from the parents of the cohort members who were interviewed by health visitors, head and class teachers completed questionnaires, the school health service carried out medical examinations on each child, and the cohort members themselves undertook ability tests (Butler et al., 1982).

The follow-up study at age sixteen was carried out in 1986 by the International Centre For Child Studies (ICCS)[2] and was then named 'Youthscan'. This sweep was a particularly ambitious project using sixteen separate survey instruments, including self-completion questionnaires, interview schedules, cognitive and behavioural assessments, diaries, a medical examination and measures of height and weight. Questionnaires were completed by the parents, and by the school class and head teacher. The young people themselves completed questionnaires as well, kept two four-day diaries (one for nutrition and one for general activity), underwent a medical examination and undertook some educational assessments. Unfortunately, this sweep was hampered by industrial action by the teachers, which coincided with the fieldwork and produced a much reduced response for some of the instruments.

In 1991 responsibility for the BCS70 cohort was assumed by the Social Statistics Research Unit (SSRU) at City University, London. This move fostered the adoption and development of an integrated approach for future sweeps of data collection in NCDS and BCS70. Paralleling the comparable NCDS basic skill survey, a 10 per cent sample survey of 1,650 cohort members was carried out in 1992, at age twenty-one, with funding from the Basic Skills Agency to investigate the development of basic skills and the circumstances influencing the transition from full-time education to employment (Bynner & Steedman, 1995). This survey was also designed to serve as a feasibility study for the next full survey that was originally planned for 1994–5, and was finally carried out in 1996 when the cohort members were twenty-six years old.

The 1996 survey aimed to provide information on the transition into early adulthood, and to parallel the NCDS survey at age twenty-three (Ferri, 1998). Because of the limited funding available, this survey was carried out using postal questionnaires. In order to maximise response, the survey questionnaire was kept as short and simple as possible, yet it covered all the key topic areas, including health and health-related behaviour, qualifications and skills, education and training, employment and earnings, relationships, marriage and children, housing and views on a range of social issues (Bynner et al., 1997).

The next full interview survey was carried out in the year 2000, when the cohort members were thirty. This survey was coordinated with the NCDS survey at forty-two using a common survey instrument and following a joint survey strategy aiming to integrate the timing, design and analysis of future surveys of NCDS and BCS70 (Bynner et al., 2000a; Ferri et al., 2003). Data was collected from the cohort members by personal interview and by using a self-completion questionnaire, including information on education and employment, income and living standards, family and housing, health and life styles, social participation, values and crime.

The most recent follow-up survey started in June 2004 involving a face-to-face interview with the BCS70 cohort members at thirty-four. The major objective of this follow-up study was to update information collected in the year 2000,

---

[2] The ICCS was set up by Professor Neville Butler to raise funds for the survey and to guarantee continuing support for the study. For over forty years, Professor Butler has played a vital role in the foundation, design, continuation and analysis of both the NCDS and BCS70 studies.

and to conduct an assessment of basic skills and dyslexia. For a one in two sample information has also been collected from and about any natural or adopted children living with the cohort member. Information is collected from the cohort member by interview and self-completion questionnaire, and from their children aged three to seventeen using child assessments. Children of the cohort members aged ten to seventeen have also been asked to complete a self-completion questionnaire (Shepherd, 2004).

All data collected for NCDS and BCS70 are held by the ESRC Data Archive at the University of Essex and are available for secondary analysis by researchers from the Data Archive directly. The deposited data sets have been fully documented, and an interactive data dictionary is available to facilitate the search for specific variables.

Useful web connections

UK Data Archive (UKDA) – http://www.data-archive.ac.uk
The UK Data Archive is a curator of the largest collection of digital data in the social sciences in the UK and houses a major collection of computerised historical material. It provides resource discovery and support for secondary use of quantitative and qualitative data in research, teaching and learning, and facilitates international data exchange.

Economic and Social Data Service (ESDS) – http://www.esds.ac.uk/
The Economic and Social Data Service is a national data service that came into operation in January 2003. ESDS provides access and support for an extensive range of key economic and social data, both quantitative and qualitative, spanning many disciplines and themes. It comprises a number of specialist data services that promote and encourage data usage in teaching and research.

Centre for Longitudinal Studies (CLS) – http://www.cls.ioe.ac.uk/
The Centre for Longitudinal Studies at the Institute of Education houses the ESRC funded Resource Centre, which provides support and facilities for those using the 1958 National Child Development Study (NCDS), the 1970 British Cohort Study (BCS 70) and the latest Millennium Cohort Study (MCS). The Centre holds responsibility for the conservation, development and dissemination of the three British Cohort Studies.

Appendix B Response rates and handling of missing data

The purpose of this appendix is to provide an account of the National Child Development Study (NCDS) and British Cohort Study (BCS70) populations and samples as they change over time, covering the major sweeps of the two cohorts until the year 2000. In the following the response rates in the two cohorts, the analytic sample and sample attrition, as well as the approaches used for handling the possible effects of missingness and non-response will be described. Another issue considered here concerns the reporting of effect sizes of observed associations.

Participation in the 1958 National Child Development Study (NCDS)

The target sample for NCDS is defined as all babies born in Great Britain during the reference week 3–9 March 1958, until they die or permanently emigrate from Great Britain. In NCDS the original target sample included altogether 17,634 babies. For the first three follow-up sweeps at ages seven, eleven and sixteen, cohort members were traced through records and the National Health Service Central Register. Throughout adulthood, tracing of the survey members was based on existing address records and was continuously updated by sending an annual birthday card.

As Table B1 shows, the overall level of response has remained high, with 10,979 cohort members taking part in the 2000 survey at forty-two. The amount of sample attrition up to the age of eleven years was quite small. Even after age eleven the attrition rate was smaller than in most panel studies (Kerckhoff, 1993; Shepherd, 1993; Shepherd, 1995). Several analyses of response bias have been conducted comparing included and missing cases on measures from earlier data points (Goldstein, 1979; Shepherd, 1993; 1995; 2004; Plewis et al., 2004; Davie et al., 1972; Ferri et al., 2003). These response bias checks have been generally reassuring, indicating that the achieved samples remain representative of the full cohort. Comparing the distribution of key characteristics, such as sex, family social class or parental education, in the achieved samples with the distribution of the same characteristics in the sample at birth shows relatively little bias (Shepherd, 2004). Even with the large sample size, most of the differences were not statistically significant. There is, however, a tendency for more women than men to continue to participate and for the most educationally disadvantaged to leave the study.

Table B1. *Achieved response to NCDS follow-ups*

Cohort age	Target sample	Achieved sample	Per cent response
Birth (PMS)	17,634	17,415	99
7 years	16,500	15,051	91
11 years	16,253	14,757	91
16 years	16,068	13,917	87
23 years	15,885	12,044	76
33 years	15,567	10,986	71
42 years	15,451	10,979	71

Participation in the 1970 British Cohort Study (BCS70)

Table B2 gives the achieved response at each full sweep of data collection of BCS70 cohort members to date. The reference population is defined as those born in Great Britain during the reference week 5–11 April 1970: altogether 17,287 babies. Tracing of cohort members was more limited than in NCDS until 1991, since when, following the joint research strategy for both cohorts, annual birthday cards have been used for tracing cohort members between surveys. The overall level of response has remained satisfactorily high, especially up to age ten. The survey conducted in 1986, at sixteen, was the most ambitious undertaking in data coverage, yet this has to be set against a poorer response rate. As already mentioned, the 1986 survey took place during a teachers' strike. Many cohort members did not receive their questionnaires, which led to a relatively low response rate. All school children were affected in the same way and the demographic characteristics of the sample at sixteen remained representative of the target population (Shepherd, 1997). The response level for the sweep conducted in 1996 was low – yet nonetheless encouraging for a postal survey of a cohort of whom many had not been traced since the last full survey in 1986 (Bynner et al., 1997). With the 2000 survey, the study has been restored to much the same response level as NCDS, and 10,833 cohort members responded at age thirty (Ferri et al., 2003).

Sample attrition

A most coherent series of tables capturing the changes in both sample populations over time can be found in Plewis et al. (2004). Although a generally acceptable response rate has been achieved, anything less than a perfect response raises the question of whether those who completed a questionnaire are representative of the sampled population. This issue has been explored in both NCDS and BCS70 by exploiting a possibility only available to longitudinal studies: comparison of the characteristics of the achieved sample – those cohort members who returned a questionnaire – with those in the target sample (Plewis et al., 2004; Shepherd, 1997; 2004). The variables chosen for comparison include data relating to demography, education, social and economic circumstances, family

Table B2. *Achieved response to BCS70 follow-ups*

Cohort age	Target sample	Achieved sample	Per cent response
Birth (BBS)	17,287	16,571	96
5 years (CHES)	16,461	12,981	79
10 years (CHES)	16,181	14,350	89
16 years (Youthscan)	15,999	11,206	70
26 years	15,726	8,654	55
30 years	15,503	10,833	70

and relationships, housing and household, as well as health. This analysis provides an important and, in the case of cohort studies, a generally encouraging insight into differential response. Absolute differences between the sampled populations and the achieved samples on the whole are small and checks of response bias at each follow-up study have been generally reassuring (Plewis et al., 2004). In BCS70 (as in NCDS) there is a small tendency for more women than men to continue with the survey, and for the most socially and educationally disadvantaged to leave the study (Butler et al., 1997). Perhaps not surprisingly, this picture is similar to that emerging from the analyses of differential response to other surveys (Shepherd, 1997).

The analytic samples and sample attrition

The actual analytic samples used in the previous chapters are slightly smaller than the ones shown in Tables B1 and B2. Only cohort members for whom complete data on two key variables (sex and parental social class) was collected at birth, have been selected for further analysis. This selection gave a sample of 16,994 cohort members for NCDS and 14,229 cohort members for BCS70. In both cohorts 52 per cent are men and 48 per cent are women. The sample is further limited by non-response for individual variables included in particular analyses. Linking data collected at birth to outcomes at later life stages is also affected by non-response in the follow-up sweeps. Longitudinal cohort studies generally suffer from missing data because of both survey loss and incomplete response, especially in analyses drawing on data from several waves.

As indicated in Tables B1 and B2 retention rates for those who responded in the first sweep of data collection have remained rather high (possibly with the exception of the 1986 and 1996 BCS70 surveys) and compares quite well with the total retention rates reported for other longitudinal studies, as for example, the National Youth Survey (NYS) or the Panel Study of Income Dynamics (PSID) (Menard, 2002).

Handling 'missingness'

To handle the possible effects of 'missingness' and non-response, maximum likelihood or multiple imputation methods plus selection models for non-response are generally recommended (Little et al., 2000; Wothke, 2000; Menard, 2002). The use of maximum likelihood methods is a feature of the structural equation modelling programme AMOS 4.01 (Arbuckle, 1999) which has been used in this study. The AMOS programme uses maximum likelihood estimation that can be based on incomplete data, known as the full information maximum likelihood (FIML) approach. FIML is preferable to estimation based on complete data (the listwise deletion (LD) approach) since FIML estimates will tend to show less bias and be more reliable than LD estimates even when the data deviate from missing at random and are non-ignorable (Arbuckle, 1999). In the LD approach, the complete data covariance matrix is the data source for the latent variable analysis. In the FIML approach, estimation is based on the many covariance matrices between observed variables for all patterns of missing data in the other observed variables.

The goodness of fit of a Structural Equation Model (SEM) is assessed by several criteria. The χ^2 statistic is overly sensitive to model misspecification when sample sizes are large or the observed variables are non-normally distributed. The root mean square error of approximation (RMSEA) gives a measure of the discrepancy in fit per degrees of freedom (Steiger, 1990). If the RMSEA is $<.05$, the model is considered a close fit to the data. The final index of choice is the Comparative Fit Index (CFI) where values above .95 indicate an acceptable fit (Bentler, 1990).

While the maximum likelihood imputation of missing data is generally the preferable method, the use of listwise deletion has been recommended in particular for ordinary least squares regression analysis and logistic regression, as it is more robust to violations of the assumption that data are missing at random than other methods (Graham & Hofer, 2000). Where the listwise deletion of missing cases was utilised in this study, results using pairwise or listwise deletion of cases with missing values have been compared. Similar results would suggest that there is little systematic sample bias related to differing rates of non-response. Results of these comparisons have been reported where they have been applied.

Effect size of parameter estimates

Another issue to be considered at this point is, that the individuals included in the studies are, in a strict sense, not a sample. They are rather the full population, or at least most of the population, and therefore the use of statistical tests of significance would be ill-advised, as they are intended to allow for sampling variation. On the other hand, it has been argued that the use of significance tests is nonetheless appropriate, because they provide systematic comparative statements about the relative sizes of the associations and thus make it easier to judge the importance of the findings (Kerckhoff, 1993). Following Kerkhoff's assertion significance tests to illustrate effect sizes are reported. Effect sizes of the parameter estimates are described as small ($r = .10$), medium ($r = .30$) and large ($r = .50$) following Cohen's power primer (Cohen, 1992).

Appendix C Description of variables used in the study

Table C1. *Overview of variables used in analyses*

Variable name	Description
Childhood experiences	
Social risk	
Parental social class	Registrar General's Social Class (RGSC)
Mother's age at birth	
Parental education	Mother's education (left school at age 15 or not)
	Father's education (left school at age 15 or not)
Material conditions	Housing Tenure (yes/no)
	Overcrowding (> 1 person per room)
	Amenities (sole use of bathroom, or not)
	Receipt of state benefits (yes/no)
Social integration	
Family moves	Number of family moves since birth
Contact with other children	Child is in regular contact with other children (yes/no)
Parental involvement in education	
Parental reading	Parents read to child on regular basis (yes/no)
Parental involvement	Parents visit school to talk to teacher (yes/no)
Parental expectations	Parents' educational expectations
Academic attainment	
Early childhood (age 5/7)	Draw-a-Man Test
	Copy-a-Design Test
	Reading Tests,
	Arithmetic Test for NCDS only
Mid-childhood (age 10/11)	Reading and Maths Tests
Adolescence (age 16)	Exam scores and highest secondary school qualifications obtained at age 16
Behavioural adjustment	
	A modified version of the Rutter 'A' Scale (Rutter et al., 1970) was used in both cohorts at all ages

Aspirations for the future
  (at age 16 only)

Education	Aspiration for further education
Occupation	Job aspirations (professional job or not)

Adult outcomes

Highest qualifications	None, some, O-level, A-level, Degree level
Social position	Social Class (RGSC as above), Cambridge Scale (Prandy, 1990)
Health and well-being	Malaise Inventory (Rutter et al., 1970)
	Satisfaction with life (0–10)
	Control over life

MEASUREMENT OF VARIABLES USED IN ANALYSES

Indicators of social risk

Socio-economic disadvantage is indicated by parental social class and material conditions in the family household. The indicator variables are measured at ages seven, eleven and sixteen for NCDS and ages five, ten and sixteen for BCS70.

Parental social class in both cohorts is measured by the Registrar General's measure of Social Class (RGSC). The RGSC is defined according to job status and the associated education, prestige (OPCS, 1980) or life style (Marsh, 1986). It is assessed by the current or last held job, which is classified according to six ordinal categories. The definitions of social classes are adopted from the British census and include the following kinds of occupations:

- Class I: Professionals and high-level managers and administrators
- Class II: Intermediate professions including lower-level managers, technicians
- Class IIInm: Clerks and other lower-level non-manual workers
- Class IIIm: Skilled manual workers and foremen
- Class IV: Semi-skilled non-manual, mainly service workers
- ClassV: Unskilled workers

Class I represents the highest level of prestige or skill and class V the lowest (Leete & Fox, 1977). Professional status refers to occupations in medicine, law, etc., or senior civil servants. The intermediate group includes a wide range of white-collar jobs, including teaching, nursing and management, which are not professional, junior clerical or sales occupations. The occupational categories used in the US census and other European countries are similarly based on the skills and status of different occupations (Krieger et al., 1997).

- *Overcrowding.* This is a dichotomous variable based on the ratio of people living in the household to the number of rooms in the household. One or more persons per room is coded (1), less than one person per room is coded (0).

- *Household amenities.* This is a dichotomous scale based on the cohort member's family having sole use of a bathroom, toilet and hot water. The same three questions were asked in both studies. Sole access to all of these amenities is coded (0) shared use or no access to any of these amenities is coded (1).
- *Housing tenure.* The tenure of the home is defined as (0) owner-occupier or (1) other.
- *State benefits.* Receipt of state benefits is an indicator of financial hardship within the family environment (Fogelman, 1983). The assessed benefits include payment of unemployment benefit, income support and housing benefit, but exclude payment of pensions or child benefit. Parents are either (0) not in receipt of benefits or (1) in receipt of benefits in last 12 months.

Social integration

Two measures of social integration or embeddedness in the community were used: the number of family moves since birth, and whether the child has regular contact with other children.

Family moves

Number of moves since birth were assessed in both cohorts at each of the measurement points at ages five, ten and sixteen in BCS70 and ages seven, eleven and sixteen in NCDS.

Child's contact with other children

The child's contact with other children was assessed at five in BCS70 and at seven in NCDS. In NCDS, parents were asked whether the child had social contact with other children on a daily basis, often, had little contact or no contact at all. In BCS70, parents were asked whether the child went to visit friends. For comparative reasons the responses to the questions were dichotomised indicating in both cohorts in regular contact with other children (1) or not (0).

Academic attainment

Academic attainment is measured by the child's academic adjustment at each measurement point. Reflecting the changing competencies of the growing child, academic attainment has been assessed differently during early childhood (age five or seven), middle childhood (age ten or eleven) and adolescence (age sixteen).

Academic attainment at age five (BCS70) and seven (NCDS)

Draw-a-Man test   The Human Figure Drawing Test used in both cohorts is a modified version of the Draw-a-Man Test originally devised by Goodenough (1926) and developed further by Harris (1963). The Harris-Goodenough

Test has a good reliability of r = 94 (Osborn et al., 1984). It correlates with conventional IQ tests such as the Binet and the Wechsler, with r averaging between .4 and .5 (Scott, 1981). The scoring of the drawings produced by the children is based on thirty developmental items and uses the Harris point system of scoring. One point is scored for each item represented in the drawing giving a maximum possible score of thirty (Harris, 1963). In both cohorts the children had to draw two figures. In BCS70, however, only one figure was coded. Thus, the maximum score in NCDS is 60, and in BCS70 it is 30. The achieved scores ranged from 0 to 53 in NCDS, and from 0 to 23 in BCS70.

Copy-a-Design test   The Copy-a-Design Test was used to assess the cohort member's perceptual-motor ability, assuming that children must have reached a certain level of conceptual development in order to be able to recognise the principles governing different geometric forms, and to reproduce them (Osborn et al., 1984). The ability to copy designs or geometric shapes is included as one element of assessment in many standard intelligence tests. The test has a satisfactory reliability of .70 (Osborn et al., 1984). In NCDS test scores ranged from 0 to 12, in BCS70 0 to 8.

Reading tests   In NCDS, the Southgate Reading Test (Southgate, 1962) was used. This is a test of word recognition and comprehension parti-cularly suited to identifying problems with reading in young children. The test has a good reliability of .94 (Southgate, 1962). The range of scores in NCDS was 0–30.

In BCS70, the English Picture Vocabulary Test (EPVT), an adaptation of the American Peabody Picture Vocabulary Test (Brimer & Dunn, 1962) was used. The test has a good reliability of .96 (Osborn et al., 1984). It consists of 56 sets of four different pictures with a particular word associated with each set of four pictures. The child is asked to indicate the one picture that corresponds to the given word, and the test proceeds with words of increasing difficulty, until the child makes five mistakes in a run of eight consecutive items. The range of scores in BCS70 was 0–51.

Arithmetic   Knowledge of arithmetic in early childhood was only assessed among seven-year-old children in NCDS, using the Problem Arithmetic Test. The test has a satisfactory reliability of .85 (Pringle et al., 1966). Scores range from 0 to 10. Cohort members in BCS70 were too young to have started formal training in arithmetic.

Academic attainment at age ten (BCS70) and eleven (NCDS)

Reading   The National Foundation for Educational Research in England and Wales (NFER) constructed a reading comprehension test specifically for use in the NCDS (Fogelman, 1983). A good test reliability of .82 has been reported (Goldstein, 1979). The scores range from 0 to 35. In BCS70 a shortened version of the Edinburgh Reading Test, a test of word recognition, was used after consultation with the test's authors (Godfrey Thomson Unit for 1978). The shortened test version contained sixty-seven items, examining vocabulary, syntax, sequencing, comprehension and retention. The test has a good reliability (.87) and the items discriminate well between good and poor readers (Butler et al., 1997). The range of scores in BCS70 was 0–65.

Mathematics The NFER developed an arithmetic-mathematics test specifically for use in the NCDS (Fogelman, 1983). The scores range from 0 to 40. The test has a good test reliability of .94 (Goldstein, 1979). In BCS70, the lack of a fully acceptable mathematics test appropriate for ten-year-olds also led to the development of a special test. It consisted of a total of seventy-two multiple choice questions and covered in essence the rules of arithmetic, number skills, fractions, measures in a variety of forms, algebra, geometry and statistics. The test has good reliability (.92) and the items have adequate discrimination (Butler et al., 1997).

Academic attainment at age sixteen (both cohorts)

Two measures of academic achievement in secondary school are used. One is the exam scores students obtained at sixteen and the second is the highest level of secondary school examinations the students passed.

In the UK during the 1970s there were essentially two types of secondary school examinations a student could pass at sixteen: the Certificate of Secondary Education (CSE) examination and the ordinary (O-level) examinations within the General Certificate of Education (GCE) examinations. The GCE was the accepted examination for children of above average intelligence and it aimed to cater for approximately 20 per cent of the total age group, while the CSE examination was designed to cover a wider range of ability than the GCE – about a further 40 per cent. Between them, the two exams were intended for some three-fifths of the population (Rutter et al., 1979). Both GCE and CSE were subject-based and grades were awarded on the basis of performance with a range from 1 to 5 (or A to E). Generally GCE grades of D and E were classified as failures. There is an accepted equivalence between the two examination systems with a grade 1 CSE being seen as equal to at least a grade C pass in GCE. For both cohorts the highest level of qualifications obtained at sixteen were recorded, ranging from none (0), CSE grades 2–5 (1) to CSE grade 1 or O-level (2).

An overall 'exam score' could be calculated from the examination performance at sixteen. The actual examination results of the NCDS cohort were collected from schools in 1978, whereas BCS70 cohort members self-reported their examination results in a follow-up study in 1986. The examination system was the same for both cohorts, with BCS70 being one of the last cohorts to sit the two-tiered examination structure of O-levels and CSEs. A simple scoring technique was applied to the results, giving a score of 7 to a grade 1 O-level and a score of 1 to a grade 5 CSE. Overall exam scores range from 0 to 106 in NCDS and from 0 to 97 in BCS70.

Behavioural adjustment

Behavioural adjustment was measured in both cohorts using a modified version of the Rutter 'A' Scale (Rutter et al., 1970). In NCDS, assessments took place at ages seven, eleven and sixteen and in BCS70, at ages five, ten and sixteen. The modified version of the Rutter 'A' Scale comprises eight items, which were completed by a parent (usually the mother) as part of the home interview. The scale has a good test–retest reliability with $r = 0.74$ (Schachar et al., 1981). Behavioural adjustment is measured by summing each of the eight items scored on a three category scale from 0 to 2 ('Does not apply', 'Applies somewhat', 'Certainly applies'). A high score indicates behaviour adjustment problems.

Factor analyses of the data revealed consistently the existence of three main factors of behaviour adjustment, namely conduct problems, emotional problems and hyperactivity problems. Alpha coefficients for factor scores were 0.83 (conduct), 0.72 (emotional) and 0.82 (hyperactivity). All three factors are positively intercorrelated (Elander & Rutter, 1996). The three subscales are assessed as follows:

- An *emotional disorder* subscore is obtained by summing the score of three items: is often tearful or distressed, is often worried/worries about many things and often appears miserable and unhappy (range 0–6).
- The *conduct disorder* subscore is obtained by summing the scores of the items: is often disobedient, often destroys own or others' belongings, and frequently fights or is extremely quarrelsome with other children (range 0–6).
- The *hyperactivity disorder* subscore is obtained by summing the scores of the items: is squirmy, fidgety child, cannot settle to anything for more than a few moments (range 0–4).

Life Plans (at sixteen only)

Educational aspirations

At sixteen both cohort members were asked whether they wanted to continue full-time education and to obtain a degree. They had to indicate at what age they were most likely to leave school and which of the following they would like to do on leaving: continue with full-time study, do a job that involved part-time study, or do a job that required no further study. The answers to these two questions have been combined to indicate whether the cohort members wanted to leave school at minimum age; to continue post-sixteen training with a job that involved part-time study; or to pursue further education after the age of eighteen years.

Occupational aspirations

Questions about occupational aspirations were asked slightly differently in the two cohorts at sixteen. NCDS cohort members were asked 'What do you expect to be your first full-time job?' The responses to the open-ended question were coded according to different categories reflecting the social status of the occupational choice. BCS70 cohort members were given a choice of occupations including professional/managerial positions, trained clerical and administrative office work, service worker, manual worker, craftsmen, farming and armed forces. In both cohorts it was possible to identify cohort members with high aspirations, i.e. those expecting to pursue a professional or managerial career (1) and those who made less ambitious occupational choices (0). For a more detailed description of the questions on occupational aspirations and their coding see Schoon and Parsons (2002a).

Parental support and involvement in education

Parents reading to the child

In both cohorts parents were asked whether they read to their child on a regular basis. The assessments were made at age five among BCS70 cohort members and at age seven among NCDS cohort members. Responses were coded as (0) do not read or do read infrequently versus (1) read at least once a week.

Parental involvement in education

Throughout the school years parental involvement in the child's education has been assessed in both cohorts with a question put to the teachers of the child (at ages five, ten and sixteen among BCS70 cohort members, and at ages seven, eleven and sixteen among NCDS cohort members). Teachers were asked to indicate whether the parents of the cohort member have been up to the school to talk to them about the progress of their child. The answers were coded on a dichotomous scale as (1) yes (0) no.

Parental educational expectations for their child

In both cohorts parents were asked about their expectations for their child regarding school leaving age and further education. At sixteen, this comprised two questions in NCDS and four questions in BCS70. The questions identified whether the parents expected that their child would continue with post-eighteen education, post-sixteen education or training, or leave school at sixteen with no further education/training.

Adult outcomes

Adult outcomes were assessed by highest qualifications obtained, measures of adult social status and of adult psychological well-being, which in combination are understood to be indicators of adult psychosocial adjustment.

Highest qualifications

Highest qualifications in adulthood were assessed in terms of a broad classification of academic and vocational qualifications based on a scale related to National Vocational Qualification (NVQ) levels (Makepeace et al., 2003). NVQ 5 covers all post-graduate qualifications. NVQ4 refers to first degree-level qualifications and diplomas. NVQ3 encompasses the attainment of two or more A-levels, or their academic or vocational equivalent. This is comparable to the baccalaureat or to a US High School degree. NVQ2 includes academic or vocational qualifications equivalent to General Certificate of Secondary Education (GCSE) or ordinary (O-level) General Certificate of Education (GCE) examinations grades A–C. NVQ1 covers other qualifications, such as lower grades of GCSE, O-level or CSE and the lowest level of vocational certificates.

Social position

Adult social status of the cohort members themselves is indicated by the same measures used to assess the social status of their parents: the Registrar General's Social Class (RGSC) already described above (OPCS (Office for Population Census and Surveys) 1980, 1990). In addition the Cambridge Scale was used to assess social position of the cohort members at thirty for BCS70 and at thirty-three for NCDS.

The Cambridge Scale

The Cambridge Scale (CS) is conceptualised as an indicator of general social advantage and life style (Prandy, 1990). It is based on the analysis of friendship choices, judged to be the most accurate indication of perceived and experienced social distance between members of different occupations. The scale is measured on a 100-point continuum, whereby high scores indicate a higher level of social advantage.

Health and well-being

A number of measures were used to assess adult health and well-being, including an instrument measuring psychological distress, as well as questions about life satisfaction and feeling in control.

The Malaise Inventory

In both cohorts the Malaise Inventory (Rutter et al., 1970) has been used to measure levels of psychological distress or depression. This self-completion measure has been widely used in both general population studies (McGee et al., 1986; Rutter & Madge, 1976; Rodgers et al., 1999) and in investigations of high-risk groups, notably informal carers (Grant et al., 1990). The twenty-four items of the inventory cover emotional disturbance and associated somatic symptoms. The internal consistency of the scale has been shown to be acceptable and the validity of the inventory applies in different socio-economic groups (Rodgers et al., 1999). Rutter et al. (1970) affirms that 'the inventory differentiates moderately well between individuals with and without psychiatric disorder' (p. 160). The overall scale score ranges from 0–24. Individuals scoring affirmatively on eight or more of the twenty-four items are considered to be at risk of depression (Rodgers et al., 1999).

In addition a measure of general *satisfaction with life* was obtained: 'On a scale from 0 to 10 how satisfied are you about the way your life has turned out so far?' (0 = extremely unsatisfied to 10 = completely satisfied). The use of one-item questions to assess life satisfaction is not optimal, yet there is evidence from other studies that life satisfaction can be reliably and validly assessed by one-item measures (Veenhoven, 1993). For reasons of expediency the typical life satisfaction measure in large-scale surveys is usually based only on a single item (Diener & Suh, 1999).

Another variable used as an indicator of positive adjustment in early adulthood assesses feelings of *being in control of one's life*. In both cohorts three dichotomous items were used to assess control beliefs: 'I usually get what I want out of life', 'I usually feel free choice and control over my life' and 'Usually I can run my life more or less as I want to'. The three items show satisfactory internal consistency with a Cronbach's alpha of .63 in NCDS and .55 in BCS70. Cohort members agreeing with all three items were identified as feeling in control of their lives.

References

ATD Fourth World (1996). *'Talk with us, not at us': How to develop partnerships between families in poverty and professionals.* London: ATD Fourth World.

Ackerman, B. P., Brown, E. D. and Izard, C. E. (2004). 'The relations between persistent poverty and contextual risk and children's behavior in elementary school', *Developmental Psychology*, 40: 367–77.

Ackerman, B. P., Schoff, K., Levinson, K., Youngstrom, E. and Izard, C. E. (1999). 'The relations between cluster indexes of risk and promotion and the problem behaviors of 6 and 7-year-old children from economically disadvantaged families', *Developmental Psychology*, 35: 1355–66.

Ainley, P. and Corney, M. (1990). *Training for the future.* London: Cassell.

Alexander, K. L., Entwisle, D. R. and Thompson, M. S. (1987). 'School performance, status relations, and the structure of sentiment – bringing the teacher back in', *American Sociological Review*, 52: 665–82.

Allan, G. (1999). *The sociology of the family: A reader.* Oxford: Blackwell.

Anthony, E. J. (1974). 'The syndrome of the psychologically invulnerable child', in E. J. Anthony and C. Koupernik (eds.), *The child in his family: Children at psychiatric risk*, Vol. 3. New York: John Wiley and Sons pp. 99–121.

(1987). 'Risk, vulnerability, and resilience: An overview', in E. J. Anthony and B. J. Cohler (eds.), *The invulnerable child*. New York: Guilford pp. 3–48.

Antonovsky, A. (1979). *Health, stress and coping.* San Francisco: Jossey-Bass Publishers.

(1987). *Unraveling the mystery of health: How people manage stress and stay well.* San Francisco: Jossey-Bass.

(1994). 'A sociological critique of the "well-being" movement', *The Journal of Mind Body Health*, 10: 6–12.

Arbuckle, J. L. (1999). *Amos for Windows. Analysis of moment structures.* Chicago: Smallwaters Corp.

Arnett, J. J. (2000). 'Emerging adulthood: A theory of development from the late teens through the twenties', *American Psychologist*, 55: 469–80.

Atkinson, A. B. (2000). 'Distribution of income and wealth', in A. H. Halsey and J. Webb (eds.), *Twentieth-century British social trends*. London: Macmillan pp. 348–81.

Atkinson, A. B. and Hills, J. (1998). *Exclusion, employment and opportunity.* London: Centre for Analysis of Social Exclusion, London School of Economics and Political Science.

Baltes, P. B. (1987). 'Theoretical propositions of life-span developmental-psychology on the dynamics between growth and decline', *Developmental Psychology*, 23: 611–26.

Baltes, P. B. and Mayer, K. U. (1999). *The Berlin aging study: Aging from 70 to 100*. Cambridge: Cambridge University Press.

Baltes, P. B., Reese, H. W. and Nesselroade, J. R. (1988). *Life-span developmental psychology: Introduction to research methods*. Hillsdale, NJ: Lawrence Erlbaum Associates.

Bamfield, L. (2004). *Life chances: The new politics of equality*. London: Fabian Society pp. 20–8.

Barry, M. (2001). *Challenging transitions: young people's views and experiences of growing up*. London: Save the Children Fund.

Bartelt, D. W. (1994). 'On resilience: Questions of validity', in M. C. Wang and E. W. Gordon (eds.), *Educational resilience in inner-city America. Challenges and prospects*. Hillsdale, NJ: Erlbaum pp. 97–108.

Bartley, M. (2004). *Health inequality. An introduction to theories, concepts, and methods*. Cambridge: Polity Press.

Bateson, M. C. (1990). *Composing a life*. New York: Plume.

Baumrind, D. (1978). 'Parental disciplinary patterns and social competence in children', *Youth and Society*, 9: 229–76.

Bebbington, P. (1996). 'The origins of sex differences in depressive disorder: Bridging the gap', *International Review of Psychiatry*, 8: 295–332.

Beck, U. (1992). *Risk society: Towards a new modernity*. London: Sage.

Belsky, J. (1980). 'Child maltreatment: An ecological integration', *American Psychologist*, 35: 320–35.

Bengston, V. L., Biblarz, T. J. et al. (2002). *How families still matter. A longitudinal study of youth in two generations*. Cambridge: Cambridge University Press.

Bentler, P. M. (1990). 'Comparative fit indexes in structural models', *Psychological Bulletin*, 107(2): 238–46.

Beresford, P. (2000). 'Service users' knowledges and social work theory: Conflict or collaboration', *British Journal of Social Work*, 31: 489–503.

Birch, H. G. and Gussow, J. D. (1970). *Disadvantaged children: Health, nutrition and school failure*. London: Grune & Stratton.

Blanchflower, D. G. and Oswald, A. J. (2004). 'Well-being over time in Britain and the USA', *Journal of Public Economics*, 88: 1359–86.

Bleuler, M. (1911, English translation 1978). *The schizophrenic disorders: Long-term patient and family studies*. New Haven: Yale University Press.

Block, J. H. and Block, J. (1980). 'The role of ego control and ego resilience in the organisation of behaviour', in W. A. Collins (ed.), *Development of cognition, affect, and social relations: The Minnesota Symposia on Child Psychology* 13: 39–101. Hillsdale, NJ: Lawrence Erlbaum.

Blossfeld, H. P. and Shavit, Y. (1993). 'Persisting barriers. Changes in educational opportunities in thirteen countries', in: Y. Shavit & H. P. Blossfeld (eds.), *Persistent inequality: Changing educational stratification in thirteen countries*. Boulder, CO: Westview Press pp. 1–23.

Bolger, K. E., Patterson, C. J., Thompson, W. W. and Kupersmidt, J. B. (1995). 'Psychosocial adjustment among children experiencing persistent and intermittent family economic hardship', *Child Development*, 66: 1107–29.

Bollen, K. A. and Long, J. S. (1993). *Testing structural equation models.* Newbury Park: Sage.

Booth, A. and Crouter, A. C. (eds.) (2001). *Does it take a village? Community effects on children, adolescents, and families.* Mahwah, NJ: Erlbaum.

Boudon, R. (1974). *Education, opportunity, and social inequality.* New York: Wiley-Interscience.

Bourdieu, P. and Passeron, J. (1977). *Reproduction in education, society and culture.* London: Sage.

Bozdogan, H. (1987). 'Model selection and Akaike information criterion (AIC) – the general-theory and its analytical extensions', *Psychometrika* 52(3): 345–70.

Brimer, M. A. and Dunn, L. M. (1962). *English Picture Vocabulary Test.* Bristol: Education Evaluation Enterprises.

Bronfenbrenner, U. (1977). 'Toward an experimental ecology of human development', *American Psychologist*, 32: 513–31.

(1979). *The ecology of human development: Experiments by nature and design.* Cambridge, MA: Harvard University Press.

(1989). 'Ecological systems theory', in R. Vasta (ed.), *Six theories of child development: Revised formulations and current issues.* Greenwich, CT: JAI Press pp. 187–250.

(1995). 'Developmental ecology through space and time: A future perspective', in P. Moen, G. H. Elder and K. Lüscher (eds.), *Examining lives in context. Perspectives on the ecology of human development.* Washington, DC: American Psychological Association pp. 619–47.

Bronfenbrenner, U. and Ceci, S. J. (1994). 'Nature-nurture reconceptualized in developmental perspective – a bioecological model', *Psychological Review*, 101: 568–86.

Bronfenbrenner, U. and Crouter, A. C. (1983). 'The evolution of environmental models in developmental research', in W. Kesson (ed), *Handbook of child psychology*, Vol. 1. History, theory, and methods (4th edn). New York: Wiley pp. 357–414.

Brooks-Gunn, J. (1995). 'Children in families and communities: Risk and interventions in the Bronfenbrenner tradition', in P. Moen, G. H. Elder and K. Lüscher (eds.), *Examining lives in context. Perspectives on the ecology of human development.* Washington, DC: American Psychological Association pp. 467–519.

Brooks-Gunn, J., Duncan Greg, J. and Britto, P. R. (1999). 'Are socioeconomic gradients for children similar to those for adults?', in P. D. Keating and C. Hertzman (eds.), *Developmental health and the wealth of the nations.* New York: The Guilford Press pp. 94–124.

Brophy, J. E. and Good, T. L. (1974). *Teacher-student relationships: Causes and consequences.* New York: Holt, Rinehart and Winston.

Brown, G. W. and Harris, T. (1978). *Social origins of depression: A study of psychiatric disorder in women.* London: Tavistock.

Bühler, C. (1933/1959). *Der menschliche Lebenslauf als psychologisches Problem.* Leipzig: Hirzel.

Burchinal, M. R., Follmer, A. and Bryant, D. M. (1996). 'The relations of maternal social support and family structure with maternal responsiveness and child outcomes among African-American families', *Developmental Psychology*, 32: 1073–83.

Butler, N., Despotidou, S. and Shepherd, P. (1997). *1970 British Cohort Study (BCS70) ten-year follow up: A guide to the BCS70 10-year data available at the Economic and Social Research Unit Data Archive.* Social Statistics Research Unit. London: City University.

Butler, N. R. and Alberman, E. D. (1969). *Perinatal problems: The second report of the 1958 British perinatal mortality survey.* Edinburgh: Livingstone.

Butler, N. R. and Bonham, D. G. (1963). *Perinatal mortality: The first report of the 1958 British perinatal mortality survey.* Edinburgh: Livingstone.

Butler, N. R., Golding, J. and Howlett, B. (1986). *From birth to five: A study of the health and behaviour of Britain's five-year-olds.* Oxford: Pergamon.

Butler, N. R., Haslum, M. N., Barker, W. and Morris, A. C. (1982). *Child health and education study. First report to the Department of Education and Science on the 10-year follow-up.* Bristol: Department of Child Health, University of Bristol.

Bynner, J. (1998). 'Education and family components of identity in the transition from school to work', *International Journal of Behavioral Development*, 22: 29–53.

(2001). 'Childhood risk and protective factors in social exclusion', *Children and Society*, 15: 285–301.

Bynner, J., Chisholm, L. and Furlong, A. (1997a). *Youth, citizenship and social change in a European context.* Aldershot: Ashgate.

Bynner, J., Elias, P., McKnight, A. and Pan, H. (1999). *The changing nature of the youth labour market in Great Britain.* York: Joseph Rowntree Foundation.

Bynner, J., Ferri, E. and Shepherd, P. (1997b). *Getting on, getting by, getting nowhere. Twenty-something in the 1990's.* Aldershot: Ashgate.

Bynner, J., Ferri, E., Shepherd, P. and Smith, K. (2000a). *The 1999–2000 surveys of the National Child Development Study and the 1970 British Cohort Study.* Centre for Longitudinal Studies, London: Institute of Education.

Bynner, J., Goldstein, H. and Alberman, E. D. (1998). 'Neville Butler and the British birth cohort studies', *Paediatric and Perinatal Epidemiology*, 12: 1–14.

Bynner, J., Joshi, H. and Tsatsas, M. (2000b). *Obstacles and opportunities on the route to adulthood.* London: The Smith Institute.

Bynner, J. and Parsons, S. (1997). 'Getting on with qualifications', in J. Bynner, E. Ferri and P. Shepherd (eds.), *Getting on, getting by, getting nowhere. Twenty-something in the 1990's.* Aldershot: Ashgate pp. 11–29.

Bynner, J. and Steedman, J. (1995). *Difficulties with basic skills.* London: Basic Skills Agency.

Cairns, R. B., Bergman, L. R. and Kagan, J. (1998). *Methods and models for studying the individual.* London: Sage.

Cairns, R. B., Cairns, B. D. and Neckerman, H. J. (1989). 'Early school dropout – configurations and determinants', *Child Development*, 60: 1437–52.

Campbell, S. B., Pierce, E. W., Moore, G., Marakovitz, S. and Newby, K. (1996). 'Boys' externalizing problems at elementary school age: Pathways from early behavior problems, maternal control, and family stress', *Development and Psychopathology*, 8: 701–19.

194   List of references

Cantor, N., Norem, J. K., Niedenthal, P. M., Langston, C. A. and Brower, A. M. (1987). 'Life tasks, self-concept ideals, and cognitive strategies in a life transition', *Journal of Personality and Social Psychology*, 53: 1178–91.

Canvin, K., Jones, C. and Whitehead, M. (2004). *How do social welfare policies and practices build or undermine resilience in poor households? An international comparative study.* ESRC Priority Network Meeting on the development and persistence of human capability and resilience in its social and geographical context, London.

Caprara, G. V. and Rutter, M. (1995). 'Individual development and social change', in M. Rutter and D. Smith (eds.), *Psychosocial disorders in young people: Time trends and their causes.* Chichester: Wiley pp. 800–23.

Caputo, T. (1999). *Hearing the voices of youth: A review of research and consultation documents: Final report.* Ottawa: Health Canada.

(2000). *Hearing the voices of youth: Youth participation in selected Canadian municipalities.* Ottawa: Health Canada.

Carlson, E. A. and Sroufe, L. A. (1995). 'Contribution of attachment theory to developmental psychology', in D. Cicchetti and D. J. Cohen (eds.), *Developmental Psychopathology. Vol 1: Theory and methods.* New York: Wiley pp. 581–617.

Carlson, E. A., Sroufe, L. A., Collins, W. A., Jimerson, S., Weinfield, N., Hennighausen, K., Egeland, B., Hyson, D. M., Anderson, F. and Meyer, S. E. (1999). 'Early environmental support and elementary school adjustment as predictors of school adjustment in middle adolescence', *Journal of Adolescent Research*, 14: 72–94.

Caspi, A., McClay, J., Moffitt, T. E., Mill, J., Martin, J., Craig, I. W., Taylor, A. and Poulton, R. (2002). 'Role of genotype in the cycle of violence in maltreated children', *Science*, 297: 851–4.

Catalano, R. F. and Hawkins, J. D. (1996). 'The social development model: A theory of antisocial behaviour', in J. D. Hawkins (ed.), *Delinquency and crime: Current theories.* Cambridge: Cambridge University Press.

Catan, L. (2004). *Becoming adult: Changing youth transitions in the 21st century.* Brighton: Trust for the Study of Adolescence.

Catsambis, S. & Beveridge, A. A. (2001). *Neighborhood and school influences on the family life and mathematics performance of eighth grade students.* Baltimore, MD: Center for Research on the Education of Students Placed at Risk.

Central Advisory Council for Education (1967). *The Plowden report.* London: HMSO.

Chamberlain, R., Chamberlain, G., Howlett, B. C. and Claireaux, A. (1973). *British births 1970. Vol. 1. The first week of life.* London: Heineman.

(1975). *British births 1970. Vol. 2. The first week of life.* London: Heineman.

Cicchetti, D. (1990). 'A historical perspective on the discipline of developmental psychopathology', in J. Rolf, A. Masten, D. Cicchetti, K. H. Nuechterlin and S. Weintraub (eds.), *Risk and protective factors in the development of psychopathology.* Cambridge: Cambridge University Press pp. 2–28.

(1993). 'Developmental psychopathology – reactions, reflections, projections', *Developmental Review*, 13: 471–502.

(1984). 'The emergence of developmental psychopathology', *Child Development*, 55: 1–7.

Cicchetti, D. and Aber, J. L. (1998). 'Contextualism and developmental psychopathology', *Development and Psychopathology*, 10: 137–41.

Cicchetti, D. and Garmezy, N. (1993). 'Prospects and promises in the study of resilience', *Development and Psychopathology*, 5: 497–502.

Cicchetti, D. and Lynch, M. (1993). 'Toward an ecological transactional model of community violence and child maltreatment – consequences for children's development', *Psychiatry-Interpersonal and Biological Processes*, 56: 96–118.

Cicchetti, D. and Rogosch, F. A. (1996). 'Equifinality and multifinality in developmental psychopathology', *Development and Psychopathology*, 8: 597–600.

Cicchetti, D., Rogosch, F. A., Lynch, M. and Holt, K. D. (1993). 'Resilience in maltreated children – processes leading to adaptive outcome', *Development and Psychopathology*, 5: 629–47.

Cicchetti, D. and Schneider-Rosen, K. (1986). 'An organisational approach to childhood depression', in M. Rutter, C. E. Izard and P. Read (eds.), *Depression in young people: Developmental and clinical perspectives*. New York: Guilford Press pp. 71–134.

Cicchetti, D. and Tucker, D. (1994). 'Development and self-regulatory structures of the mind', *Development and Psychopathology*, 6: 533–49.

Clark, R. (1983). *Family life and school achievement: Why poor black children succeed or fail*. Chicago: University of Chicago Press.

Clarke, A. D. B. and Clarke, Ann M. (2000). *Early experience and the life path*. London: Jessica Kingsley.

Clarke, A. M. and Clarke, A. D. B. (2003). *Human resilience: A fifty year quest*. London: Jessica Kingsley.

Clausen, J. A. (1993). *American lives: Looking back at the children of the great depression*. Berkeley: University of California Press.

Cohen, J. (1992). 'A power primer', *Psychological Bulletin*, 112(1): 155–9.

Coie, J. D., Watt, N. F., West, S. G., Hawkins, J. D., Asarnow, J. R., Markman, H. J., Ramey, S. L., Shure, M. B. and Long, B. (1993). 'The science of prevention – a conceptual framework and some directions for a national research-program', *American Psychologist*, 48: 1013–22.

Colby, A. (1998). 'Crafting life course studies', in J. Z. Giele and G. H. Elder (eds.), *Methods of life course research: Qualitative and quantitative approaches*. London: Sage pp. viii–xiii.

Coleman, D. (2000a). 'Population and family', in A. H. Halsey and J. Webb (eds.), *Twentieth-century British social trends*. London: Macmillan pp. 27–93.

Coleman, J. (2000b). 'Young people in Britain at the beginning of a new century', *Children & Society*, 14: 230–42.

Coleman, J. S. (1988). 'Social capital in the creation of human-capital', *American Journal of Sociology*, 94: S95–S120.

Coles, B. (2000). *Joined-up youth research, policy and practice: A new agenda for change?* Leicester: Youth Work Press.

Coles, B. and Macdonald, R. (1990). 'The new vocationalism to the culture of enterprise', in C. Wallace and M. Cross (eds.), *Youth in transition*. London: Falmer.

Coll, C. G., Lamberty, G., Jenkins, R., McAdoo, H. P., Crnic, K., Wasik, B. H. and Garcia, H. V. (1996). 'An integrative model for the study of developmental competencies in minority children', *Child Development*, 67: 1891–914.

Conger, R. D., Conger, K. J., Elder, G. H., Lorenz, F. O., Simons, R. L. and Whitbeck, L. B. (1992). 'A family process model of economic hardship and adjustment of early adolescent boys', *Child Development*, 63: 526–41.

(1993). 'Family economic-stress and adjustment of early adolescent girls', *Developmental Psychology*, 29: 206–19.

Conrad, M. and Hammen, C. (1993). 'Protective resilience factors in high and low risk children: A comparison of children of unipolar, bipolar, medically ill and normal mothers', *Development and Psychopathology*, 5: 593–607.

Cooper, H. (1979). 'Pygmalion grows up: A model for teacher expectations, communication and performance influence', *Review of Educational Research*, 49: 389–410.

Cowen, E. L., Wyman, P. A., Work, W. C., Kim, J. Y., Fagen, D. B. and Magnus, K. B. (1997). 'Follow-up study of young stress-affected and stress-resilient urban children', *Development and Psychopathology*, 9: 565–77.

Crijnen, A. A. M., Achenbach, T. M. and Verhulst, F. C. (1997). 'Comparisons of problems reported by parents of children in 12 cultures: Total problems, externalizing, and internalizing', *Journal of the American Academy of Child and Adolescent Psychiatry*, 36: 1269–77.

Curtis, J. W. and Cicchetti, D. (2003). 'Moving research on resilience into the 21st century: Theoretical and methodological considerations in examining the biological contributors to resilience', *Development and Psychopathology*, 15: 773–810.

Davidson, R. J. (2000). 'Affective style, psychopathology, and resilience: Brain mechanisms and plasticity', *American Psychologist*, 55: 1196–214.

Davie, R., Butler, N. R. and Goldstein, H. (1972). *From birth to seven: The second report of the National Child Development Study (1958 cohort)*. London: Longman, in association with the National Children's Bureau.

Deater-Deckard, K., Dodge, K. A., Bates, J. E. and Pettit, G. S. (1998). 'Multiple risk factors in the development of externalizing behavior problems: Group and individual differences', *Development and Psychopathology*, 10: 469–93.

Department of Education and Science (1983). *Statistical Bulletin*. London: HMSO.

(1993). *Statistical Bulletin*. London: HMSO.

Department of Health (2001). *The expert patient: A new approach to chronic disease management for the 21st century*. London: Department of Health.

Dex, S. and Joshi, H. (eds.) (2004). *The Millennium cohort: first descriptive findings*. London: Institute of Education.

Dilnot, A. and Emmerson, C. (2000). 'The economic environment', in A. H. Halsey and J. Webb (eds.), *Twentieth-century British social trends*. London: Macmillan pp. 324–47.

Dodge, K. A., Pettit, G. S. and Bates, J. E. (1994). 'Socialization mediators of the relation between socioeconomic status and child conduct problems', *Child Development*, 65: 649–65.

Duncan, G. J. (2002). 'The PSID and me', in E. Phelps, F. F. Furstenberg and A. Colby (eds.), *Looking at lives. American longitudinal studies of the twentieth century.* New York: Russel Sage Foundation.

Duncan, G. J. and Brooks-Gunn, J. (1997). *Consequences of growing up poor.* New York: Russell Sage Foundation.

Duncan, G. J., Brooks-Gunn, J. and Klebanov, P. K. (1994). 'Economic deprivation and early childhood development', *Child Development*, 65: 296–318.

Duncan, G. J. and Rodgers, W. L. (1988). 'Longitudinal aspects of childhood poverty', *Journal of Marriage and the Family*, 50: 1007–21.

Duncan, G. J., Yeung, W. J., Brooks-Gunn, J. and Smith, J. R. (1998a). 'How much does childhood poverty affect the life chances of children?', *American Sociological Review*, 63: 406–43.

Easterlin, R. A. (1974). 'Does economic growth improve the human lot? Some empirical evidence', in P. A. David and M. W. Reder (eds.), *Nations and households in economic growth: Essays in honor of Moses Abramovitz.* New York; London: Academic Press pp. 98–125.

(1995). 'Will raising the incomes of all increase the happiness of all?', *Journal of Economic Behavior and Organization*, 27: 35–47.

Eccles, J. S. and Harold, R. D. (1993). 'Parent-school involvement during the early adolescent years', *Teachers College Record*, 94: 568–87.

Eccles, J. S. and Wigfield, A. (1985). 'Teacher expectations and student motivation', in J. B. Dusek (ed.), *Teacher expectancies.* Hillsdale, NJ: Erlbaum pp. 85–220.

Eckenrode, J., Rowe, E., Laird, M. and Brathwaite, J. (1995). 'Mobility as a mediator of the effects of child maltreatment on academic performance', *Child Development*, 66: 1130–42.

Egeland, B., Carlson, E. and Sroufe, L. A. (1993). 'Resilience as process', *Development and Psychopathology*, 5: 517–28.

Egeland, B. and Kreutzer, T. (1991). 'A longitudinal study of the effects of maternal stress and protective factors on the development of high risk children', in E. M. Cummings, A. L. Greene and K. H. Karraker (eds.), *Life-span developmental psychology: Perspectives on stress and coping.* Hillsdale, NJ: Erlbaum pp. 61–85.

Egerton, M. and Halsey, A. H. (1993). 'Trends by social-class and gender in access to higher-education in Britain', *Oxford Review of Education*, 19: 183–96.

Ekinsmyth, C. B. J., Montganery, S. and Shepherd, P. (1992) *An integrated approach to the design and analysis of the 1970 British Cohort Study (BCS70) and the National Child Development Study (NCDS).* London: City University.

Elander, J. and Rutter, M. (1996). 'Use and development of the Rutter parents' and teachers' scales', *International Journal of Methods in Psychiatric Research*, 6: 63–78.

Elder, G. H. (1968). 'Achievement motivation and intelligence in occupational mobility: A longitudinal analysis', *Sociometry*, 327–54.

(1974/1999). *Children of the great depression: Social change in life experience.* Boulder, CO: Westview Press.

(1985). *Life course dynamics.* Ithaca, NY: Cornell University Press.

(1994). 'Time, human agency, and social change: Perspectives on the life course', *Social Psychology Quarterly*, 57: 4–15.

(1998). 'The life course as developmental theory', *Child Development*, 69: 1–12.

Elder, G. H. and Caspi, A. (1988a). 'Economic stress in lives: developmental perspectives', *Journal of Social Issues*, 44: 25–45.

(1988b). 'Human development and social change: An emerging perspective on the life course', in N. Bolger, A. Caspi, G. Downey and M. Moorehouse (eds.), *Persons in context: Developmental processes*. Cambridge: Cambridge University Press pp. 77–113.

Elder, G. H., Parke, R. D. and Modell, J. (1993). *Children in time and place: Developmental and historical insights*. Cambridge: Cambridge University Press.

Elder, G. H. and Shanahan, M. J. (2006). 'The life course and human development', in *The handbook of child psychology. 6th edition*. New York: Wiley (forthcoming).

Emslie, C., Hunt, K. and MacIntyre, S. (1999). 'Gender differences in minor morbidity among full time employees of a British university', *Journal of Epidemiology and Community Health*, 53: 465–75.

Entwistle, D. R., Alexander, K. L. and Olson, L. S. (2002). 'Baltimore beginning school study in perspective', in E. Phelps, F. F. Furstenberg and A. Colby (eds.), *Looking at lives. American longitudinal studies of the twentieth century*. New York: Russell Sage Foundation pp. 167–93.

Epstein, J. (1990). 'School and family connection: Theory, research, and implications for interpreting sociologies of education and family', *Marriage and Family Review*, 15: 99–126.

Erikson, E. H. (1959). *Identity and the life cycle: Selected papers*. New York: International Universities Press.

Erikson, R. and Jonsson, J. O. (1996). 'Explaining class inequality in education: The Swedish test case', in R. Erikson and J. O. Jonsson (eds.), *Can education be equalized?: The Swedish case in comparative perspective*. Boulder, CO; Oxford: Westview Press pp. 1–63.

Ermisch, J. and Francesconi, M. (2000). 'Patterns of family and household formation', in R. Berthoud and J. Gershuny (eds.), *Seven years in the lives of British families*. Bristol: The Policy Press.

Essen, J. and Wedge, P. (1978). *Continuities in disadvantage*. London: Heinemann.

Evans, K. (2002). 'Taking control of their lives? Agency in young adult transitions in England and the New Germany', *Journal of Youth Studies*, 5: 245–71.

Evans, K. and Furlong, A. (1997). 'Metaphors of youth transitions: Niches, pathways, trajectories or navigations', in J. Bynner, L. Chisholm and A. Furlong (eds.), *Youth, citizenship and social change in a European context*. Aldershot: Ashgate pp. 17–41.

Featherman, D. L. and Lerner, R. M. (1985). 'Ontogenesis and sociogenesis – problematics for theory and research about development and socialization across the lifespan', *American Sociological Review*, 50: 659–76.

Feinstein, L. (2003). Inequality in the early cognitive development of British children in the 1970 cohort. *Economica*, 70: 73–98.

Feiring, C. and Lewis, M. (1996). 'Finality in the eye of the beholder: Multiple sources, multiple time points, multiple paths', *Development and Psychopathology*, 8: 721–33.

Felner, R. D., Brand, S., Dubois, D. L., Adan, A. M., Mulhall, P. F. and Evans, E. G. (1995). 'Socioeconomic disadvantage, proximal environmental experiences, and socioemotional and academic adjustment in early adolescence – investigation of a mediated effects model', *Child Development*, 66: 774–92.

Fergus, S. and Zimmerman, M. A. (2005). 'Adolescent resilience: A framework for understanding healthy development in the face of risk', *Annual Review of Public Health*, 26: 13.1–13.21.

Fergusson, D. M. and Horwood, L. J. (2003). 'Resilience to childhood adversity: Results of a 21-year study', in S. S. Luthar (ed.), *Resilience and vulnerability: Adaptation in the context of childhood adversities.* Cambridge: Cambridge University Press pp. 130–55.

Fergusson, D. M., Horwood, L. J. and Lawton, J. M. (1990). 'Vulnerability to childhood problems and family social background', *Journal of Child Psychology and Psychiatry and Allied Disciplines*, 31: 1145–60.

Fergusson, D. M., Horwood, L. J. and Lynskey, M. (1994). 'The childhoods of multiple problem adolescents – a 15-year longitudinal-study', *Journal of Child Psychology and Psychiatry and Allied Disciplines*, 35: 1123–40.

Fergusson, D. M. and Lynskey, M. T. (1996). 'Adolescent resiliency to family adversity', *Journal of Child Psychology and Psychiatry and Allied Disciplines*, 37: 281–92.

Ferri, E. (1993). *Life at 33: The fifth follow-up of the National Child Development Study.* London: National Children's Bureau.

(1998). 'Forty years on: Professor Neville Butler and the British cohort studies', *Paediatric and Perinatal Epidemiology*, 12: 31–44.

Ferri, E., Bynner, J. and Wadsworth, M. (2003). *Changing Britain, changing lives. Three generations at the turn of the century.* London: Institute of Education.

Ferri, E. and Smith, K. (1996). *Parenting in the 1990s.* London: Family Policy Studies Centre supported by Joseph Rowntree Foundation.

(2003a). 'Partnership and parenthood', in E. Ferri, J. Bynner and M. Wadsworth (eds.), *Changing Britain, changing lives. Three generations at the turn of the century.* London: Institute of Education pp. 105–32.

(2003b). 'Family life', in E. Ferri, J. Bynner and M. Wadsworth (eds.), *Changing Britain, changing lives. Three generations at the turn of the century.* London: Institute of Education pp. 133–47.

Finley, M. K. (1984). 'Teachers and tracking in a comprehensive high-school', *Sociology of Education*, 57: 233–43.

Fogelman, K. (1983). *Growing up in Great Britain: Collected papers from the National Child Development Study.* London: Macmillan.

Fraser, M. W., Richman, J. M. and Galinsky, M. J. (1999). 'Risk, protection, and resilience: Toward a conceptual framework for social work practice', *Social Work Research*, 23: 131–43.

Furlong, A. (1992). *Growing up in a classless society.* Edinburgh: Edinburgh University Press.

Furlong, A. and Cartmel, F. (1997). *Young people and social change.* Buckingham: Open University Press.

Furlong, A. and Raffe, D. (1989). *Young people's routes into the labour market.* Edinburgh: Industry Department for Scotland.

Furnham, A. and Gunter, B. (1989). *The anatomy of adolescence: young people's social attitudes in Britain*. London: Routledge.

Furstenberg, F. F., Cook, T. D. et al. (1999). *Managing to make it: Urban families and adolescent success*. Chicago: University of Chicago Press.

Fussell, E. and Greene, M. E. (2002). 'Demographic trends affecting youth around the world', in B. B. Brown, R. Larson and T. S. Saraswathi (eds.), *The world's youth: Adolescence in eight regions of the globe*. Cambridge: Cambridge University Press pp. 21–60.

Gallie, D. (2000). 'The labour force', in A. H. Halsey and J. Webb (eds.), *Twentieth-century British social trends*. London: Macmillan pp. 281–323.

Gallie, D., White, M., Cheng, Y. and Tomlinson, M. (1998). *Restructuring the employment relationship*. Oxford: Clarendon Press.

Garmezy, N. (1970). 'Process and reactive schizophrenia: Some conceptions and uses', *Schizophrenia Bulletin*, 2: 30–74.

(1971). 'Vulnerability research and the issue of primary prevention', *American Journal of Orthopsychiatry*, 41: 101–16.

(1974). 'The study of competence in children at risk for severe psychopathology', in E. J. Anthony and C. Koupernik (ed.), *The child in his family: Children at psychiatric risk*, Vol. 3. New York: Wiley pp. 77–97.

(1985). 'Stress-resistant children: The search for protective factors', in J. E. Stevenson (ed.), *Recent research in developmental psychopathology*. Oxford: Pergamon Press pp. 213–33.

(1991). 'Resiliency and vulnerability to adverse developmental outcomes associated with poverty', *American Behavioral Scientist*, 34: 416–30.

Garmezy, N. and Masten, A. (1994). 'Chronic adversities', in M. Rutter, L. Hertov and E. Taylor (eds.), *Child and adolescent psychiatry*. Oxford: Black Scientific Publications pp. 191–208.

Garmezy, N., Masten, A. S. and Tellegen, A. (1984). 'The study of stress and competence in children – a building block for developmental psychopathology', *Child Development*, 55: 97–111.

Garmezy, N. and Rutter, M. L. (1983). *Stress, coping, and development in children*. New York: McGraw-Hill.

Giddens, A. (1991). *Modernity and self-identity: Self and society in the late modern age*. Cambridge: Polity Press.

Giele, J. Z. and Elder, G. H. (1998). *Methods of life course research: Qualitative and quantitative approaches*. London: Sage.

Ginzberg, E., Ginzberg, S. W., Axelrad, S. and Herma, J. L. (1951). *Occupational choice. An approach to a general theory*. New York: Columbia University Press.

Ginzberg, E. and Herma, J. L. (1964). *Talent and performance*. New York: Columbia University Press.

Glantz, M. D. and Sloboda, Z. (1999). 'Analysis and reconceptualisation of resilience', in M. D. Glantz and J. L. Johnson (eds.), *Resilience and development: Positive life adaptations*. New York; London: Kluwer Academic/Plenum pp. 109–26.

Glass, N. (1999). 'Sure Start: The development of an early intervention programme for young children in the United Kingdom', *Children and Society*, 13: 257–64.

Glenn, N. (1977). *Cohort analysis*. London: Sage.

Godfrey Thomson Unit (1978). *Edinburgh Reading Test.* Sevenoaks: Hodder & Stoughton.

Goldstein, H. (1979). 'Some models for analysing longitudinal data on educational attainment', *Journal of the Royal Statistical Society, Series A,* 142: 402–47.

Goodenough, F. L. (1926). *Measurement of intelligence by drawings.* New York: Harcourt, Brace & World.

Gordon, E. W. and Song, L. D. (1994). 'Variations in the experience of resilience', in M. C. Wang and E. W. Gordon (eds.), *Educational resilience in inner-city America: Challenges and prospects.* Hillsdale, NJ: Erlbaum pp. 27–43.

Gottfredson, L. S. (1981). 'Circumscription and compromise – a developmental theory of occupational aspirations', *Journal of Counseling Psychology,* 28: 545–79.

Gottlieb, G., Wahlsten, D. and Lickliter, R. (1998). 'The significance of biology for human development: A developmental psychobiological systems view', in R. M. Lerner and W. Damon (eds.), *Handbook of child psychology,* Vol 1. *Theoretical models of human development.* New York: Wiley pp. 233–74.

Goulet, L. R. and Baltes, P. B. (1970). *Life-span developmental psychology: Research and theory.* New York: Academic Press.

Graber, J. A. and Brooks-Gunn, J. (1996). 'Transitions and turning points: Navigating the passage from childhood through adolescence', *Developmental Psychology,* 32: 768–76.

Graham, J. R. and Barter, K. (1999). 'Collaboration: A social work practice model', *Families in Society,* 80: 6–13.

Graham, J. W. and Hofer, S. M. (2000). 'Multiple imputation in multivariate research', in T. D. Little, K. U. Schnabel and J. Baumert (eds.), *Modeling longitudinal and multilevel data.* Mahwah, New Jersey: Lawrence Erlbaum Associates pp. 201–18.

Grant, G., Nolan, M. and Ellis, N. (1990). 'A reappraisal of the Malaise Inventory', *Social Psychiatry and Psychiatric Epidemiology,* 25: 170–8.

Greenberg, M. T., Lengua, L. J., Coie, J. D. and Pinderhughes, E. E. (1999). 'Predicting developmental outcomes at school entry using a multiple-risk model: Four American communities', *Developmental Psychology,* 35: 403–17.

Gregg, P. and Machin, P. (1997). 'Blighted lives: Disadvantaged children and adult unemployment', *Centrepiece,* 2: 14–18.

Griffin, C. (1993). *Representations of youth: The study of youth and adolescence in Britain and America.* Cambridge, England: Polity Press.

Haggerty, R. J., Sherrod, L. R., Garmezy, N. and Rutter, M. (eds.) (1994). *Stress, risk, and resilience in children and adolescents: Processes, mechanisms, and interventions.* Cambridge: Cambridge University Press.

Halsey, A. H. (2000). 'Introduction: Twentieth-century Britain', in A. H. Halsey and J. Webb (eds.), *Twentieth-century British social trends.* London: Macmillan Press pp. 1–23.

Halsey, A. H., Heath, A. and Ridge, J. (1980). *Opening wide the doors of higher education.* London: National Commission of Education.

Hammen, C. (1992). 'Cognitive, life stress, and interpersonal approaches to a developmental psychopathology model of depression', *Development and Psychopathology*, 4: 189–206.

Hammer, T. (1997). 'History dependence in youth unemployment', *European Sociological Review*, 14.

Harris, D. B. (1963). *Children's drawings as measures of intellectual maturity: A revision and extension of the Goodenough draw-a-man test*. New York: Harcourt, Brace & World.

Hart, P. E. (1988). *Youth unemployment in Great Britain*. Cambridge: Cambridge University Press.

Hartup, W. W. and Laursen, B. (1991). 'Relationships as developmental contexts', in F. Cohen and A. Siegel (eds.), *Context and development*. Hillsdale, NJ: Erlbaum pp. 253–79.

Haskey, J. (1996). 'Population review: Families and households in Great Britain', *Population Trends*, 85: 7–24.

Haveman, R. H. and Wolfe, B. (1994). *Succeeding generations: On the effects of investments in children*. New York: Russell Sage Foundation.

Heckhausen, J. (1999). *Developmental regulation in adulthood: Age-normative and sociostructural constraints as adaptive challenges*. Cambridge: Cambridge University Press.

Heinz, W. R. (2002). 'Transition discontinuities and the biographical shaping of early work careers', *Journal of Vocational Behavior*, 60: 220–40.

Hertzman, C. (1999). 'Population health and human development', in D. P. Keating and C. Hertzman (eds.), *Developmental health and the wealth of nations*. New York: Guilford Press pp. 21–40.

Heyns, B. (1974). 'Social selection and stratification within school', *American Journal of Sociology*, 79: 1434–51.

Hinde, R. A. (1998). 'Through categories toward individuals: Attempting to tease apart the data', in R. B. Cairns, L. R. Bergman and J. Kagan (eds.), *Methods and models for studying the individual*. London: Sage pp. 11–31.

Hobcraft, J., Hango, D. and Sigle-Rushton, W. (2004). 'The childhood origins of adult socio-economic disadvantage: Do cohort and gender matter?' London: London School of Economics, Centre for Analysis of Social Exclusion.

Hobsbawm, E. J. (1995). *Age of extremes: The short twentieth century, 1914–1991*. London: Abacus.

Holland, J. L., Gottfredson, G. D. et al. (1990). 'Validity of vocational aspirations and interest inventories – extended, replicated, and reinterpreted', *Journal of Counseling Psychology*, 37(3): 337–42.

Holtz, G. T. (1995). *Welcome to the jungle: the why behind 'Generation X'*. New York: St. Martin's Griffin.

Horowitz, F. D. (2000). 'Child development and the pits: Simple questions, complex answers, and developmental theory', *Child Development*, 71: 1–10.

Huston, A. C., McLoyd, V. C. and Coll, C. G. (1994). 'Children and poverty – issues in contemporary research', *Child Development*, 65: 275–82.

Huttenlocher, P. R. (2002). *Neural plasticity: The effects of environment on the development of the cerebral cortex*. Cambridge, MA: Harvard University Press.

Iacovou, M. and Berthoud, R. (2001). *Young people's lives: A Map of Europe.* Colchester: University of Essex, Institute for Social and Economic Research.

Jausovec, N. & Jausovec, K. (2000). 'Correlations between erp parameters and intelligence: A reconsideration', *Biological Psychology,* 55: 137–54.

Jencks, C. and Petersen, P. (1992). *The urban underclass.* Washington, DC: Brookings Institution.

Jenkins, R., Lewis, G., Bebbington, P., Brugha, T., Farrell, M., Gill, B. and Meltzer, H. (1997). 'The national psychiatric morbidity surveys of Great Britain – initial findings from the household survey', *Psychological Medicine,* 27: 775–89.

Jones, G. (2002). *The youth divide: diverging paths to adulthood.* York: Joseph Rowntree Foundation.

Jones, G. and Wallace, C. (1992). *Youth, family and citizenship.* Buckingham: Open University Press.

Joshi, H. (2002). 'Production, reproduction and education: women, children and work in contemporary Britain' *Population and Development Review,* 28: 445–74.

Joshi, H. Cooksey, E. Wiggins, R. D., McCulloch, A., Verropoulou, G. and Clarke, L. (1999). 'Diverse family living situations and child development: a multilevel analysis comparing longitudinal evidence from Britain and the United States' *International Journal of Law, Policy and the Family,* 13: 292–314.

Joshi, H. and Paci, P. (1998). *'Unequal pay for men and women: Evidence from the British birth cohort studies.* London: MIT Press.

Kaplan, H. B. (1999). 'Toward an understanding of resilience: A critical review of definitions and models', in M. D. Glantz and J. L. Johnson (eds.), *Resilience and development: Positive life adaptations.* New York: Kluwer Academic pp. 17–83.

Keating, D. P. and Hertzman, C. (1999a). *Developmental health and the wealth of nations.* New York: Guilford Press.

(1999b). 'Modernity's paradox', in Daniel P. Keating and C. Hertzman (eds.), *Developmental health and the wealth of nations.* New York: The Guilford Press pp. 1–17.

Kerckhoff, A. C. (1993). *Diverging pathways: Social structure and career deflections.* Cambridge: Cambridge University Press.

Kiernan, K. E. and Estaugh, V. (1993). *Cohabitation: Extra-marital childbearing and social policy.* London: Family Policy Studies Centre.

Kobasa, S. C., Maddi, S. R. and Kahn, S. (1982). 'Hardiness and health; A prospective study', *Journal of Personality and Social Psychology,* 42: 168–77.

Krieger, N., Williams, D. R. and Moss, N. E. (1997). 'Measuring social class in US public health research: Concepts, methodologies, and guidelines', *Annual Review of Public Health,* 18: 341–78.

Kuh, D. and Ben-Shlomo, Y. (eds.) (1997). *A life course approach to chronic disease epidemiology: Tracing the origins of ill-health from early to adult life.* Oxford: Oxford University Press.

Kuh, D. J. L., Power, C., Blane, D. and Bartley, M. (1997). 'Social pathways between childhood and adult health', in D. Kuh and Y. Ben-Shlomo (eds.), *A life course approach to chronic disease epidemiology: Tracing the origins of ill-health from early to adult life.* Oxford: Oxford University Press pp. 169–98.

Lakin, C. (2001). 'The effects of taxes and benefits on household income, 1999–2000', *Economic Trends*, 569: 35–74.

Laub, J. H. and Sampson, R. J. (2003). *Shared beginnings, divergent lives. Delinquent boys to age 70.* Cambridge, MA: Harvard University Press.

Lee, V. E. and Croninger, R. G. (1994). 'The relative importance of home and school in the development of literacy skills for middle-grade students', *American Journal of Education*, 102: 286–329.

Leete, R. and Fox, J. (1977). 'Registrar general's social classes: Origins and users', *Population Trends*, 8: 1–7.

Lerner, R. M. (1984). *On the nature of human plasticity.* New York: Cambridge University Press.

(1991). 'Changing organism-context relations as the basic process of development: A developmental contextual perspective', *Developmental Psychology*, 27: 27–32.

(1996). 'Relative plasticity, integration, temporality, and diversity in human development: A developmental contextual perspective about theory, process, and method', *Developmental Psychology*, 32: 781–6.

Little, B. R. (1983). 'Personal projects – a rationale and method for investigation', *Environment and Behavior*, 15: 273–309.

Little, T. D., Schnabel, K. U. and Baumert, J. (eds.) (2000). *Modeling longitudinal and multilevel data: Practical issues, applied approaches, and specific examples.* Mahwah, NJ: Lawrence Erlbaum.

Loehlin, J. C. (1998). *Latent variable models: An introduction to factor, path, and structural analysis.* London: Lawrence Erlbaum Associates.

Lundberg, O. (1991). 'Causal explanations for class-inequality in health – an empirical-analysis', *Social Science and Medicine*, 32: 385–93.

Lurie, A. and Monahan, K. (2001). 'Prevention principles for practitioners: A solution or an illusion?', *Social Work in Health Care*, 33: 69–86.

Luthar, S. S. (1991). 'Vulnerability and resilience – a study of high-risk adolescents', *Child Development*, 62: 600–16.

(1993). 'Methodological and conceptual issues in research on childhood resilience', *Journal of Child Psychology and Psychiatry and Allied Disciplines*, 34: 441–53.

(1995). 'Social competence in the school setting – prospective cross-domain associations among inner-city teens', *Child Development*, 66: 416–29.

(1997). 'Socioeconomic disadvantage and psychosocial adjustment: Perspectives from developmental psychopathology', in S. S. Luthar, J. A. Burack, L. Cicchetti and J. R. Weisz (eds.), *Developmental psychopathology: Perspectives on adjustment, risk, and disorder.* Cambridge: Cambridge University Press pp. 459–85.

(1999). *Poverty and children's adjustment.* Thousand Oaks, CA: Sage.

(ed.) (2003). *Resilience and vulnerability: Adaptation in the context of childhood adversities.* Cambridge: Cambridge University Press.

Luthar, S. S., Burack, J. A., Cicchetti, D. and Weisz, J. R. (eds.) (1997). *Developmental psychopathology. Perspectives on adjustment, risk, and disorder.* Cambridge: Cambridge University Press.

Luthar, S. S. and Cicchetti, D. (2000). 'The construct of resilience: Implications for interventions and social policies', *Development and Psychopathology*, 12: 857–85.

Luthar, S. S., Cicchetti, D. and Becker, B. (2000). 'The construct of resilience: A critical evaluation and guidelines for future work', *Child Development*, 71: 543–62.

Luthar, S. S. and Cushing, G. (1999). 'Measurement issues in the empirical study of resilience: An overview', in M. D. Glantz and J. L. Johnson (eds.), *Resilience and development: Positive life adaptations*. New York: Kluwer Academic pp. 129–60.

Luthar, S. S., D'Avanzo, K. and Hites, S. (2003). 'Maternal drug abuse versus other psychological disturbances: Risks and resilience among children', in S. S. Luthar (ed.), *Resilience and vulnerability: Adaptation in the context of childhood adversities*. Cambridge: Cambridge University Press pp. 104–29.

Luthar, S. S. and Zelazo, L. B. (2003). 'Research on resilience: An integrative view', in S. S. Luthar (ed.), *Resilience and vulnerability: Adaptation in the context of childhood adversities*. Cambridge: Cambridge University Press pp. 510–49.

Machin, S. (2003). 'Unto them that hath. . .', *Centre Piece*, 8: 4–9.

Macoby, E. E. (1980). *Social development: Psychological growth and the parent-child relationship*. San Diego, CA: Harcourt Brace Jovanovich.

Magnusson, D. (1995). 'Individual development: A holistic integrated model', in P. Moen, G. H. Elder and K. Lüscher (eds.), *Linking lives and contexts: Perspectives on the ecology of human development*. Washington: APA Books pp. 19–60.

Magnusson, D. and Bergman, L. R. (1988). 'Individual and variable-based approaches to longitudinal research on early risk factors', in M. Rutter (ed.), *Studies of psychosocial risk: The power of longitudinal data*. Cambridge: Cambridge University Press pp. 44–61.

Makepeace, G., Dolton, P., Woods, L., Joshi, H., and Galinda-Rueda, F. (2003). 'From school to the labour market', in E. Ferri, J. Bynner and M. Wadsworth (Eds.), *Changing Britain, Changing Lives. Three Generations at the Turn of the Century*. London: Institute of Education pp. 29–70.

Marsh, C. (1986). 'Social class and occupation', in R. G. Burgess (ed.), *Key variables in social investigation*. London: Routledge.

Marwick, A. (1982). *British society since 1940*. London: Pelican.

Massey, S., Cameron, A., Ouellette, S. and Fine, M. (1998). 'Qualitative approaches to the study of thriving: What can be learned?', *Journal of Social Issues*, 54: 337–55.

Masten, A. (1994). 'Resilience in individual development: Successful adaptation despite risk and adversity', in M. C. Wang and E. W. Gordon (eds.), *Educational resilience in inner-city America: Challenges and prospects*. Hillsdale, NJ: L. Erlbaum Associates pp. 3–25.

(1999). 'Resilience comes of age: Reflections on the past and outlook for the next generation of research', in M. D. Glantz and J. L. Johnson (eds.), *Resilience and development: Positive life adaptations*. New York: Kluwer Academic pp. 281–96.

Masten, A. and Coatsworth, J. D. (1995). 'Competence, resilience and psychopathology', in D. Cicchetti and D. J. Cohen (eds.), *Developmental psychopathology: Vol 2. Risk, disorder and adaptation*. New York: J. Wiley pp. 715–52.

Masten, A., Morison, P., Pellegrini, D. S. and Tellegen, A. (1990a). 'Competence under stress: Risk and protective factors', in J. Rolf, A. Masten, D. Cicchetti, K. H. Nuechterlin and S. Weintraub (eds.), *Risk and protective factors in the development of psychopathology* Cambridge: Cambridge University Press pp. 236–56.

Masten, A. S. (2001). 'Ordinary magic – resilience processes in development', *American Psychologist*, 56: 227–38.

Masten, A. S., Best, K. M. and Garmezy, N. (1990b). 'Resilience and development: Contributions from the study of children who overcome adversity', *Development and Psychopathology*, 2: 425–44.

Masten, A. S. and Coatsworth, J. D. (1998). 'The development of competence in favorable and unfavorable environments – lessons from research on successful children', *American Psychologist*, 53: 205–20.

Masten, A. S., Garmezy, N., Tellegen, A., Pellegrini, D. S., Larkin, K. and Larsen, A. (1988). 'Competence and stress in school-children – the moderating effects of individual and family qualities', *Journal of Child Psychology and Psychiatry and Allied Disciplines*, 29: 745–64.

Masten, A. S., Hubbard, J. J., Gest, S. D., Tellegen, A., Garmezy, N. and Ramirez, M. (1999). 'Competence in the context of adversity: Pathways to resilience and maladaptation from childhood to late adolescence', *Development and Psychopathology*, 11: 143–69.

Masten, A. S and Powell, J. L. (2003). 'A resilience framework for research, policy, and practice', in S. S. Luthar (ed.), *Resilience and vulnerablity: Adaptation in the context of childhood adversities*. Cambridge: Cambridge University Press pp. 1–25.

McClelland, D. C. (1961). *The achieving society*. Princeton, NJ: Van Nostrand.

McCulloch, A., Wiggins, R. D., Joshi, H. E. and Sachdev, D. (2000). 'Internalising and externalising children's behaviour problems in Britain and the US: Relationships to family resources', *Children and Society*, 14: 368–83.

McGee, R., Williams, S. and Silva, P. A. (1986). 'An evaluation of the Malaise Inventory', *Journal of Psychosomatic Research*, 30: 147–52.

McLeod, J. and Shanahan, M. J. (1993). 'Poverty, parenting and children's mental health, *American Sociological Review*, 58: 351–66.

McLoyd, V. C. (1990). 'The impact of economic hardship on black families and children – psychological distress, parenting, and socioemotional development', *Child Development*, 61: 311–46.

    (1994). 'The strain of living poor: Parenting, social support, and child mental health', in A. C. Huston (eds.), *Children in poverty*. Cambridge: Cambridge University Press pp. 105–35.

    (1998). 'Socioeconomic disadvantage and child development', *American Psychologist*, 53: 185–204.

McMillen, J. C. (1999). 'Better for it: How people benefit from adversity', *Social Work*, 44: 455–68.

McRae, S. (ed.) (1999). *Changing Britain: Families and households in the 1990s*. Oxford: Oxford University Press.

Meltzer, H., Gatward, R., Goodman, R. and Ford, F. (2000). *Mental health of children and adolescents in Great Britain*. London: The Stationery Office.

Menard, S. (2002). *Longitudinal research*. London: Sage.

Modell, J., Furstenberg, G. and Hershberg, T. (1976). 'Social change and transitions to adulthood in historical perspective', *Journal of Family History*, 1: 7–32.

Moen, P., Elder, G. H. and Lüscher, K. K. (1995). *Examining lives in context: Perspectives on the ecology of human development*. Washington, DC: American Psychological Association.

Moffitt, T. E. and Caspi, A. (2001). 'Childhood predictors differentiate life-course persistent and adolescence-limited antisocial pathways, among males and females', *Development and Psychopathology*, 13: 355–75.

Moffitt, T. E., Caspi, A., Rutter, M. L. and Silva, P. A. (2001). *Sex differences in antisocial behaviour: Conduct disorder, delinquency*. Cambridge: Cambridge University Press.

Montgomery, S. M. and Schoon, I. (1997). 'Health and health behaviour', in J. Bynner, E. Ferri and P. Shepherd (eds.), *Getting on, getting by, getting nowhere. Twenty-something in the 1990s*. Aldershot: Ashgate pp. 77–96.

Mortimer, J. T. and Larson, R. (2002). 'Macrostructural trends and the reshaping of adolescence', in J. T. Mortimer and R. Larson (eds.), *The changing adolescent experience: Societal trends and the transition to adulthood*. Cambridge: Cambridge University Press pp. 1–19.

Mortimer, J. T. and Shanahan, M. J. (2003). *Handbook on the life course*. New York: Plenum.

Müller, W. (1996). 'Class inequalities in educational outcomes: Sweden in comparative perspective', in R. Erikson and J. O. Jonsson (eds.), *Can education be equalized?: The Swedish case in comparative perspective*. Boulder, CO: Westview Press pp. 145–82.

Murphy, M. (1993). 'The contraceptive pill and women's employment as factors in fertility change in Britain 1963–1980: A challenge to the conventional view', *Population Statistics*, 47: 221–43.

Murphy, M. and Wang, D. (1999). 'Forecasting British families into the twenty-first century', in S. McRae (ed.), *Changing Britain: Families and households in the 1990s*. Oxford: Oxford University Press pp. 100–37.

Nelson, C. A. (1999). 'Neural plasticity and human development', *Current Directions in Psychological Science*, 8: 42–5.

Nolen-Hoeksema, S. (1990). *Sex differences in depression*. Stanford, CA: Stanford University Press.

Nuffield Foundation (2002). *14–19 education: Papers arising from a seminar series held at the Nuffield Foundation, December 2001–January 2002*. London: Nuffield Foundation.

Nurmi, J. E. (1993). 'Adolescent development in an age-graded context – the role of personal beliefs, goals, and strategies in the tackling of developmental tasks and standards', *International Journal of Behavioral Development*, 16: 169–89.

O'Connor, T. G. and Rutter, M. (1996). 'Risk mechanisms in development: Some conceptual and methodological considerations', *Development and Psychopathology*, 5: 567–79.

Office of Population, Censuses and Surveys (1980). *Classification of occupations and coding index*. London: HMSO.

Office of Population, Censuses and Surveys (1990). *Standard occupational classification*. London: HMSO.

Office for National Statistics (2003). Labour market trends. London: ONS.

Ogbu, J. U. (1981). 'Origins of human competence – a cultural-ecological perspective', *Child Development*, 52: 413–29.

—— (1985). 'A cultural ecology of competence among inner-city blacks', in M. B. Spencer, G. K. Brookins and W. R. Allen (eds.), *Beginnings: The social and affective development of black children*. Hillsdale, NJ: L. Erlbaum pp. 45–66.

Osborn, A. F. (1990). 'Resilient children: A longitudinal study of high achieving socially disadvantaged children', *Early Child Development and Care*, 62: 23–47.

Osborn, A. F., Butler, N. R. and Morris, A. C. (1984). *The social life of Britain's five-year-olds: A report of the child health and education study*. London: Routledge & Kegan Paul.

Osborn, A. F. and Milbank, J. E. (1987). *The effects of early education*. Oxford: Oxford University Press.

Owens, E. B. and Shaw, D. S. (2003). 'Poverty and early childhood adjustment', in S. S. Luthar (ed.), *Resilience and vulnerability: Adaptation in the context of childhood adversities*. Cambridge: Cambridge University Press pp. 267–92.

Parsons, J. E., Kaczala, C. M. and Meece, J. L. (1982). 'Socialization of achievement attitudes and beliefs – classroom influences', *Child Development*, 53: 322–39.

Peck, M. N. (1994). 'The importance of childhood socioeconomic group for adult health', *Social Science and Medicine*, 39: 553–62.

Pianta, R. C. and Walsh, D. J. (1996). *High-risk children in schools: Constructing sustaining relationships*. London: Routledge.

Pilling, D. (1990). *Escape from disadvantage*. London: Falmer Press.

Pittman, K., Diversi, M. and Ferber, T. (2002). 'Social policy supports for adolescence in the twenty-first century: Framing questions', *Journal of Research on Adolescence*, 12: 149–58.

Pittman, K., Irby, M., Tolman, J., Yohalem, N. and Ferber, T. (2001). *Preventing problems, promoting development, encouraging engagement: Competing priorities or inseparable goals?* Takoma Park, MD: The Forum of Youth Investment, International Youth Foundation.

Plewis, I., Calderwood, L., Hawkes, D. and Nathan, G. (2004). *National Child Development Study and 1970 British Cohort Study Technical Report: Changes in the NCDS and BCS70 populations and samples over time*. London: Institute of Education, Centre for Longitudinal Studies.

Plomin, R. and Daniels, D. (1987). 'Why are children in the same family so different from one another?', *Behavioral and Brain Sciences*, 10: 1–16.

Poole, M. (1983). *Youth: expectations and transitions*. London: Routledge and Kegan Paul.

Poole, M. (1990). 'Attitudes to school, careers and the future', in P. C. L. Heaven and V. J. Callan (eds.), *Adolescence: an Australian perspective*. Marrickville, NSW: Harcourt Brace Jovanovich.

Power, C. (1991). 'Social and economic background and class inequalities in health among young-adults', *Social Science & Medicine*, 32: 411–17.

Power, C. and Hertzman, C. (1999). 'Health, well-being, and coping styles', in D. P. Keating and C. Hertzman (eds.), *Developmental health and the wealth of nations*. New York: Guilford Press pp. 41–54.

Power, C., Matthews, S. and Manor, O. (1998). 'Inequalities in self-rated health: Explanations from different stages of life', *Lancet*, 351: 1009–14.

Prandy, K. (1990). 'The revised Cambridge scale of occupations', *Sociology*, 24: 629–55.

Pringle, M. K., Butler, N. R. and Davie, R. (1966). *11,000 seven-year-olds: First report of the national child development study (1958 cohort)*. London: Longman.

Pulkkinen, L. (1996). 'Female and male personality styles: A typological and developmental analysis', *Journal of Personality and Social Psychology*, 70: 1288–306.

Pulkkinen, L. and Caspi, A. (2002). 'Personality and paths to successful development: An overview', in L. Pulkkinen and A. Caspi (eds.), *Paths to successful development. Personality in the life course*. Cambridge: Cambridge University Press pp. 1–18.

Pulkkinen, L., Nygren, H. and Kokko, K. (2002). 'Successful development: Childhood antecedents of adaptive psychosocial functioning in adulthood', *Journal of Adult Development*, 9: 251–65.

Pungello, E. P., Kupersmidt, J. B., Burchinal, M. R. and Patterson, C. J. (1996). 'Environmental risk factors and children's achievement from middle childhood to early adolescence', *Developmental Psychology*, 32: 755–67.

Quinton, D. and Rutter, M. (1988). *Parenting breakdown: The making and breaking of intergenerational links*. Aldershot: Avebury.

Reynolds, A. J. and Walberg, H. J. (1991). 'A structural model of science achievement', *Journal of Educational Psychology*, 83: 97–107.

Richters, J. and Weintraub, S. (1990). 'Beyond diathesis: Toward an understanding of high-risk environments', in J. Rolf, A. Masten, D. Cicchetti, K. H. Nuechterlin and S. Weintraub (eds.), *Risk and protective factors in the development of psychopathology*. Cambridge: Cambridge University Press pp. 67–96.

Rigsby, L. C. (1994). 'The Americanization of resilience: Deconstructing research practice', in M. C. Wang & E. W. Gordon (eds.), *Educational resilience in inner-city America. Challenges and prospects*. Hillsdale, NJ: Erlbaum.

Rist, R. C. (2000). 'Student social class and teacher expectations: The self-fulfilling prophecy in ghetto education', *Harvard Educational Review*, 70: 257–65.

Roberts, K. (1995). *Youth and employment in modern Britain*. Oxford: Oxford University Press.

Roberts, K. P. G. (1992). 'The stratification of youth training', *British Journal of Education and Work*, 5: 65–83.

Robins, L. N. and Rutter, M. (1990). *Straight and devious pathways from childhood to adulthood*. Cambridge: Cambridge University Press.

Rodgers, B., Pickles, A., Power, C., Collishaw, S. and Maughan, B. (1999). 'Validity of the Malaise Inventory in general population samples', *Social Psychiatry and Psychiatric Epidemiology*, 34: 333–41.

Rolf, J., Masten, A., Cicchetti, D., Nuechterlin, K. H. and Weintraub, S. (eds.) (1990). *Risk and protective factors in the development of psychopathology*. Cambridge: Cambridge University Press.

Rossi, A. S. (1983). *Seasons of a woman's life: A self-reflective essay on love and work in family, profession, and politics*. Amherst: University of Massachusetts, Social and Demographic Research Institute.

Routh, G. (1981). *Occupation and pay in Great Britain*. Cambridge: Cambridge University Press.

Ruskin, J. (1867). *Time and tide*, Letter 8.

Rutter, M. (1970). 'Sex differences in children's response to family stress', in E. J. Anthony and C. Koupernik (eds.), *The child in his family*. New York: Wiley pp. 165–96.

(1981). 'Stress, coping and development – some issues and some questions', *Journal of Child Psychology and Psychiatry and Allied Disciplines*, 22: 323–56.

(1985). 'Resilience in the face of adversity – protective factors and resistance to psychiatric-disorder', *British Journal of Psychiatry*, 147: 598–611.

(1987). 'Psychosocial resilience and protective mechanisms', *American Journal of Orthopsychiatry*, 57: 316–31.

(1988). *Studies of psychosocial risk: The power of longitudinal data* (ed.). Cambridge: Cambridge University Press.

(1989). 'Pathways from childhood to adult life', *Journal of Child Psychology and Psychiatry and Allied Disciplines*, 30: 23–51.

(1990). 'Psychosocial resilience and protective mechanisms', in J. Rolf, A. S. Masten, D. Chichetti, K. H. Nuechterlin and S. Weintraub (eds.), *Risk and protective factors in the development of psychopathology*. New York: Cambridge University Press pp. 181–214.

(1996). 'Transitions and turning points in developmental psychopathology: As applied to the age span between childhood and mid-adulthood', *International Journal of Behavioral Development*, 19: 603–26.

(1998). 'Developmental catch-up, and deficit, following adoption after severe global early privation', *Journal of Child Psychology and Psychiatry and Allied Disciplines*, 39: 465–76.

(1999). 'Resilience concepts and findings: Implications for family therapy', *Journal of Family Therapy*, 21: 119–44.

(2000). 'Psychosocial influences: Critiques, findings, and research needs', *Development and Psychopathology*, 12: 375–405.

(2003). 'Genetic influences on risk and protection: Implications for understanding resilience', in S. S. Luthar (ed.), *Resilience and vulnerability. Adaptation in the context of childhood adversities*. Cambridge: Cambridge University Press pp. 489–509.

Rutter, M., Cox, A., Tulping, C., Berger, M. and Yule, W. (1975a). 'Attainment and adjustment in two geographical areas. I: The prevalence of psychiatric disorder', *British Journal of Psychiatry*, 126: 493–509.

Rutter, M., Giller, H. and Hagell, A. (1998). *Antisocial behaviour by young people*. Cambridge: Cambridge University Press.

Rutter, M. and Madge, N. (1976). *Cycles of disadvantage: A review of research*. London: Heinemann Educational Books.

Rutter, M., Maughan, B., Mortimore, P. and Ouston, J. (1979). *Fifteen thousand hours: Secondary schools and their effects on children*. London: Open Books.

Rutter, M. and Quinton, D. (1984). 'Long-term follow-up of women institutionalised in childhood: Factors promoting good functioning in adult life', *British Journal of Developmental Psychology*, 15: 225–34.

Rutter, M., Tizard, J. and Whitmore, K. (1970). *Education, health and behaviour*. London: Longmans.

Rutter, M., Yule, B., Morton, J. and Bagley, C. (1975b). 'Children of West Indian immigrants. III: Home circumstances and family patterns', *Journal of Child Psychology and Psychiatry*, 16: 105–23.

Rutter, M., Yule, B., Quinton, D., Rowlands, O. and Yule, W. (1975c). 'Attainment and adjustment in two geographical areas. III: Some factors accounding for area differences', *British Journal of Psychiatry*, 126: 520–33.

Rutter, M. L. (1966). *Children of sick parents: An environmental and psychiatric study*. Oxford: Oxford University Press.

Sacker, A., Schoon, I. et al. (2002). 'Social inequality in educational achievement and psychosocial adjustment throughout childhood: magnitude and mechanisms', *Social Science and Medicine* 55: 863–80.

Sacker, A. and Wiggins, R. D. (2002). 'Age-period-cohort effects on inequalities in psychological distress 1981–2000', *Psychological Medicine*, 32: 977–90.

Sameroff, A. J. (1983). 'Developmental systems: Contexts and evolution', in W. Kesson (Vol. ed.) and P. H. Mussen (ed.), *Handbook of child psychology*, Vol. 1. *History, theory and methods*. New York: Wiley pp. 237–94.

(1999). 'Ecological perspectives on developmental risk', in J. D. Osofsky and H. E. Fitzgerald (eds.), *WAIMH handbook of infant mental health*, Vol 4: *Infant mental health groups at risk*. New York: Wiley pp. 223–48.

Sameroff, A. J., Bartko, W. T., Baldwin, A., Baldwin, C. and Seifer, R. (1998). 'Family and social influences on the development of child competence', in M. Lewis and C. Feiring (eds.), *Families, risk and competence*. Mahwah, NJ: Erlbaum pp. 161–85.

Sameroff, A. J. and Chandler, M. J. (1975). 'Reproductive risk and the continuum of caretaking casualty', in F. D. Horowitz, E. M. Hetherington, G. M. Siegel and S. Scarr-Salapatek (eds.), *Review of child development research*. Chicago: University of Chicago Press pp. 187–244.

Sameroff, A. J. and Seifer, R. (1990). 'Early contributors to developmental risk', in J. Rolf, A. Masten, D. Cicchetti, K. H. Nuechterlin and S. Weintraub (eds.), *Risk and protective factors in the development of psychopathology*. Cambridge: Cambridge University Press pp. 52–66.

Sameroff, A. J., Seifer, R., Baldwin, A. and Baldwin, C. (1993). 'Stability of intelligence from preschool to adolescence – the influence of social and family risk-factors', *Child Development*, 64: 80–97.

Sampson, R. J. and Laub, J. H. (1994). 'Urban poverty and the family context of delinquency – a new look at structure and process in a classic study', *Child Development*, 65: 523–40.

Scarr, S. (1992). 'Developmental theories for the 1990s – development and individual-differences', *Child Development*, 63: 1–19.

Schachar, R., Rutter, M. and Smith, A. (1981). 'The characteristics of situationally and pervasively hyperactive-children – implications for syndrome definition', *Journal of Child Psychology and Psychiatry and Allied Disciplines*, 22: 375–92.

Schaie, K. W. (1965). 'A general model for the study of developmental problems', *Psychological Bulletin*, 64: 92–107.

Schneider, B. and Stevenson, D. (1999). *The ambitious generation: America's teenagers, motivated but directionless*. New Haven: Yale University Press.

Schoon, I., Bynner, J., Joshi, H., Parsons, S., Wiggins, R. D. and Sacker, A. (2002). 'The influence of context, timing, and duration of risk experiences for the passage from childhood to mid-adulthood', *Child Development*, 73: 1486–504.

Schoon, I., McCulloch, A., Joshi, H., Wiggins, R. D. and Bynner, J. (2001). 'Transitions from school to work in a changing social context', *Young*, 9: 4–22.

Schoon, I. and Parsons, S. (2002a). 'Teenage aspirations for future careers and occupational outcomes', *Journal of Vocational Behavior*, 60: 262–88.

(2002b). 'Competence in the face of adversity: The influence of early family environment and long-term consequences', *Children and Society*, 16: 260–72.

Schoon, I., Parsons, S. and Sacker, A. (2004). 'Socioeconomic adversity, educational resilience, and subsequent levels of adult adaptation', *Journal of Adolescent Research*, 19: 383–404.

Schoon, I., Sacker, A. and Bartley, M. (2003). 'Socio-economic adversity and psychosocial adjustment: A developmental-contextual perspective', *Social Science and Medicine*, 57: 1001–15.

Schulenberg, J. E., Vondracek, F. W. and Crouter, A. C. (1984). 'The influence of the family on vocational development', *Journal of Marriage and the Family*, 46: 129–43.

Scott, J. (2004). 'Family, gender, and educational attainment in Britain: A longitudinal study', *Journal of Comparative Family Studies*, 35: 565.

Scott, L. H. (1981). 'Measuring intelligence with the Goodenough-Harris drawing test', *Psychological Bulletin*, 89: 483–505.

Seccombe, K. (2002). "Beating the odds" versus "changing the odds": Poverty, resilience, and family policy', *Journal of Marriage and the Family*, 64: 384–94.

Seifer, R., Sameroff, A. J., Baldwin, C. P. and Baldwin, A. (1992). 'Child and family factors that ameliorate risk between four years and 13 years of age', *Journal of the American Academy of Child and Adolescent Psychiatry*, 31: 893–903.

Sennett, R. (2003). *Respect: The formation of character in a world of inequality*. London: Allen Lane.

Shanahan, M. J. (2000). 'Pathways to adulthood in changing societies: Variability and mechanisms in life course perspective', *Annual Review of Sociology*, 26: 667–92.

Shanahan, M. J., Mortimer, J. T. and Krüger, H. (2002). 'Adolescence and adult work in the twenty-first century', *Journal of Research on Adolescence*, 12: 99–120.

Shavit, Y. and Müller, W. (1998). *From school to work: A comparative study of educational qualifications and occupational destinations*. Oxford: Clarendon Press.

Shepherd, P. (1993). 'Analysis of response bias', in E. Ferri (ed.), *Life at 33: The fifth follow-up of the National Child Development Study*. London: National Children's Bureau and City University pp. 184–8.

Shepherd, P. (1995). *The National Child Development Study: An introduction, its origins and the methods of data collection*. London: National Children's Bureau and City University pp. 184–8.

Shepherd, P. (1997). 'Survey and Response. Getting on, getting by, getting nowhere', in J. Bynner, E. Ferri and P. Shepherd (eds.), *Twenty-something in the 1990's*. Aldershot: Ashgate pp. 129–36.

Shepherd, P. (2004). 'NCDS and BCS70 update', in *Kohort. CLS Cohort studies newsletter*. London: Institute of Education.

Silbereisen, R. K. (2005). 'Social change and human development: Experiences from German unification', *International Journal of Behavioral Development*, 29: 2–13.

Silbereisen, R. K. and Eye, A. V. (eds.) (1999). *Growing up in times of social change*. New York: Walter de Gruyter.

Singh, K. Bickley, Trivette, P., Keith, P. & Anderson, E. (1995). 'The effects of four components of parental involvement on eighth grade student achievement. Structural analysis of NELS-88 data', *School Psychology Review*, 24: 299–317.

Smith, G. D., Hart, C., Blane, D., Gillis, C. & Hawthorne, V. (1997a). 'Lifetime socioeconomic position and mortality: Prospective observational study', *British Medical Journal*, 314: 547–52.

Smith, J. (1996). 'Planning about life: Toward a social-interactive perspective', in P. B. Baltes and U. M. Staudinger (eds.), *Interactive minds. Life-span perspectives on the social foundation of cognition*. Cambridge: Cambridge University Press. pp. 242–75.

Smith, J. R., Brooks-Gunn, J. and Klebanov, P. K. (1997b). 'Consequences of living in poverty for young children's cognitive and verbal ability and early school achievement', in G. J. Duncan and J. Brooks-Gunn (eds.), *Consequences of growing up poor*. New York: Russell Sage Foundation pp. 132–89.

Social Exclusion Unit (1999). *Bridging the gap: New opportunities for 16–18 year olds not in education, employment or training*. London: The Stationery Office.

(2000a). *Report of policy action team 12: Young people*. London: The Stationery Office.

(2000b). *National strategy for neighbourhood renewal: Report of policy action team 8: Anti-social behaviour*. London: The Stationery Office.

Southgate, V. (1962). *Southgate Reading Tests: Manual of instructions*. London: University of London Press.

Spring, J. H. (1976). *The sorting machine: National educational policy since 1945*. London: Longman.

Sroufe, L. A. (1979). 'The coherence of individual development: Early care, attachment, and subsequent developmental issues', *American Psychologist*, 34: 834–41.

Sroufe, L. A., Egeland, B. and Kreutzer, T. (1990). 'The fate of early experience following developmental change – longitudinal approaches to individual adaptation in childhood', *Child Development*, 61: 1363–73.

Sroufe, L. A. and Rutter, M. (1984). 'The domain of developmental psychopathology', *Child Development*, 55: 17–29.

Steiger, J. H. (1990). 'Structural model evaluation and modification – an interval estimation approach', *Multivariate Behavioral Research*, 25(2): 173–80.

Steinberg, L., Elmen, J. D. and Mounts, N. S. (1989). 'Authoritative parenting, psychosocial maturity, and academic success among adolescents', *Child Development*, 60: 1424–36.

Steinberg, L. D., Brown, B. B. and Dornbusch, S. M. (1996). *Beyond the classroom: Why school reform has failed and what parents need to do*. New York: Simon & Schuster.

Stouthamer-Loeber, M., Loeber, R., Farrington, D. P., Zhang, Q. W., van Kammen, W. and Maguin, E. (1993). 'The double edge of protective and risk-factors for delinquency – interrelations and developmental patterns', *Development and Psychopathology*, 5: 683–701.

Surridge, P. and Raffe, D. (1995). *The participation of 16–19 year olds in education and training: Recent trends*. Edinburgh: Edinburgh University Press.

Szatmari, P., Shannon, H. S. and Offord, D. R. (1994). 'Models of multiple risk – psychiatric disorder and poor school performance', *International Journal of Methods in Psychiatric Research*, 4: 231–40.

Tarter, R. E. and Vanyukov, M. (1999). 'Re-visiting the validity of the construct of resilience', in M. D. Glantz and J. L. Johnson (eds.), *Resilience and development: Positive life adaptations*. New York: Kluwer Academic pp. 85–100.

Tizard, J. (1976). 'Psychology and social policy', *British Psychological Society Bulletin*, 29: 225–34.

Townsend, P., Davidson, N. and Black, D. A. K. S. (1982). *Inequalities in health: The Black report*. Harmondsworth: Penguin.

Trice, A. D. and Knapp, L. (1992). 'Relationship of children's career aspirations to parents' occupations', *Journal of Genetic Psychology*, 153(3): 355–7.

Ungar, M. (2004). *Nurturing hidden resilience in troubled youth*. Toronto: University of Toronto Press.

—— (2004b). 'A constructionist discourse on resilience. Multiple contexts, multiple realities among at-risk children and youth', *Youth & Society*, 35: 341–65.

United Nations Development Programme (UNDP) (1998). *Human Development Report*. New York: Oxford University Press.

Utting, D. (1999). *Communities that care: A guide to promising approaches*. London: Communities that Care.

Vaillant, G. E. (1977). *Adaptation to life*. Boston: Little, Brown.

van de Mheen, H., Stronks, K., vandenBos, J. and Mackenbach, J. P. (1997). 'The contribution of childhood environment to the explanation of socio-economic inequalities in health in adult life: A retrospective study', *Social Science and Medicine*, 44: 13–24.

Veenhoven, R. (1993). *Happiness in nations: Subjective appreciation of life in 56 nations 1946–1992*. Rotterdam: Erasmus University Press.

von Bertalanffy, L. (1968). *General system theory: Foundations, development, applications*. New York: Braziller.

Vondracek, F. W., Lerner, R. M. and Schulenberg, J. E. (1986). *Career development: A life-span developmental approach*. Hillsdale, NJ: Erlbaum.

Wadsworth, M. (1991). *The imprint of time*. Oxford: Oxford University Press.

Wadsworth, M., Butterworth, S., Montgomery, S. M., Ehlin, A. and Bartley, M. (2003). 'Health', in E. Ferri, J. Bynner and M. Wadsworth (eds.), *Changing Britain, changing lives. Three generations at the turn of the century*. London: Institute of Education pp. 207–36.

Walsh, F. (1998). *Strengthening family resilience*. New York: Guilford Press.

Warr, P. (1999). 'Well-being and the workplace', in D. Kahneman, E. Diener and N. Schwarz (eds.), *Well-being. The foundations of hedonic psychology*. New York: Russell Sage Foundation pp. 392–412.

Wedge, P. (1969). 'The second follow-up of the National Child Development Study', *Concern*, 3: 34–9.

Werner, E. E., Bierman, J. M. and French, F. E. (1971). *The children of Kauai: A longitudinal study from the prenatal period to age ten*. Honolulu: University of Hawaii Press.

Werner, E. E. and Smith, R. S. (1977). *Kauai's children come of age*. Honolulu: University of Hawaii Press.

(1982). *Vulnerable but invincible: A longitudinal study of resilient children*. New York: McGraw-Hill.

(1992). *Overcoming the odds: High risk children from birth to adulthood*. Ithaca, NY: Cornell University Press.

(2001). *Journeys from childhood to midlife: Risk, resilience, and recovery*. Ithaca, NY: Cornell University Press.

West, P. (1991). 'Rethinking the health selection explanation for health inequalities', *Social Science and Medicine*, 32: 373–84.

White, M. and Smith, D. J. (1994). 'The causes of persistently high unemployment', in A. C. Petersen and J. T. Mortimer (eds.), *Youth unemployment and society*. Cambridge: Cambridge University Press pp. 95–144.

(1996). *Unhealthy societies: The afflictions of inequality*. London: Routledge.

Wilkinson, R. (1996). Unhealthy societies: The afflictions of inequality. London: Routledge.

Willis, P. E. (1977). *Learning to labour: How working class kids get working class jobs*. Aldershot: Gower.

Wilson, W. J. (1987). *The truly disadvantaged: The inner city, the underclass, and public policy*. Chicago: University of Chicago Press.

(1991). 'Studying inner-city social dislocations: The challenge of public agenda research', *American Sociological Review*, 56: 1–14.

Wolke, D., Sohne, B., Ohrt, B. and Riegel, K. (1995). 'Follow-up of preterm children – important to document dropouts', *Lancet*, 345– 447.

Woods, L., Makepeace, G., Joshi, H. and Dolton, P. (2003). 'The world of paid work', in E. Ferri, J. Bynner and M. Wadsworth (eds.), *Changing Britain, changing lives* (pp. 71–104). London: Institute of Education.

Wothke, W. (2000). 'Longitudinal and multigroup modeling with missing data', in T. D. Little, K. U. Schnabel and J. Baumert (eds.), *Modeling longitudinal and multilevel data*. Mahwah, NJ: Erlbaum pp. 219–40.

Wyman, P. A., Cowen, E. L., Work, W. C. and Parker, G. R. (1991). 'Developmental and family milieu: Correlates of resilience in urban children who have experienced major life stress', *American Journal of Community Psychology*, 19: 405–26.

Zellman, G. & Waterman, J. (1998). 'Understanding the impact of parent–school involvement on children's educational outcomes', *Journal of Education Research*, 91: 370–80.

Zoccolillo, M. (1993). 'Gender and the development of conduct disorder', *Development and Psychopathology*, 5: 65–78.

Index